THE EUROPEAN PUZZLE

THE EUROPEAN PUZZLE

The Political Structuring of Cultural Identities
at a Time of Transition

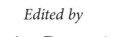

Edited by

Marion Demossier

Berghahn Books
NEW YORK • OXFORD

Published in 2007 by
Berghahn Books

www.berghahnbooks.com

© 2007 Marion Demossier

Library of Congress Cataloging-in-Publication Data

The European puzzle : the political structuring of cultural identities at a time of
transition / edited by Marion Demossier.
p. cm.
Includes bibliographical references and index.
ISBN 978-1-57181-626-9 (hardcover : alk. paper)
1. Group identity—European Union countries. 2. Group identity—Cross-
cultural studies. 3. Nationalism—European Union countries. 4. Nationalism—
Cross-cultural studies. 5. European Union. I. Demossier, Marion.

HN373.5.E823 2007
306.2094'090511—dc22

2007022855

British Library Cataloguing in Publication Data

A catalogue record for this book is available from
the British Library.
Printed and bound by CPI Antony Rowe, Eastbourne

To Margot and Louisa

Contents

Abbreviations

CC	City of Culture
CDU	Christlich-Demokratische Union (Christian Democratic Union)
CSU	Christlich-Soziale Union (Christian Social Union)
CoE	Council of Europe
CNRS	Centre National de la Recherche Scientifique
EC	European Community
ECSC	European Coal and Steel Community
EEC	European Economic Community
EFA-DPPE	European Free Alliance-Democratic Party of the Peoples of Europe
EFGP	European Federation of Green Parties
ELDR	European Liberal Democrat and Reform Party
EMU	Economic and Monetary Union
ENA	Ecole Nationale d'Administration
EP	European Parliament
EPP	European People's Party
ESRC	Economic and Social Research Council
EU	European Union
GATT	General Agreement of Tariffs and Trade
GDP	Gross Domestic Product
IGC	Intergovernmental Conference
IHTP	Institut d'Histoire du Temps Présent
ILP	Independent Labour Party
NATO	North Atlantic Treaty Organisation
PCI	Partito Comunista Italiano (Italian Communist Party)
PNV	Partido Nacionalista Vasco (Basque Nationalist Party)
SI	Socialist International
SPD	Sozialdemokratische Partei Deutschlands (Social Democratic Party of Germany)
TNP	Transnational Parties
EUL-NGL	European United Left-Nordic Green Left
UKIP	United Kingdom Independence Party

Key Dates of European Integration

1948
    17 March   Treaty on Western Union (Brussels Pact) signed
    7–11 May   The Hague Congress
1949
    5 May   Treaty of St James establishing the CoE
1950
    9 May   Schuman Plan announced. Since this date can be regarded as the birthday of the European Union, 9 May is now celebrated annually as Europe Day.
1951
    18 April   Treaty establishing the European Coal and Steel Community (ECSC) is signed by six countries: Belgium, France, Germany, Italy, Luxembourg and the Netherlands.
1957
    25 March   Treaties of Rome
1962
    30 July   The Common Agricultural Policy (CAP) is introduced. Second stage of ECC begins.
1966
    29 January   The Luxembourg Compromise
1972
    19–21 October Paris summit of EC Nine
1973
    1 January   Denmark, Ireland and the United Kingdom join the European Communities.
1979
    28 May   The European Communities sign a treaty of accession with Greece.
1981
    1 January   Greece joins the European Communities, bringing the number of member states to 10.

1985

12 June   The European Communities sign accession treaties with Spain and Portugal.

1986

1 January   Spain and Portugal join the European Communities, bringing their membership to 12.

17, 28 February   The Single European Act is signed in Luxembourg and The Hague. It comes into force on 1 July 1987.

1987

15 June   Start of the Erasmus programme, set up to help young Europeans study abroad in other European countries

1989

9 November   Fall of the Berlin Wall

1990

19 June   The Schengen Agreement, aimed at abolishing checks at the borders between member states of the European Communities, is signed.

3 October   Germany is reunited.

1991

9–10 December   At a European Council Summit in Maastricht, a draft of the Treaty on European Union is adopted.

1992

7 February   The Treaty on European Union is signed at Maastricht. It enters into force on 1 November 1993.

1993

1 January   The Single Market is created.

1995

1 January   Austria, Finland and Sweden join the EU, bringing its membership to 15. Norway stays out, following a referendum in which most people voted against membership.

1997

16–17 June   The European Council, meeting in Amsterdam, agrees on a draft treaty giving the European Union new powers and responsibilities.

2 October   The Amsterdam Treaty is signed. It comes into force on 1 May 1999.

1998

3 May   The Brussels European Council decides that 11 EU member states (Austria, Belgium, Finland, France, Germany, Ireland, Italy, Luxembourg, the Netherlands, Portugal and Spain) meet the requirements for adopting the single currency on 1 January 1999. Greece will join later.

31 December   Fixed and irrevocable exchange rates are set between the currencies that are to be replaced by the euro.

1999

1 January   Start of the third stage of EMU: the currencies of 11 EU countries are replaced by the euro. The single currency is launched on the money markets.

2000

7–8 December   In Nice, the European Council reaches agreement on the text of a new treaty changing the EU's decision-making system so that the Union will be ready for enlargement. The presidents of the European Parliament, the European Council and the European Commission solemnly proclaim the EU Charter of Fundamental Rights.

2001

26 February   The Treaty of Nice is signed. It comes into force on 1 February 2003.

2002

1 January   People in the euro-area countries begin using euro notes and coins.

31 May   All 15 EU member states simultaneously ratify the Kyoto Protocol, the worldwide agreement to reduce air pollution.

13 December   The European Council, meeting in Copenhagen, agrees that 10 of the candidate countries (Cyprus, the Czech Republic, Estonia, Hungary, Latvia, Lithuania, Malta, Poland, Slovakia and Slovenia) can join the EU on 1 May 2004. Bulgaria and Romania are expected to join in 2007.

2003

16 April   In Athens, the EU signs accession treaties with Cyprus, the Czech Republic, Estonia, Hungary, Latvia, Lithuania, Malta, Poland, Slovakia and Slovenia.

10 July   The Convention on the Future of Europe completes its work on the draft of the European Constitution.

2004

1 May   Cyprus, the Czech Republic, Estonia, Hungary, Latvia, Lithuania, Malta, Poland, Slovakia and Slovenia join the European Union.

10, 13 June   The sixth direct elections to the European Parliament

16–17 December   Decision to start accession talks with Croatia and Turkey in 2005 if certain conditions are met

2005

25 April   In Luxembourg, the EU signs accession treaties with Bulgaria and Romania.

2007

1 January   Date set by the European Council, meeting in Copenhagen in 2002, for Bulgaria and Romania to join the EU.

For additional information, see http://europa.eu/abc/12lessons/key_dates_en.htm.

ACKNOWLEDGEMENTS

The idea behind this book came from my years as an anthropologist teaching in a European studies department at a time when a politics section was being created. Over the years, the postgraduate students in my classes of Euromasters (postgraduate programme in European politics, optional module and identity in Europe) have been the most important influence on this edited book because it was written mainly with the expectations of students in mind, and also because I always had to justify my intellectual position with respect to my colleagues from politics. I would like to thank, in particular, the first cohort of my Greek, German, French and American students, who made me think hard about what it means to be European.

The index for this volume was compiled with the help of Chris Reynolds. I would like to thank him for his work. In addition, I would like to thank the Berghahn editorial team with Melissa Spinelli, and especially their copy-editor Shawn Kendrick and her husband who have provided invaluable editorial assistance that went beyond mere proofreading.

The book is dedicated to my husband, Julian, and my father-in-law, Ron, who have been over the years the most engaged opponents of European integration and with whom I have debated about European identity with passion.

Finally, my thanks to Margot, who was born in April 1998 when I was starting to think about this project. She has been truly European since the beginning, combining French conviction with English Euro-scepticism.

— *Marion Demossier*

European Union Member States as of January 2007   Non-Member States

MAP OF EUROPE

European Union Member States as of 2007 and Date of Accession

Austria, 1995	Germany, 1951	Netherlands, 1951
Belgium, 1951	Greece, 1981	Poland, 2004
Bulgaria, 2007	Hungary, 2004	Portugal, 1986
Cyprus, 2004	Ireland, 1973	Romania, 2007
Czech Republic, 2004	Italy, 1951	Slovakia, 2004
Denmark, 1973	Latvia, 2004	Slovenia, 2004
Estonia, 2004	Lithuania, 2004	Spain, 1986
Finland, 1995	Luxembourg, 1951	Sweden, 1995
France, 1951	Malta, 2004	United Kingdom, 1973

INTRODUCTION

Marion Demossier

Since 1 May 2004, when the European Union was enlarged from 15 to 25 countries and then to 27,[1] the issues of European culture and identity have resurfaced, becoming more acute than ever before. Following the entry of Bulgaria and Romania in 2007, over 490 million people now belong to this unique and challenging project that is called the European Union. Twenty-seven countries, 23 official languages and a strong sense of cultural diversity provide a real challenge to any attempt to construct a viable political edifice. The expansion into a wider political structure regulated by treaties and a common legal framework, which has occurred against the background of globalisation and growing multiethnicity, has posed a major challenge to national, cultural and historic roots of identity. This cultural heterogeneity, an important element of modern political communities, has called into question the nature of the new demos at the base of the European political process. According to Nezar Alsayyad and Manuel Castells (2002: 4), 'In the long term, the emergence of a European network state and a fully integrated European economy without a European identity (overlayered on national and regional identities) seems to be an unsustainable situation.'

As integration has proceeded and nation-states have lost some of their importance and economic sovereignty to the benefit of the European Union, members of individual nation-states have started to question the nature of their own identity. Under new pressure from both external and internal forces, identities have been radically transformed and in some instances radicalised. For example, being Corsican has taken on a new resonance as Europe has progressively created an arena for the expression of regional identities. Thus, the definitions of what it meant to be Corsican at the end of the 1960s, when intense nationalist voices were dominating a disrupted civil society, now have little in common with contemporary Corsican identity, even if some cultural elements have been presented as permanent and unchanging.

Notes for this section begin on page 11.

At the national level, the key issues of integration and what it means to be French, British, Italian or German have been called into question under the impact of economic and social change and in response to the new threats associated with global terrorism. Emigration from former colonies and new waves of migrants escaping poverty and political persecution, associated with new forms of democratic representation and rights, have all contributed to the rise of the politics of identity. The various models of integration – e.g. multiculturalism, assimilation – have failed to resolve the question of identity for a great number of citizens. The politics of difference that emerged in the 1960s had a major impact on the notion of culture that became the defining feature of specific groups and the means by which one group differentiated itself from others. Diverse groups, such as French peasants and the descendants of Algerian immigrants, claimed to have a specific culture rooted in their own history and experiences; since then, globalisation has homogenised the cultural features of their uniqueness. Modernity, social fragmentation and individualism attached to consumerism have entrenched these altered conceptions of identity as stable and traditional forms of being. New questions about the nature and role of religion and culture have arisen in this globalised context, and the European Union (EU) has been confronted by the challenge of international terrorism, the rise of ethno-political identities and the so-called Islamic threat.

The new and even more fragmented state of cultural diversity in Europe gives a voice to certain groups to the detriment of others, and notions of power, political representation and bargaining are becoming essential to these groups and their identity, be they in the area of local or regional cultures or migrants' rights. With enlargement and the successive treaties, especially Maastricht and Amsterdam, citizenship has become more important than before, especially in the context of the integration of countries which have a different history and conception of the nation and its membership. Citizenship and the concepts of identity that are attached to it are notions that remain inseparable from the EU as a political object. The narratives about the supposed decline of the nation-state, further political integration and the extension of a certain form of globalisation and economic liberalism are part of the current values shaping the future development of the EU. If it is undeniable that the nation-state has lost its influence and primacy in a number of key areas such as economy, policy making and justice, it is equally true that major changes are taking place to shift power from the centre to the periphery. Even in highly centralised France, decisions are now taken at the regional and local level, thus chipping away at the vast edifice represented by the French state. Yet the anti-nationalist tenet has been a constant in European debates to the extent that social anthropologists have encountered this obsessive rejection of the nation in the discourse of EU civil servants (Abélès 1996: 33–45). The EU could be seen as a progressive and ahistorical institution defined by a type of cosmopolitan and elitist culture. But politics still remains confined almost exclusively to the nation-state and is tied to the locality and issues of parochial concern.

In 2003, as part of a search for political legitimacy, the EU sought to introduce a European constitution. This was not the first attempt by the EU to respond to the growing uncertainties expressed by European civil society. Enlargement, in this context, is, according to European political leaders, 'the first attempt to create a new type of citizenship on a continental scale'.[2] Yet the attempt to impose a European constitution has failed because basic questions about the nature of representation and political rights still divide the members of the Union. The 2004 referenda on the constitution in France and the Netherlands, where the 'no' vote triumphed, seemingly struck a blow against further political integration and raised questions about the future of European identity. Public opinion in member states is also deeply divided over the development of the EU itself, and many doubt its democratic credentials. The current economic position is also controversial, and disputes continue to rage about the financial participation of specific countries in the euro and the economic consequences for those who have already adopted it. In terms of political achievement, it could be argued that since 1989, the European project has helped to heal the split between the free-world democracies and the former communist states. A more stable political context and a liberalised economy seem to offer the best guarantee of a new, peaceful European order. Yet European identity remains to be defined.

Before starting to explore further the complex and multifaceted nature of identity in Europe, it is necessary to recall the main processes and elements forming the modern EU. Emerging from the economic crisis of the 1930s and the catastrophe of the Second World War, the EU has developed, through a long series of treaties, into a unique pan-European political entity based upon five key institutions (the European Parliament, the Council of the EU, the European Commission, the Court of Justice, the Court of Auditors) and five other significant bodies (the European Economic and Social Committee, the Committee of the Regions, the European Central Bank, the European Ombudsman, the European Investment Bank). The culture of the EU could be defined by its multicultural and multilingual nature (albeit one that has so far failed to integrate religious or ethnic minorities), by the fundamental rule of law which makes it a bureaucratic transnational network, by its emphasis upon specific economic and political values and by its common set of socio-economic issues to address, such as unemployment and immigration.

Many commentators have noted that unity in diversity is the leitmotiv of the Union. As in other institutions, relationships between groups, individuals and levels of governance are highly complex and are shaped by the specificities of the tasks they have to face. Until recently, the approach to European identity in the context of the EU has been dominated by the French neo-functionalist school associated with Jean Monnet; it has lately been challenged by a more

Anglo-Saxon managerial approach.[3] On the one hand, the political machine imposes and dictates what European identity is or must be (Shore 2000), while on the other, the cultural realm of European societies in their fluid, many-stranded, perpetually negotiated and ambiguous nature challenges any attempt to generate a sense of belonging. The reconciliation between these conflicting processes can successfully occur only if it is based upon a set of common values which are presented in an inclusive and democratic way and which will address the challenges posed by fragmented and complex European societies.

The major issues at stake concern the reconciliation of civil society with the political sphere and the question of defining who does and does not belong to the EU. The very existence of a multiplicity of ethnic communities and identities – already in crisis at the national level – makes it imperative that the EC minimise the importance of ethno-cultural criteria for determining membership in the political community. The so-called crisis of politics, the decline of major ideologies and the increasingly common destiny Europe has to face requires a new polity based upon values shared by a majority of Europeans. However, these values, be they democratic or humanitarian, still remain to be defined.

* * * * *

This book aims to contribute to the debate on European identity by locating the various conceptual meanings attached to it, and by contrasting them with the broader more gradual process of Europeanisation and the wider fragmentation affecting postmodern societies. The puzzle created by these political changes needs to be examined by situating them within a theoretical and ideological framework, that is to say, in relation to the variety of discourses produced by institutions, groups and actors on culture and identity.[4] The political structuring of cultural identity is a fruitful way of examining the nature and content of the debates surrounding the making of Europe and could be viewed as a *face à face* between European integration as a political process and European societies as an arena engaged with the negotiation of cultural identities, which could be constrained by European integration or could, in turn, constrain the political process. However, these negotiations are also transformed by external forces such as the impact of globalisation and the effect of convergent liberalism. Although the countries composing the EU have all been affected differently by these pressures, they have reacted in ways that reflect their historical and cultural specificity. They have also given forms to common patterns of political behaviour and have created spaces for the expression of new identities. All these processes have to be taken into account when looking at issues of identity, culture and politics. European integration has played a major role in reshaping cultural identities at the national level. However, it has led to greater differentiation between social groups at the micro-level. Moreover, the bitter divisions in some European countries over questions such as the treatment of immigrants, the place of Muslims, and political and economic integration are powerful points of tension involving complicated alternative cultural constructions of what it means to be French, German or British (Ross 2000).

Two processes will be at the core of our discussion: the idea of European identity as a top-down process and the bottom-up manifestations of political and cultural identities in the European Union, be they cultural, ethnic, professional or political in nature. Both processes ought to inform our approach towards Europe as a political construction. The tensions which emerge when cultures meet are essential to the construction of a European identity as they offer an insight into the causes of conflict and the shortcomings of the democratic process. One of the aims of this volume is to address the process of European integration from different cultural and political perspectives and in relation to existing or newly created cultural identities. The contributors also endeavour to examine the contradictions, tensions and dynamic elements which make the construction of a European identity an ongoing and difficult process. Yet European integration remains a fragmented and incomplete project in political terms, and any attempt to generate a sense of belonging and a specific allegiance to this imperfect body is fraught with difficulty. The book does not intend to address all of the issues attached to the question of European identity/identities, but rather focuses on the complicated and contradictory processes that have accompanied the flux of cultures. Thus, questions of a European identity have to be addressed in the plural, in a wider perspective, and not solely on a political basis.

Political Constructs, or the Obstacles to the Making of Europe

In the first section of the volume, we embark on discussions of obstacles where the commonly used notions of nations, national identity, history and European identity are further explored. Most studies on European identity have been conducted with the framework of the nation-state in mind – its history, its 'imagined community' and its boundaries. This top-down approach has often been cited as an efficient way to create European citizens. However, while the economic and political processes at the core of this construction have often been endorsed, cultural processes and especially the question of regional and ethnic identity and cultures have been downplayed or ignored. Yet recent studies have emphasised the dual processes – national construction versus regional identities and ethnic identity versus global identity – at the centre of the establishment of specific nations.

As Anne-Marie Thiesse argues in her chapter, the recent and largely unsuccessful attempts to create a European identity have provoked fierce debate in contemporary societies. The existence of strong national identities which seem to represent a major obstacle to the process of Europeanisation cannot be doubted. However, for Thiesse, three major issues need to be addressed. Firstly, nations are much younger than their official histories would have us believe; most are recent creations, barely two centuries old. Secondly, they were literally invented, resulting from a conscious political project. Thirdly, the construction of national identities in the nineteenth century was part of a broader pan-European movement and not a purely national affair. As a result, a list of the symbolic and material items defining national identities was drawn up: a history establishing a nation's continuity through the ages, a set of heroes embodying its national values, a language, cultural monuments, folklore, historic sites, distinctive geographical features, a specific mentality and a number of picturesque labels, such as national costumes, dishes and animal emblems. In her conclusion, Thiesse opens the debate by suggesting that new cultural forms are currently emerging in Europe, such as the *métissage*, or mixed heritage, of regional traditions which are integrating the contribution of extra-European migrants, and that they may provide the embryo of a new European identity. Her view is echoed by research conducted on new forms of social identities developed by authors such as Jürgen Habermas.

It is therefore undeniable that any attempt to forge a new European sphere needs to take into account that which makes each nation unique in a historical sense. History is a primary factor in the making of Europe and in the way European identity is conceptualised by nations, families, groups, political parties and even the EU. Yet as Richard Vinen demonstrates in his chapter, peoples talk about their history in different ways and to different extents. The break-up of big narratives and the changes affecting the world of history are very rarely taken into account. Historically, European identity was created in opposition to others who were 'infidels' or 'barbarians' (Alsayyad and Castells 2002: 4). The defence of Christianity was the impetus for setting up the existence of a so-called European culture. However, examining Europe and its more recent past, Vinen emphasises the diversity of national situations regarding their own history, as well as the common processes attached to the definition of the historical profession and its public status.

It is only comparatively recently that popular history, memory and history from below have been brought into the equation, offering a new vision of European history and culture. Twentieth-century attitudes to the law are also a major element in the emergence of history as the unique truth. The multiplication of trials and the new place accorded to historians as witnesses in the process of historical truth have changed the political landscape by placing more emphasis upon the individual to the detriment of the collective. The collapse of Communism has accompanied this political and moral dimension of the making of the EU, and the rethinking of the colonial experience is also part of the same process of reinvesting and assessing the contribution of each actor in the political process. The rise of new forms of narratives which have been legitimised through a variety of mediums – history being one – has accompanied the expression of new forms of identities, and in the making, history has played a major role in providing a new cultural resource or base for the consolidation of identity. Yet the EU has not yet provided its members with such an opportunity to realise a collective and more inclusive historical narrative; in a sense, its history is also still under construction.[5]

However, the national framework often represents an obstacle to the examination of Europe as a new political object and to its scenarios of future development as a 'true' democratic transnational order. When looking at the political structuring of cultural identities in the European Union, the question of European identity can be examined in a critical way by discussing the juxtaposition of top-down and bottom-up processes and the relationship between culture and politics. Marion Demossier's chapter on the political structuring of cultural identities is one such attempt to rethink European identity by looking at various expressions of identities in European societies. Bringing the work of political scientists and anthropologists together, she argues that the possible emergence of such an identity is likely to be dependent upon new definitions of citizenship. The major issue is to find a common framework of values to enable all European members to adopt a project whereby questions of active participation at each level of the political process – local, regional, national and European – could be encouraged. Debates over European identity have to be in tune with the democratic and modern nature of identities at both national and European levels. The question remains as to whether such a type of identity could emerge independently or whether it has to be encouraged.

Some of the changes affecting history as a discipline are also at the core of the challenges facing European integration and the making of Europeans as citizens of Europe. In his chapter, Ralph Grillo examines European identity in light of the debate on multiculturalism versus universalism/secularism. Addressing the notion of European identity by reviewing the anthropological literature, Grillo shows clearly the polemical nature of any attempt to define European identity. Focusing on the CoE (Council of Europe) colloquia held in Strasbourg in 2002, Grillo confirms some of the conclusions already raised by anthropologists such as Shore, Abélès and McDonald concerning the promotion of a European identity presented as Christian, white and democratic. Attempts to provide an acceptable definition of European identity have failed, and according to some politicians, the future lies in the political culture of the EU and especially in the liberal values it wishes to promote. However, for Grillo the main issue remains the question of ethnic identity and national sense of belonging. Can conceptualisations of European identity transcend nationalism and provide alternatives to the crisis of the nation-state? Various scenarios have been put forward by European intellectuals to reconcile the multicultural nature of our societies with the European project, and intercultural dialogue seems to be one of the most viable options. Yet the concept of the nation and the nature of the EU itself remain major obstacles to the construction of these new Europeans.

Cultural and Political Identities in Transition

The view from below has started to challenge some of the mainstream ideas or ideologies attached to Europe, and in this context, history is no longer synonymous with fixed traditions and immutable cultures. What this section will explore is the complexity of the cultural realm and, above all, its changing nature. Starting from the notions of 'traditions' and 'heritage', cultural identities are presented as contextualised, actively operationalised by diverse social actors, deeply rooted in mythical representations but also largely modern in their bearings. Cultural identities, or cultural elements of identities, can be reactivated or operationalised for political purposes, and, to the same extent, political identities might become more cultural in their expression, as Benedict Anderson (1983) has demonstrated in his work *Imagined Communities*.

The chapter by Ullrich Kockel is a perfect example of the interaction between local/regional identities and the use of cultural resources provided indirectly by the EU. Indeed, discourses on local culture have been constructed around counter-reactions to intense processes of globalisation, and local cultures are presented as the provider of new resources for social and economic growth. In his analysis, Kockel examines processes where culture and identity are utilised under the banner of 'heritage' for tourist development. The ambiguous rise of 'public identities' – defined in opposition to 'home identities' – is seen as holding the potential for inclusion and cohesion. By using tradition and heritage as differentiated but progressive forces, the EU, according to Kockel, may find itself in a difficult position as identities will not simply respond to political processes. Examining a wide range of cases, such as the Pays Cathare or the Ulster-Scots heritage, he concludes that many cultural traditions can be seen as progressive forces challenging the fixation of cultural heritage. The idea of a so-called European culture and its corollary European heritage must therefore be treated with caution. From a public policy perspective, treating identities as merely public identities makes sense and works up to a point. However, Kockel argues that the heart of identity politics lies in the private and domestic sphere, as demonstrated by the Basque example. The expanding EU will therefore find it increasingly difficult to engineer a coherent European-heritage identity perceived as based on a common past, and this will be even more difficult where European heritage is viewed as fluid, undefined and ambiguous in its expression. By focusing on the Karelian experience, Kockel suggests that identity may be based on excellence in a field of contemporary international culture, such as music, rather than on a glorious past.

Cinema offers another example where European identity in all its complexity and contradictions could be displayed in a constructive manner at the international level. For Wendy Everett, within the ongoing debate about the complex and multiple identities of Europe, the role of European cinema must be acknowledged as particularly significant because of its crucial and original contribution in creating, articulating and shaping identities in our postmodern societies. Moreover, the problems of fragmentation and difference defining Europe are perhaps nowhere more deeply and uncompromisingly etched than in its cinema as a 'volatile meeting place of art and commerce'. While cinema is seen as a commodity in the United States, Europeans fight to protect it as part of their material and symbolic heritage. Because of the domination of the Hollywood industry, European cinema is often associated with problems relating to audience attendance and revenue. However, Everett argues in her chapter that European cinema plays a major role in interrogating and creating our individual understanding of ourselves and of the world we live in. Autobiography, new voices, gender issues, sexuality, immigration, exile, conflict and change are all ingredients of the European film industry, and they assume an essential function in communicating about us and others in the context of multicultural and postmodern societies. These new themes that characterise the recent developments of European cinema illustrate, according to Everett, the multiplicity, instability and fragmentation of identity which could be seen here as an open-ended process. In this context, they contribute in a constructive fashion to the evolutive nature of the narratives confronting Europe in the twenty-first century.

Yet, as Christian Bromberger argues, modern societies are still immersed in their own history, and new forms of passion, which could arguably be seen as European, reveal some of the values and contradictions that post-industrial societies now have to face. In his chapter, Bromberger recalls the history of football as the illustration of social class struggles, political activism and cultural boundaries in Europe. The popularity of such sports resides in their capacity to transcend social barriers and to represent the ideal of democratic societies. Succeeding through one's own merits and competition between equals illustrate the values endorsed by the public at large. However, the other side of the story is the increasing power of money, the corruption and the violent behaviour of essentialist forms of expressions by football fans and players alike. As does politics, football symbolises some of the values at the core of our modernity, and the exaltation of identities accompanying it reveals the nature of local, regional and national antagonisms. Not only has football been simply a form of peacetime mobilisation for nation-states, but also it has been – and remains – a powerful catalyst of aspirations for autonomy and independence. The site of multiple antagonisms, it also combines the *mise-en-scène* of multiple identities which act as a factor of identification for individuals and groups. The nation, community, collective identities and supporters' groups are the main sites of allegiance displayed during the game. Even if the nature of the public has changed by becoming more socially fragmented and mixed, football still tells us a lot about contemporary identities and their celebration. As Bromberger concludes, it constitutes a new genre, a diapason of the contradictions of our time. But how to generate a new type of citizenship which would embrace all the contradictions of our post-industrial societies remains another question.

Towards a European Identity:
Challenges to Existent Forms of Belonging

The last section of the book explores levels of governance and the emergence of new forms of citizenship and belonging (Cesarani and Fulbrook 1996; Habermas 1992; Neveu 2000), while discussing in a critical way current debates concerning the issue of European citizenship and the rise of new identities. The idea of European citizenship has been promoted by the EU since the 1980s as a means of building a 'Euro-polity' and creating political allegiances towards it. The status of the 'citizens of the Union' was enshrined in the Maastricht Treaty, which granted to these citizens the right to vote in local government and European parliamentary elections in their country of residence, regardless of their nationality. However, European citizenship still remains a pale shadow of its national counterpart. This section will examine whether or not a bottom-up process can generate a European identity and will discuss the effectiveness of the policies that have sought to encourage its development.

In his chapter, David Hanley examines the possibility of fostering a sense of European identity through political parties. Hanley argues that political parties are not traditionally seen as agencies that have helped form the imagined communities of European nations, and yet the role of Europarties or transnational parties (TNP) in fostering identities remains largely unexplored. Analysing the historical development of traditional political parties in nation-states, Hanley argues that Europe provides a new arena for political parties, enabling them to take advantage of currently evolving opportunities. However, political parties remain of limited use in fostering alternative identities at the transnational level. As followers and adapters to circumstances rather than active players, they do not have a strong voice in creating European allegiances.

Like party identity, regional identity in Europe seems to occupy a paradoxical and ambiguous position in the search for a new European allegiance. In his chapter, Peter Wagstaff notes the tensions between the quest for unity that underlies the European project and the tendency towards uniqueness and difference offered by regionalism. If regional identities could be seen as a way forward in the making of new Europeans, it is only as part of a set of multiple identities which will supplement national identity as a single focus of affiliation. In the new European context, there is a growing preoccupation with the region at both a political and a symbolic level. A regional sense of belonging has increased, illustrating individuals' recourse to local, culturally homogeneous allegiances in the physical territory they inhabit. However, for Wagstaff, the notion of migration and the disappearance of national boundaries make the notion of Europeanness more likely to emerge, as it is based on the realities of human experiences of space. Several attempts have been made to foster transnational networks at the European level in the hope of creating a new sense of belonging amongst the population. Peter Wagstaff questions these initiatives, as they could lead to new forms of tribalism based on identity vacuum.

As pointed out by Susan Milner in her concluding chapter, the city could also be seen as a form of organisation which is central to European identity. Discussing recent developments affecting cities in the context of increasing competition for public funding, she argues that successive social and cultural policies have contributed to an emergent European civic space. However, the impact of these policies provides examples of the tension between various levels of governance – between local and global, roots and networks, places and flows. This tension results in the strengthening of existing forms of identities and thus the reinforcement of existentialist versus constructivist types of identities, in the end leading to exclusion, racial and ethnic problems, and economic and social segregation. The variety of situations affecting European cities – their centres and their peripheries – illustrates a contrasting mapping out of new forms of identities based upon economic regeneration. Yet cultural policies remain limited in their scope to transform cities into new places for collective European identity.

Despite the variety of approaches and themes developed in this volume, the principal aim has been to reconcile unity and diversity by offering an interdisciplinary approach to questions of European identity/identities. What these chapters have in common is an emphasis on the new challenges involved in the making of complex identities in a multinational Europe and above all the need to take them into account when creating new political spheres and affiliations. Secondly, the book suggests that intercultural communication, whatever its forms, could provide a way forward towards further integration. It is only by accepting diversity, developing ways of communicating, understanding the language and culture of others, and acknowledging the changes affecting our contemporary societies that a meaningful European identity is likely to emerge. Yet the political structuring of cultural identities tells us that any attempt to police them from above is likely to end in failure, as further fragmentation and resistance are liable to result.

Notes

1. In referring to Europe, I mean the ongoing political construct as it could be defined at the time of writing, which includes the European Union with its 27 member states (Belgium, France, Germany, Italy, Luxembourg, the Netherlands, Denmark, Ireland, the United Kingdom, Spain, Portugal, Greece, Austria, Finland, Sweden; after 2004, Cyprus, the Czech Republic, Estonia, Hungary, Latvia, Lithuania, Malta, Poland, Slovakia, Slovenia; and in January 2007, Bulgaria and Romania) and the various elements forming the European political space, such as the European Commission, the European Parliament and the Council of Europe.
2. Speech by Romano Prodi to the European Parliament, Strasbourg, 6 November 2002.

3. See, for example, McDonald (1996) and Shore (1998).
4. As a starting point to the idea of tensions in the construction of Europe, see the very stimulating article by McDonald (1996).
5. The controversy surrounding the creation of a Museum of Europe in the 1990s is a telling example of the various problems attached to defining the entity 'Europe'.

References

Abélès, M. 1996. 'La communauté européenne: Une perspective anthropologique'. *Social Anthropology* 4, no. 1: 33–46.

Alsayyad, N. and Castells, M. 2002. 'Introduction'. In *Muslim Europe or Euro-Islam: Politics, Culture and Citizenship in the Age of Globalization*, ed. N. Alsayyad and M. Castells, 1–6. Lanham, MD: Lexington Books.

Anderson, B. 1983. *Imagined Communities*. London: Verso.

Cesarani, D. and Fulbrook, M., eds. 1996. *Citizenship, Nationality and Migration in Europe*. London: Routledge.

Habermas, J. 1992. 'Citizenship and National Identity: Some Reflections on the Future of Europe'. *Praxis International* 12, no. 1: 1–19.

McDonald, M. 1996. 'Unity in Diversities: Some Tensions in the Construction of Europe'. *Social Anthropology* 4, no. 1: 47–60.

Neveu, C. 2000. 'European Citizenship, Citizens of Europe and European Citizens'. In *An Anthropology of the European Union: Building, Imagining and Experiencing the New Europe*, ed. I. Bellier and T. M. Wilson, 119–36. Oxford: Berg.

Ross, M. 2000. 'Culture and Identity in Comparative Political Analysis'. In *Culture and Politics: A Reader*, ed. L. Crothers and C. Lockhart, 39–70. New York: St. Martin's Press.

Shore, C. 1998. 'Creating Europeans: The Politicization of Culture in the European Union'. *Anthropology in Action* 5, no. 1 and 2: 11–16.

_____. 2000. *Building Europe: The Cultural Politics of European Integration*. London: Routledge.

PART I

European Political Constructs

Chapter 1

THE FORMATION OF NATIONAL IDENTITIES

Anne-Marie Thiesse

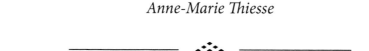

If the debate about the composition and form of a European identity has become so complex today, it is because the nature of that identity is still unclear. There cannot, however, be any doubt about the existence of national identities. And these national identities, so solidly entrenched, often appear to be the principal obstacle, as an expression of ancient and irreducible differences between nations, to any sort of union on the Continent (Thiesse 1999).

Three points should nevertheless be kept in mind. Firstly, the different European nations are all far younger than their official histories would have us believe. Secondly, these national identities are not facts of nature or history, nor have their origins been lost in the mists of time. They are recent constructions, the result of conscious thought and action. Thirdly, this creation of national identities was the fruit of an enormous transnational workshop that was active across the whole of the Continent throughout the nineteenth century.

The Nation: A Modern and Transnational Concept

All national history derives from centuries-old stories. Yet the idea of the nation in its modern sense – that is to say, its political sense – is of very recent vintage. It did not exist before the ideological revolution, launched in the eighteenth century, which conferred power and political legitimacy on the people. The nation was initially a new and subversive concept that challenged the society of orders and monarchical power that justified itself through the principles of the divine right of kings or the right of conquest. The child of a great political and intellectual revolution, the nation was conceived of as a community of birth, establishing the principles of equality and fraternity between its members. The nation, in contrast to a group of peoples defined by their allegiance to the same monarch, was presented as independent of dynastic and military history: it existed before and after its prince. What made the nation was a sense of sharing the same collective history and the transmission through the ages of a shared and inalienable heritage. The creation of national identities involved a process of preparing an inventory of this shared patrimony, that is to say, in reality, of inventing it.

Today, the nation is defined as a relatively large group of people characterised by a sense of social, cultural and historical unity and a desire to live together. But to express that ambition to live together, it was first necessary for each nation not only to develop its consciousness of that unity but also to construct it. However, at the end of the eighteenth century, the idea of the nation was merely a theory in total contrast with the most basic social realities. As Ernest Gellner (1983) has noted, cultural heterogeneity was the rule in the states of the early modern period. The points of reference for individual identity, determined by social status, religion and belonging to a local community, were rich with all kinds of particularities. Everything, or nearly everything, separated a Prussian Junker from a Bavarian artisan, a Hungarian aristocrat from a peasant on his estates, a Milanese bourgeois from a Sicilian shepherd. If today we can say that German, Hungarian and Italian national identities exist, it is evidence of an enormous work of creation of identity and of education in the sense of national belonging that has been achieved during the last two centuries.

In order that these 'imagined communities' (Anderson 1983) that are nations could be born, it was first necessary to give them a common history, language and culture. This was a major undertaking which mobilised the energies of scholars, writers and artists for decades (Smith 1991). An intense creative activity was required to form the national identity of the Germans, Italians and French, and that of their European cousins. That process implied, if not the eradication of existing identities founded on social status, religion or a sense of belonging to a smaller local community, at least a redefinition in which these identities would come to be seen as secondary to the national identity. The spatial and hierarchical organisation of national identities has consisted not only of the elaboration of new collective references but also of a vast educational program in order that ever larger groups of a given population would be aware of them and recognise themselves in that mirror. What is perhaps most remarkable is that the formation of national identities was less the result of national introspection than a large-scale international exchange of ideas, theories and savoir-faire. The various national identities which exist today, while individually specific, are in reality similar in their conception.

The list of attributes that any self-respecting nation should possess is well established and includes the following: founding fathers, a historical narrative that provides a sense of continuity across the vicissitudes of history itself, a series of heroes, a language, cultural and historic monuments, sites of shared memory, a typical landscape, a folklore, not to mention a variety of more pic-turesque features, such as costumes, gastronomy and an emblematic animal or beast. This list is prescriptive: the nations that have achieved recognition after the dismantling of Yugoslavia, Czechoslovakia and the USSR never cease to proclaim that they conform perfectly to these criteria. As for the Padania of the Italian separatist Umberto Bossi, it has been endowed with a 'delegate of cultural identity' charged with watching over its implementation. This 'identity checklist', to borrow the provocative expression of the sociologist Orvar Lofgren (1989), is the matrix of all the representations of a nation. It supplies the first chapter of tourist guides, the iconography of banknotes and the scene for the festivities accompanying the visit of a foreign head of state or a national holiday.[1] Yet no ambassador or foreign traveller of the eighteenth century would have recognised these features, not even in those states that today like to think of themselves as the most ancient. Although the first signs of the emergence of this identity checklist can be detected in the Europe of the Enlightenment, the real work of construction took place, brick by brick, during the nineteenth century.

The Nation and Its Ancestors

Logically enough, the construction of nations as communities defined by birth began with the identification of particular founding fathers. The claim of belong-ing to the nation was accompanied by an emphasis on the role of tradition in conserving, in a more or less perfect way, the original culture of the nation across the centuries. Knowledge of popular culture was therefore a means of displaying the relics of an ancestral culture and, after a process of reconstitution, of establishing the foundations of a modern national culture. The ethnographic approach can therefore be seen as the key to unlocking the archaeology of the nation. As it was consistent with the revolutionary ideology which cast the peo-ple as the only legitimate source of power, this promotion of popular culture also served to impose a form of universalism. In eighteenth-century Europe, the cultural hegemony of France, which posed as the privileged guardian of a com-mon Graeco-Roman heritage, inspired English, German and Swiss scholars to question how to create national cultures that were not simply imitations and, as a result, inferior versions of French culture. The answer they produced stressed the plurality of European cultures, arguing that the civilisations of their 'barbar-ian' ancestors could rival those of Greece or Rome. In opposition to the existing universalism that postulated the existence of a dominant culture, they offered a particularistic universalism that denied the existence of a hierarchy amongst nations. Each peoples became the guardians of a particular heritage, equal in value and in dignity to that of others. The loyalty shown to this heritage was held to be the only valid measure of the value of the nation.

This interpretation was first elaborated in the second half of the eighteenth century, in parallel with the first excavations of the primitive cultures supposedly conserved in the bosom of the people. The most remarkable example was the alleged discovery of a Caledonian Homer, identified by the name of Ossian, to whom two epics were attributed: *Fingal* and *Temora*, published in 1760 and 1763, respectively. The young James Macpherson claimed to have discovered them and translated them from Gaelic on the basis of his research into Scottish folk songs. A long-running polemic started almost immediately about the veracity or otherwise of Macpherson's claims, pitting those who wished to believe in the existence of Ossian's works at all costs against those who maintained on the basis of philological arguments that they were forgeries. Yet the belief in the existence of national cultural relics was so strong that the Ossian epics exerted a real fascination across Europe, launching an intensive collection of folk songs and other expressions of popular culture. It is, however, important to note that the popular culture which was promoted in this way, as the basis of national culture, had little in common with the reality of the living culture of the peasantry. It was instead a process of reconstruction which borrowed, it is true, certain elements from this popular culture, but above all was destined, at the cost of a major work of adaptation, to inspire a renewal of high culture. Thus, groups of young Germans, Swedes and Russians, inspired by the precedent of Ossian, would collect and publish epic songs, sagas and ballads that would serve as the foundations for modern national cultures.

The German theologian Johann-Gottfried Herder, a great admirer of Ossian, delivered numerous exhortations to his compatriots as well as other European scholars to collect the ingredients of their cultures. In what would become a famous formula, Herder (1983: 532) declared that 'folksongs are the archives of the people, the treasure of its science, its theology and its cosmology. They are the treasure of our fathers' achievements, retracing their history, carrying the mark of their hearts, illustrating their domestic lives, their joy and pain, from the conjugal bed to the grave'. The author of an anthology of folksongs (*Volkslieder*, 1778–89), wherein he collected a series of texts from a wide range of provenance, Herder developed a philosophy of history which presented the new universalism, that of equal value and dignity of different incarnations of the same essence. Condemning the artificiality of states constituted by right of conquest, he declared that the only legitimate political formation was that constituted by people possessing a national character. He also insisted strongly on the importance of a language that was common territorially and socially, as an expression of the constantly renewed communion of the nation.

The Creation of National Languages

Today, the French speak French, the Germans German, the Italians Italian and so on. Each nation is distinguished by a language which is generally specific to it, and the linguistic map usually corresponds to that of the state. Yet the linguistic panorama of the eighteenth century was completely different. Within the boundaries of a particular state, several languages co-existed together, with the language spoken depending upon the social status of the individual or the context of the conversation. The languages of the court, of religion, of the administration or of education could all vary, and they also co-existed with a variety of local dialects. In the German Protestant states, the language of religious instruction and of primary education was German, secondary education was dominated by Latin, while the language of the court and of cultural life was French. The *Actes* of the Berlin Academy were drafted in French on the orders of Frederick II of Prussia, who was contemptuous of the German language, and Herder felt it necessary to reproach the aristocracy for only speaking German to their servants and their horses. French was the preferred language of the European elite, but many of the inhabitants of the French kingdom were incapable of speaking or understanding it because they spoke Breton, Basque, Flemish, German or *langue d'Oc* (southern French).

Such linguistic diversity did not pose any major problems for the early modern state. It was the nationalist ideal which brought with it the notion that a single language – common to all members of the nation – was a necessary symbol and a means of participating in the national community. From this perspective, a national language has as its principal function to assure the totality of communication of all the members of the nation, whatever their social or geographic background. Everyone should understand it and use it, regardless of the circumstances or situation. It should permit the expression of any idea or reality, from the most ancient to the modern, from the abstract to the concrete. Through a common language, the nation should incarnate and illustrate itself, a function that other languages or dialects should not be able to fulfil. The actual national languages are for the most part the result of philological scholarship, often of a quite substantial nature, which was pursued through common methods and based upon scholarly exchange. The Grimm brothers, in particular, played a major role in setting up a body of learned references that was copied throughout Europe, with the codification of language and the collection of popular literature as constituents in the construction of a national cultural patrimony.

Since the formation of national languages was connected to political, social and international conflicts, philological choices about a language's linguistic material, dialect, ancient written language and alphabet sometimes provoked fierce debate requiring careful arbitration (Baggioni 1997: 70). The creation of a language for the South Slavs was achieved only on the basis of a dialect, the Stokavien, used by the Serbs, the Muslim Montenegrins and some Croats, which was distinct from the Kajkavien dialect initially used by a cultural movement formed in Zagreb. Vuk Karadzic, who played an important role in the development of the new language, was encouraged in his endeavours by the philologists of the Habsburg Empire and by Jacob Grimm. Codified by a convention signed in Vienna in 1850 by a group of Croatians, Serbian scholars and a Slovene, Serbo-Croat was defined as a single language, written with two alphabets: Cyrillic for Orthodox Serbs, Latin for Catholic Croats. The Romanian language, whose codification into Latin form was part of a purge of Turkish and Slavic elements, was written with Cyrillic characters until the middle of the nineteenth century. The decision to adopt a Latin alphabet was part of a conscious distancing from the Slavic world. Norway, on the other hand, found itself with two national languages: the first (the current Nynorsk) was based on the dialect spoken by the peasants of the West; the second (the current Bokmal) was administrative Danish, which was spoken in the capital and became progressively 'Norwegianised'. The creation of the modern Greek language involved a lengthy conflict between partisans of the Demotic dialect, which refers to popular parlance, and those of Kathaveroussa, a purified version more closely tied to the Greek of antiquity. A similar argument can be observed in the case of the modern Israeli language, with the quarrel between supporters of a refined Yiddish and opponents who favoured a modernised Hebrew.

This philological research was not limited to the finer points of grammar or the completion of dictionaries. On occasion, it was also necessary to engage in intense promotional campaigns for the new language. The national awakening in the majority of Slav countries and in Finland was associated with a period of literary and linguistic creativity, involving the production of books in the new language and the foundation of associations designed to finance and promote the dissemination of books and periodicals. The aim was to form a public, and literary salons and the theatre also played a critical role in the refinement of the vocabulary of the new language. The diffusion of the language to the population as a whole was, however, achieved only gradually, notably through rural emigration to the cities, the establishment of a system of national education and the impact of the mass media.

National Histories

The first national histories, generally written from a liberal perspective, appeared during the early decades of the nineteenth century. These new histories, which challenged the traditional accounts of the lives of monarchs, coincided with a new form of narration and with the constitution of documentary sources that initially placed great emphasis on the origins of the nation, especially the barbarian ancestors who were contemporaneous with the Roman Empire or who had appeared during the mediaeval period (Geary 2002). The historiography of the nation, differing markedly from that of a dynasty, was intended to retrace the continuity of a collective body through the ages, from its ancient founders to the present. A nation was expected to maintain its unity despite the vicissitudes of history. It suffers and can be oppressed or vanquished, yet it continues to resist and struggle for its liberty, led by heroes belonging to all sections of society. A nation never attacks its neighbours; it is instead defending the territory bequeathed by its ancestors or recovering that which has been wrongly taken from it. National histories were widely diffused amongst the population and became the model for the struggles of the present.

A new literary genre, the novel, which is no older than the concept of the nation, was another model for the diffusion of an idealised vision of the past. The books published by Sir Walter Scott after 1814 inspired a generation of young writers, who discovered in his works the model of a history that was both a resurrection and an explanation of times gone by. The major expansion of the printing industry helped to encourage an ever wider dissemination of national history, a movement that was assisted by the opera and the theatre. They were accompanied by the creation of an iconography of the great scenes of the national past, presented on everything from paintings and engravings to everyday objects such as crockery. It is particularly noteworthy that the different national iconographies actually have a great deal in common, not only stylistically, but also thematically.

An exhibition presented at the German Historical Museum of Berlin in the spring of 1998, under the title 'Mythen der Nationen: Ein europäisches Panorama' (Flacke 1998: 143), made this point very clearly by placing the national iconographies of 17 European nations alongside each other. As the historians Etienne François and Hagen Schultze (1998: 20) noted on this occasion: 'These national myths appear to us, from one to another, as remarkably similar, if not interchangeable. The difference from one country to the next, which seemed unbridgeable to contemporaries, appears today as little more than nuance, a question of degree, the variations in a pattern of a perfectly coherent whole.' These similarities bear witness to the constant exchange of ideas and inspiration amongst scholars, writers and artists engaged in the cultural construction of national identities. Critical observation of the initiatives of others and imitation of their successes were an essential part of the process. Patriotic intellectuals never ceased to bemoan the alleged backwardness of their nation relative to others that seemed more advanced in one area or another, calling on the state (where it existed) or their fellow citizens to supply the moral and financial support for their efforts.

The creation of national histories was complemented by another substantial cultural movement: the definition and protection of national monuments. The emergence of the idea of the nation gave birth to a new conception, that of national patrimony (Poulot 1997). Individual ownership in this case became subjected to national interest. Previously, the owner of an old building was perfectly entitled to do with it whatever he or she wished. In general, if the funds were available, the owner was likely to modernise it to reflect current fashion, while making it more comfortable to live in. Many royal palaces or great aristocratic houses have thus experienced successive waves of modernisation, while Gothic churches have been altered to incorporate baroque altars or chapels. If the building was not suitable for modernisation or if its restoration was too costly, it was liable to be abandoned or to have its stones sold off for other purposes. Countless numbers of chateaux or ancient churches suffered this fate before the ideas of a nation and a national history brought it to a halt. These concepts completely changed the situation because they instilled the notion that certain buildings were intrinsically linked to the history and the culture of the nation and that their very age was part of their value. The idea of a kind of national collective right over these monuments was propagated, and this, in turn, implied a duty to conserve them. However, it was first necessary to determine the composition of this national patrimony and to make it known. Amongst the immense collection of ancient buildings, which were those with a particular value for the nation?

From the early nineteenth century onwards, there was a real attempt to answer this question by attaching particular buildings to national history and investing them with special significance. English antiquarians were to the fore in the study of ancient buildings, the majority of which were mediaeval, inventing a new vocabulary to describe them and to explain their aesthetics. This knowledge was quickly exported to the Continent. In Paris in 1831, a historical novel appeared whose eponymous heroine was a cathedral. The author of *Notre-Dame de Paris* gave his readers a course in architecture and national history before launching an appeal for action in favour of education in national architectural patrimony. 'Save our national monuments. Inspire, if we can, in the nation a love of national architecture', exclaimed Victor Hugo in his novel. Remarkably, in the same year, the scholar Sulpiz Boisserée published his *Domwerk* in praise of the cathedral of Cologne. An association was formed to complete, following the recently discovered fourteenth-century plans, the Rhineland Cathedral, which had become a metaphor for the German nation. Indeed, throughout Europe there would be examples of patriotic and lavish movements to restore a rich collection of buildings with the aim of making them more authentic. The progressivist determination of national architecture also supplied a point of reference for the construction of modern buildings: at the end of the nineteenth century, countless town halls, post offices and railway stations were built in the national Gothic or Renaissance style.

The Construction of a National Landscape

It is possible today to evoke a nation simply by reference to its landscape: advertising agencies and tourism posters do this all the time. If it is possible to read these messages quickly and unambiguously, it is because there was such an effective campaign to provide a national codification of nature in the nineteenth century. It was through the combined efforts of poets, writers and artists that this work of constructing national landscapes was achieved. They chose imagery according to a coherent, aesthetic scenic view charged with a specific sensibility and conveying a specific sentiment. Yet how was it possible to represent a nation when choosing between mountains, plains, rivers, lakes or forests, knowing that many of these countries possessed a broad range of topographical possibilities?

This was achieved through the principle of differentiation that was brought into play. To mark a clear distinction from Austria and its Alpine summits, Hungarian writers and painters extolled the virtues of the unprepossessing landscape of the great plain (the *Puszta*). Switzerland, on the other hand, whose national territory was much smaller in size than that of its neighbours, was illustrated with prodigious and breathtaking peaks. The Norwegian national landscape took the form of a fjord surrounded by pristine white snow, the very whiteness and verticality of which contrasted with the lush green pastures of Norway's ancient Danish overlords and the no less green forests of its more recent Swedish masters. A national landscape has often been associated with a particular season: the Mediterranean countries were rarely represented in winter, whereas those of the north were more often depicted in autumn or winter. The choice of a national emblem (pine cones for Finland, silver birches for Russia, oaks for Germany and cypresses for Italy) tended to confirm this stereotype.

The emergence of genre painting effectively ran in parallel with another form of national representation which put great emphasis on something that was eminently picturesque but recent – namely, the national costumes of the different countries. Once again, this involved modifications of the cartography which established a vestimentary code that was no longer social but rather national. The various styles and collections of engravings of peasant costumes multiplied from the end of the first decade of the nineteenth century. The influence of historical illustrations and of theatrical costuming and stage design helped to accentuate certain quite spectacular features, such as ever higher hairdressings or more vibrant colours. These supposedly peasant costumes were in reality totally incompatible with the demands of rural life and labour; indeed, realistic artists continued to depict those toiling in the countryside dressed in dull and totally unoriginal clothing. But the aim of these traditional national costumes was symbolic rather than functional or social. From this collection of picturesque costumes, merchants and stylists could create an ostentatious sign for a rich clientele. In nations in the process of construction, the wearing of this type of national dress could play the role of a political manifesto, for example, on the occasion of patriotic balls which were organised in both Central and Eastern Europe. Upper-class women dressed in these picturesque and supposedly peasant costumes to go to a social event or had their portrait painted in them. The urban bourgeoisie and even the well-to-do peasantry gradually adopted these fashions, especially for festivals and special occasions. The most original of national costumes, the Scottish kilt, was the subject of intense promotion and was encouraged by Sir Walter Scott.[2] Even the English royal family adopted the habit of wearing it when residing in Balmoral.

Collections of traditional costumes provided the basis for the first ethnographic exhibitions, such as the ones in the universal exhibitions that became so popular from the mid-nineteenth century onwards and which were not limited to showing would-be buyers the latest technical innovations and industrial products. They were also exhibitions of identity at which each nation could display itself and its ancestral patrimony to advantage. The concept of archaism was honoured as equally as that of modernity. At the universal exhibition held in Paris in 1878, the Swedish section presented dozens of costumed mannequins in the reconstituted interiors of peasant dwellings that had been ornamented with paintings of national landscapes on the walls. The exhibit enjoyed enormous success, and the European ethnographic museology of subsequent decades was inspired by it. The Swedish display was assembled by the philologist Artur Hazelius, who had opened his collection of costumes and traditional artefacts to the public in 1872 with the explicit aim of using the objects of the patrimony to awaken and stimulate the patriotic sentiments of the visitor. The Nordiska Museet would serve as the model for the Danish National Museum of Ethnography, opened in 1885 by Bernard Olsen, illustrator and artistic director of the Tivoli in Copenhagen. He was also copied in the Salle de France of the Museum of Ethnology in Paris, inaugurated in 1884, and in the Museum of German Folkloric Costumes and Craft, which was opened in 1889. The different European capitals were rapidly provided with national museums of ethnography, and Oslo in 1894 and Prague in 1895 were even endowed with exhibitions of national ethnography before the establishment of Norwegian or Czechoslovak states. At the same time, national ethnographic societies were founded and produced their own periodicals, explaining to a literate and cultivated public how to collect and understand popular culture from a patriotic perspective.

By the end of the nineteenth century, the principal elements of national identity were in place and the means of acquiring them well known, enabling newly emergent nations to catch up with their longer established contemporaries. For the majority of European nations, the national ancestry was identified, the national language fixed, the national history written and illustrated, the national landscape described and painted. The major national music scores, which in some cases were presented as symphonies of the national history and landscape, had been composed, for example, *Ma Vlat* (My Country) by Smetana and *Finlandia* by Sibelius. The great national monuments had been recorded and restored. National literatures had been provided with a history and were in full expansion. Folklore had been collected and deposited in specially designed museums. Moreover, the material and symbolic output of a pre-national age had become the object of a retroactive policy of nationalisation.

National Limits

The genuinely common patrimony of European nations undoubtedly resides in this process of creation in the nineteenth century, which permitted the rapid spread of a new model of political organisation. The national principle gradually imposed itself as the only legitimate form of state formation first in Europe and then, after decolonisation, over the entire planet, with the anti-colonial movements presenting themselves as vehicles for national liberation. The initial institution representing the states of the planet was the League of Nations and since then the United Nations. While the diversity of the types of states, whether kingdoms, empires or republics, and the cultural heterogeneity of their populations had never been called into question before the eighteenth century, the nation-state progressively became the norm, with other forms henceforth perceived as anomalies or archaic. The undeniable success of the national principle, however, brought real problems in its wake – firstly, because it never ceased to pose a crucial question: how should the territory and the frontiers of a nation be decided?

The foundations of the idea of the national implied an equality between authentic nations and, in theory, offered no justification for one to annex the patrimony of another. A nation worthy of the name had the right to fight only to protect its heritage and to recover that of which it had been despoiled.[3] Philology, ethnography, history, archaeology and physical anthropology were all frequently employed to back a claim for an ancestral right to a territory, and this was officially the case in the peace treaties drafted at the end of the First World War. From these developed claims and counterclaims about the presence of ancestors and controversies about the continuity of their presence. Indeed, very recently the history of Europe has demonstrated this mobilisation of distant ancestors in tragic contemporary conflicts. The nationalist Serbian leaders, assisted by academics, film directors and public demonstrations, have trumpeted the importance of the battle of the Field of Blackbirds, in which their ancestors were defeated by the forces of the Ottoman Empire before leaving the province of Kosovo. According to this scenario, the Albanian population did no more than take advantage of this forced abandonment of 'the cradle of their nation'. The regime of Enver Hoxha, on the other hand, developed a thesis of national Communism, according to which the ancestors claimed by the Albanians, the Illyrians, had occupied the regions for centuries, even thousands of years, before the arrival of the invading Slavs in the Balkan peninsula. And archaeologists, anthropologists and philologists were expected to supply the proof. The question of whether Hungary or Romania had a legitimate claim to Transylvania has been the source of fierce controversy, especially since the 1920 Treaty of Trianon. This debate continues to rumble on, especially on Internet sites, concerning the alleged link between the Romanians and the ancient Daces or Géto-Daces, as well as the continuity of their presence: had the ancestors of Romanians abandoned their territory or not when the ancestors of the Hungarians arrived? We can also cite the controversy between French and German historians and archaeologists about the ethnographic characteristics of Alsace in the pre-Christian era: was it Gallic or German?

On the other hand, the community of culture postulated in the midst of a population is intrinsically arbitrary, passing beyond a strong initial linguistic and cultural heterogeneity. In the context of the formation of European states, great efforts have been made to emphasise the fundamental unity of the nation, even when accepting a certain part of its diversity. That has led principally to the construction of regional identities, which simplify the extremely diverse nature of the national territory and which were conceived of in such a manner that they appear as components of a harmonious whole. A spectacular material translation of this concept, which presented the nation as the sum total of these diverse but complementary entities, was offered by the 'ethnographic villages' presented at national or international exhibitions, in which a nation was represented by a series of rural buildings, theoretically coming from each region of the national territory and forming a complete village. Another similar theme was present in the processions of folklore, with dancers in traditional costumes and each region forming part of a joyful and peaceful national choreography. However, national constructions such as language, history, culture and particular landscapes have also been used by those who contest the rights of the nation. The majority of the nation-states created during the nineteenth century have seen their unity contested in the name of nations within nations that had not been recognised. The persistence of micro-nationalisms offers further evidence of the growing inability of nation-states to play their traditional social and political role and an indication of the collapse of the competing principle of internationalism.

Europe, initially the crucible of national identities, has also provided the historical context for the creation of a competing principle of collective identity. The Industrial Revolution, which began to be felt at about the same time as the national principle, gave birth to new social groups and raised serious doubts about the principle of equality within the heart of the nation. Internationalism was founded on the basis of the competing claim of class solidarity against that of national unity. Although this opposition constituted one of the fundamental axes of European history in the twentieth century, there was often co-existence between class identity and national identity. That one was put forward in a particular political situation did not necessarily mean the rejection of the other. The collapse of political regimes claiming to be based upon Marxist internationalism, on the other hand, has subsequently given considerable impetus to the idea of the nation as a point of collective solidarity in which each individual is assured a place that is not simply determined by economic status. Although the forces of globalisation today restrict the control of nation-states over the production of wealth and its distribution, the nation still appears as a refuge. Its disappearance would betoken a terrible menace that would affect social cohesion and the living conditions of the less well-off, as is demonstrated by the continued presence of populist political movements.

Conclusion

The current European situation carries within it extreme examples of the original paradoxes of the national model. The formation of nations was intrinsically linked to economic and social modernity, the transformation of modes of production, the growth of markets, the unification and rationalisation of knowledge, the new means of exchange. It is not a coincidence that these national identities are the result of the same model – one that was fundamentally transnational. This standardisation was probably a major factor in the success and the generalisation of this new form of collective identity. Yet it has been even more effective in the sense that it has eliminated the conditions of its formation: national identities are not perceived of as the product of a reconfiguration that homogenised differences but as creations *sui generis*, as perfectly autonomous. National identities have the particularity of being founded on a denial of change that glorifies archaism and the immutability of a long-lived community that has existed since time began. It is clear that the cult of tradition and the celebration of an ancestral patrimony have been effective counterweights allowing Western societies to achieve, over the last two centuries, radical change without collapsing into chaos. But this fracture between representation and reality constitutes without doubt one of the great weaknesses of contemporary societies, now confronted by another phase of drastic technological and economic modernisation. The construction of new collective identities, expressed through political projects in line with these transformations, implies the realisation of the historicity of the national model and its representations.

– Translated from the French by Julian Swann

Notes

1. The series of national characteristics could be interpreted as caricatured or distanced representations. The success of the *Axtérix* cartoons by Goscinny and Uderzo relies on a comical and anachronistic vision that projects the French checklist on the Gauls, the French ancestors.
2. Other examples can be found in Hobsbawm and Ranger (1983).
3. This principle was completely ignored during the period of colonial conquest, the colonised having been declared to be at a stage of civilisation greatly inferior to that of nations worthy of the name.

References

Anderson, B. 1983. *Imagined Communities*. London: Verso.

Baggioni, D. 1997. *Langues et nations en Europe*. Paris: Payot.

Flacke, M., ed. 1998. *Mythen der Nationen: Ein europaïsches panorama*. Berlin: Deutsche Historisches Museum.

François, E. and Schulze, H. 1998. 'Das emotionale Fundament der Nationen'. In Flacke 1998, 17–32.

Geary, P. 2002. *The Myth of Nations: The Medieval Origins of Europe*. Princeton: Princeton University Press.

Gellner, E. 1983. *Nations and Nationalisms*. Oxford: Blackwell.

Herder, J.-H. 1983. 'Von der Ähnlichkeit der mittleren englishen und deustchen Dichtkunst'. Originally in *Deutsche Museum*, November 1977. Reprint in *Sämtliche Werke*, book 9, ed. B. Suplan. Berlin: Weidmann.

Hobsbawm, E. and Ranger, T., eds. 1983. *The Invention of Tradition*. Cambridge: Cambridge University Press.

Lofgren, O. 1989. 'The Nationalization of Culture'. *Ethnologia Europaea* 19, no. 1: 5–24.

Poulot, D. 1997. *Musée, Nation et Patrimoine 1789–1815*. Paris: NRF Gallimard.

Smith, A. 1991. *National Identity*. Harmondsworth: Penguin Books.

Thiesse, A.-M. 1999. *La création des identités nationales en Europe – XVIIIème–XIXème siècles*. Paris: Seuil.

Chapter 2

'More Than Its Fair Share of History'
Europe and Its Recent Past

Richard Vinen

> And now Croatia, a land without history, meets Germany – a country that's
> seen more than its fair share of history.
>
> – English commentator, Euro 96 football competition

Whether or not countries have different shares of history, it is certainly true
that they talk about their histories in very different ways and to different
extents. The aim of this chapter is not to describe European history since
1945 but rather to suggest various ways in which recent history impinges on
Europe's present and to say something about the mechanisms through which
an awareness of history is transmitted.

The first point to be made is that discussion of the recent past has varied a
great deal from one European country to another. Compare, for example, views
of the recent past in France and Spain. From the late 1940s, French politicians
made an explicit attempt to push the divisive subject of Vichy out of public
debate. It seemed that they had succeeded by the time that Georges Pompidou
became president in 1969 (indeed, Pompidou enthusiastically embraced the virtues of forgetting). But by the time that Pompidou died in 1974, historians (especially Robert Paxton) and film makers (Marcel Ophüls and Louis Malle) had
propelled Vichy back to the centre of debate. By the end of the twentieth century,
Vichy was talked about in France so obsessively that Henry Rousso, the head of
the Institut d'Histoire du Temps Présent (a man who had spent his whole life
studying the subject), complained that politicians and journalists gave it excessive attention (Rousso 1987; Rousso and Conan 1994). Spanish discussion of the

past has moved in exactly the opposite direction. Until the mid-1970s, Spanish official discourse recalled the Spanish Civil War (or certain aspects of it) with great insistence. After the death of Franco in 1975, Spanish politics revolved around an officially sponsored policy of forgetting, a policy that ended 30 years later on 20 November 2002 (the anniversary of the death of Franco) when Parliament condemned the regime of el Caudillo.

England (this would be much less true for Scotland, Wales and, a fortiori, Ireland) is less conscious of its history than most Continental countries. The English have a vague sense of the past, linked to the (often invented) traditions of stately homes, royal funerals and Oxbridge colleges, but almost no awareness of specific historical events. All French citizens know the significance of 14 July 1789 (the storming of the Bastille), 11 November 1918 (Armistice Day, which in turn became an occasion for resistance demonstrations during the Second World War) and 8 May 1945 (the end of the Second World War in Europe). English people have none of this; indeed, attempts by the Thatcher government in the 1980s to create specifically 'national' holidays failed because no one understood the significance of, say, Trafalgar Day. Over 70 years ago, Sellar and Yeatman (1930) pointed out that there are only two 'memorable' dates in English history – 55 BC and AD 1066. Significantly, these are the dates of the last two successful foreign invasions of England. The difference between the French and English attitudes to their pasts can illustrated by one date – 18 June. Every French person knows that on 18 June 1940, de Gaulle issued his 'call to honour' in which he exhorted the French not to accept their defeat by the Germans. The date is so embedded in French collective memory that the campaign to legalise cannabis celebrates 'le 18 joint'. How many English people, by contrast, know that 18 June 1940 was the date of Winston Churchill's most self-consciously historical speech, in which he said 'if the British Empire and its Commonwealth last for a thousand years, men will still say, "This was their finest hour"'. For that matter, how many English citizens are aware that 18 June is the anniversary of the Battle of Waterloo?

Is it possible to transcend the national peculiarities outlined above and make any generalisations about Europe's relation to its recent past at the beginning of the twenty-first century? In one of the most influential works about history published in recent years, Pierre Nora (1984–91) suggested that in the mid-1970s France had undergone a 'crisis of memory' that was associated with the death of de Gaulle, the rapid economic growth that had transformed France from a rural to an industrial society, the revival of discussion about Vichy, the loss of faith in Communism and even the end of the 'long middle ages', which was brought about by the abolition of the Latin Mass.

Nora's interpretation conspicuously fails to work for many European countries: Britain, for instance, ceased to be an agricultural economy in the eighteenth century and abandoned the Latin Mass in the sixteenth. It is even questionable whether Nora's interpretation works very well for France, but what is certain is that it struck a chord in France itself. The leitmotif of his work, 'lieux de mémoire', entered the Robert dictionary in 1993 and was used by politicians and also by historians of other countries, such as Christina Dupláa (2000: 29–42) in Spain and Raphael Samuel (1989) in Britain. Whatever the reason, everyone seems to agree that Europe's relation to the past has shifted in recent years. What all this suggests is that certain broad changes can be identi-fied about the ways in which Europeans think about their past, even if those changes do not produce the same results in all European countries.

Historians

One crucial change in the way that Europe perceives its past has come from the historical profession. Although this may sound a gratuitously perverse remark, academic history is more influential now than at any time in the past. Hardly a week goes by in the Anglo-Saxon world (French historians tend to be less agitated) without a book or an article lamenting the 'crisis of history'.[1] Eminent historians claim that their discipline is losing touch with its wider public; that it is becoming divided into ever more specialised sub-disciplines that discuss their research in an increasingly impenetrable jargon; that political correctness has undermined a political narrative that revolves around dead white men; that the 'linguistic turn' has undercut the certainties of social history and that postmodernism has subverted all notion of an objective historical truth (Evans 2000). These laments, however, need to be put in three kinds of context.

First, paradoxically, the alarms about the 'crisis of history' actually reflect the discipline's centrality; national newspapers do not often contain articles about the 'crisis' of geography or chemistry. Discussion of history's alleged decline provides leading historians with a means of putting their own disci-pline, and themselves, at the centre of wider debates in the humanities. Sec-ondly, in material and institutional terms, the study of history today is much better placed than it was even 40 years ago. Universities expanded greatly in post-war Europe; by the early 1990s there were more university teachers than coal miners in Great Britain. Retaining their grip on institutional power, his-torians are much more heavily represented in the British Academy and even the Collège de France than scholars from any other discipline. Thirdly, the changing intellectual climate, about which historians so often complain, has actually given historians more power. Certainty about the past made historians the servants of a historical narrative. When history seemed to be clearly about one thing (the rise of parliamentary government, for example), the individual historian could only hope to describe his or her particular part of the story in a more or less competent fashion. The present-day historian can choose amongst an almost infinite variety of potential narratives and has a degree of power that Macaulay or Ranke could never have dreamed of. This change has coincided with a shift in the relationship between historians and the historical actors about whom they write. When historians wrote about great historical individuals, they were implicitly accepting that they themselves, the mere writers of history, played a subordinate role to their heroes, its makers. Even the rebellious A. J. P Taylor devoted much of his writing to lauding the achievements of the statesman Richard Cobden, Winston Churchill and, most of all, his own patron, Lord Beaverbrook.

This situation has changed partly because the definition of historical actors has changed as a result of the expansion of social history during the 1960s. This expansion meant a new interest in people drawn from outside the elite and also in forces beyond the control, or even understanding, of any single historical figure. All this placed historians in new positions of power. They came to believe that they themselves, and not the personages whom they studied, saw the real picture.

The interest in subjective experience and identity, which came to influence many historians during the 1970s, might have been expected to put historical actors, albeit different kinds of historical actors, back at the centre of the stage. This period saw an expansion in oral history, greatly assisted by the availability of portable tape recorders. The emphasis on 'popular memory' sometimes went with an apparent humility on the part of historians; they presented themselves as servants of communities and often expressed the ambition to 'give voice' to the inarticulate. In practice, however, it was often the power of historians themselves that was increased by oral history. The historian who sought out witnesses to interview and chose which questions to ask was exercising more explicit control than the historian who chose which parts of a written record to emphasise. Furthermore, the inarticulacy of the people who were the subjects of this new history underlined the power of the historians. Consider, for example, the situation of Luisa Passerini (1987), who wrote a famous book, *Fascism in Popular Memory*. Passerini belonged, in almost every possible way, to the privileged classes: she was young, highly educated and, most importantly in the Italy of the early 1970s, strongly identified with the 'right' political side (i.e. the left). The people whom she interviewed were at the opposite end of the spectrum. Mostly drawn from old people's homes in Turin, they were aged, penniless and poorly educated, and most of them had been compromised to some extent by the fascist regime.

The emphasis on memory as an artificial construction underwrote this shift in power relations between historians and historical actors. If memory was something that was constructed in retrospect, then that took power from the historical actor, who had previously been regarded as the bearer of memory, and gave it to the historian, who was now the analyst of the memory's construction. A striking example of changing power relations is provided by the history of the French resistance. Once, this history was very much controlled by people (mostly men) who had been members of the resistance. These individuals had great moral authority as well as the practical advantage of being able to say what had happened in organisations that had left few written records. Resistance veterans ran the Institut d'Histoire du Temps Présent (IHTP, Research Centre on Contemporary History), and when historians wrote books about resistance networks, they usually asked former resistance leaders to preface those books.

Since the 1980s, this situation has been reversed. People who were actively involved in the resistance are now older and more scarce, and this inevitably means that they have less power. However, historians are also less deferential. One cannot imagine that any leading historian in the 1950s would have dared to do what Olivier Wieviorka did in the 1990s – entitle a book on resistance leaders *Nous entrerons dans la carrière* (We'll Make a Career in the Resistance) (1994). Historians are also much more interested in 'memories', 'mythologies' and post-war images of the resistance, and are more likely to be sceptical about accounts provided by resistance veterans themselves. Two episodes in the debate about the career of the resistance leader Jean Moulin illustrate this change. One is the fate of Raymond and Lucie Aubrac, two of the most famous resistance veterans in France, who were accused of having betrayed Jean Moulin. In May 1997, the newspaper *Libération* convoked a 'jury' of historians (largely, people born after 1945) to assess the Aubracs' case. The jury interrogated the Aubracs in an aggressive manner and repeatedly called into question their recollection of events. The second episode that illustrates the change in attitude is the decision of Daniel Cordier to publish a biography of Jean Moulin, whose secretary he had once been. Cordier was not a professional historian, but in order to obtain some credibility with them, he entirely abandoned reliance on memory – his own or that of other veterans – and based his books (which sometimes read like a parody of old-style doctoral research) entirely on written documents (Cordier 1989–9).

A more complicated example of the changing balance of power between historical actors and historians is provided by Charles de Gaulle. De Gaulle was intensely conscious of his place in history, and his memoirs were designed to secure this place.[2] The composition of de Gaulle's memoirs also illustrates the subordinate role of historians: Georgette Elgey, an eminent scholar of the Fourth Republic, worked as his research assistant. However, important changes took place in the course of de Gaulle's career. In 1940, and again to some extent from 1958 to 1962, de Gaulle worked in circumstances in which his individual decision could make an important difference. He was concerned with issues of war and foreign policy, and the projection of his personality mattered a great deal. However, after 1962, de Gaulle worked in circumstances where gradual economic and social changes that were beyond the control of any single individual governed the fate of France. He himself recognised this when he commented on the success that his political opponents had in governing France during the late 1940s. Again after 1962, France was changed by the successes of a certain kind of capitalism rather than by the actions of the general himself. De Gaulle himself was bored. He complained that 'il n'y a plus rien de difficile, ni d'héroïque à faire' (there is no longer anything difficult or heroic to do) (Le Goff 1998: 30). Perhaps most humiliatingly, his enemies ceased to hate him. The rebellion of the *soixante-huitards* (68ers) was directed against a series of abstractions – imperialism, monopoly, capitalism – rather than against the authority of individuals (Debray 1990). De Gaulle, who had been the victim of numerous assassination attempts during his better days, was able to lay a wreath on the Tomb of the Unknown Soldier in the middle of the student riots without being bothered (Jackson 1994).

The tone of de Gaulle's (1989–99) own memoirs reflects this change. The early volumes have a strong authorial voice. They are written in crisp, classical French and are full of Gaullist leitmotivs: *espoir, honneur, salut* (hope, honour, salvation). The later volumes are less strongly marked by the general's personality. They are largely composed of lists of figures and accounts of economic planning, and it is obvious that large parts of them – like large parts of de Gaulle's policy – were devised by the graduates of the Ecole Nationale d'Administration (ENA) who came to surround to de Gaulle.[3]

The fate of de Gaulle's memoirs is further complicated by the fact that a new edition was brought out in 2000 as part of the *Pléiade* series. This new edition epitomised the view that de Gaulle's memoirs were to be read as literature – alongside the works of Proust or Gide – rather than as unproblematic representations of historical fact. The new edition also provided a great deal information about how de Gaulle composed his memoirs and showed how he moulded and remoulded the books as he constructed his own mythology. In short, the *Pléiade* edition completed the shift in perception from one that saw de Gaulle as a historical actor in charge of his own, and his nation's, fate to one that portrayed his destiny as a *lieu de mémoire* (realm of memory) to be interpreted by historians. *Pléiade* is, of course, published by Gallimard, and the most influential individual at Gallimard is the historian, Pierre Nora.

Historians have become more conscious of the way in which the memoirs of historical figures are artificial constructions. The relationship between autobiographer, biographer and ghostwriter has changed. The fact that many politicians' memoirs are not written by their 'authors' is more openly acknowledged (when the first volume of Margaret Thatcher's autobiography was published, reviewers noted with surprise that the Iron Lady herself appeared to have had quite a large role in its composition). This acknowledgment goes with a certain scepticism about memoirs as historical sources. Nicholas Ridley (1991: 48) became notorious for writing in 'his' memoirs that he had a 'clear memory of the first Cabinet in 1986 after the Christmas recess on 16 January'; this was the meeting at which Defence Secretary Michael Heseltine resigned. As unkind reviewers pointed out, the first Cabinet meeting of 1986 actually occurred on 9 January. Well-informed readers would also have known that Ridley's memoirs had, in large part, been written by a historian at London University. When Heseltine published his memoirs, he was quite open about the fact that they were written 'in collaboration' with the journalist Antony Howard (Heseltine 2000).

It is significant that as historians became more dubious about accounts written by powerful figures, they became obsessed with historiography. In the jargon of their trade, they started to *write about* meta-narrative rather than *writing* meta-narrative. Indeed, a historian who referred to the 'great men' of the nineteenth century was now more likely to mean historians, such as Ranke or Michelet,[4] rather than historical actors, such as Gladstone or Napoleon. The turning of the historical profession in on itself was also reflected in a sudden explosion of autobiographies penned by historians themselves. At the very moment when they were becoming sceptical about accounts by politicians, historians were more likely to record their own experiences. Nora, the engineer of so much historiographical realignment, was in the forefront of this development as the editor of *Essais d'ego-histoire* (1987), a collection of brief autobiographical essays by leading French historians. Annie Kriegel (1991), Pierre Goubert (1996) and Jacques Le Goff (1996) soon published their memoirs. Before the late 1980s, those few historians who wrote autobiographies usually presented their efforts in a relatively modest way. Either they justified the recollection of their lives by stressing their own links to larger political events, the line taken by Emmanuel Le Roy Ladurie (1982) in the 1960s, or they adopted a deliberately self-mocking style, the approach of A. J. P Taylor (1983). The historical autobiographers of the 1980s were much more likely to present their lives as significant in themselves. Noel Annan (1990) in England and Luisa Passerini (1996) in Italy explicitly presented their own lives as being emblematic of a whole generation. Eric Hobsbawm wrote his memoirs largely in the first person plural, thus producing passages such as 'after 1956 many of us did leave the Party. Why, then, did we remain?'

Lawyers and History

Lawyers were almost as important as historians in the construction of Europe's history at the end of the twentieth century. Law mediated European relations with the recent past in many ways. The use of law to confront the past is a relatively new idea, or at least one that was little used between the 1790s and 1945. For most of the nineteenth and early twentieth centuries, deposed rulers were allowed to retire peacefully in exile. Neither Napoleon nor, for all the threats, Kaiser William II were put on trial. The Nuremberg trials that followed the defeat of Nazism and the subsequent trials of collaborators in many countries that had been occupied by the Germans brought new issues to public attention. However, in many ways, these trials were a political parenthesis. Those men who were fortunate enough to escape execution in the immediate aftermath of the war were often free within a few years. Amnesty laws were passed in France in 1951 and 1953. The French government also passed an amnesty law concerning events that took place during the Algerian war in 1962, and the Spanish government passed such a law with regard to the crimes of the Franco regime in 1977.

However, the culture of amnesty did not last. It was changed, in the first instance, by an intense interest in pursuing the authors of crimes associated with the Third Reich. In many cases, this meant new, sometimes retroactive legislation and a refusal to recognise statutes of limitations where crimes against humanity were concerned. The first, and by far the most dramatic, of these trials was held in 1961 when Adolf Eichmann, the Nazi official who had coordinated the mass extermination of the Jews, was kidnapped from Argentina to be tried in Israel. The trial produced a great burst of reflection on Nazism, including, most notably, that of Hannah Arendt (1963). In France, the trials of Klaus Barbie in 1987 and of Maurice Papon in 1997 and 1998 helped rekindle interest in the wartime occupation and the Vichy regime's collaboration with the Nazis.

The use of legal process to confront the European past went with a new degree of prestige for the judiciary, particularly on the left of the political spectrum. George Orwell and Albert Camus had regarded judges as the incarnation of bourgeois hypocrisy and injustice; their disdain was rendered all the more intense by the fact that judges still passed death sentences. A brief exchange in the 1994 film *Red* by the Polish-French director Krzysztof Kieslowski captures conventional views of the judiciary. A girl asks an old man about the past of which he is so ashamed:

Tu étais flic [You were a cop].
Pire, j'étais juge [Worse, I was a judge].

In the last few years of the twentieth century, attitudes to the law changed dramatically. Judges became heroes of the left rather than its villains. On the evening that the British Law Lords decided that Chilean military commander Augusto Pinochet could be held responsible for his actions and issued an arrest warrant for his extradition, Daniel Cohn-Bendit (the French student leader of 1968) declared, 'Nous sommes tous les lords anglais' (We are all English lords).

The left's view of the judiciary was changed partly due to the perception that the law might be a useful weapon against a powerful and unchallenged state and partly due to the struggle against corruption and organised crime, especially in Italy. Italian judges acquired a new degree of independence in the 1980s, and some, such as Giovanni Falcone and Paolo Borsellino, began to make aggressive use of this independence to investigate the Mafia, the Christian Democrats and the affairs of Italy's wealthiest businessmen.

The use of trials as a means of confronting the past raised some awkward questions. Many of those tried were comparatively minor figures, and they were often very old by the time they reached the dock. Papon's trial in France seems to have happened precisely because he and his friends were no longer powerful. Furthermore, the fact that Papon was tried for his role as a comparatively minor cog in a very large machine in 1943, whereas he was never prosecuted for the very significant role that he had played as prefect of the Paris police when large numbers of Algerian demonstrators were murdered by the police in 1961, struck many observers as peculiar.

The use of legal process to get at historical truth produced some odd contortions. Trials often confronted historical fact in roundabout ways. The British historian David Irving was not brought to trial for denying the Holocaust, which is not a crime in Britain; instead, his trial was initiated when he sued another author for having alleged that he denied the Holocaust (Evans 2002). French General Paul Aussaresses was not on trial for having tortured and murdered during the Algerian war; these crimes were covered by amnesty laws. Rather, Aussaresses was being tried for attempting to justify such crimes.

Some historians felt that these trials, with their rigid standards of proof and interest in precise questions of fact, were not likely to produce interesting historical information. It is striking that the kinds of issues that preoccupied historians at the end of the twentieth century – social and cultural rather than political or military history, and the ambiguities of memory rather than the certainties of archival research – often fitted poorly with legal process. Henry Rousso, the key historian of Vichy memory, refused to testify at the Papon trial.

Attitudes to trials revealed an interesting divergence between professional historians and the wider societies in which they worked. Historians were less and less likely to be interested in ideas of absolute truth and often regarded the construction of memory with an almost playful interest. Raphael Samuel, for instance, wrote of 'theatres of memory'. By contrast, those outside the historical profession often regarded 'memory' as a matter of reconstituting a real past and thought of this task as one of moral urgency. Journalists, lawyers and politicians were increasingly prone to talk of memory as a 'duty'.

History in Eastern and Central Europe

Recollection of the past in the former Communist countries of Eastern and Central Europe took a rather different form from that in the West. Historians of these countries, at least those whose political or physical exile made them something other than instruments of state propaganda, often seemed methodologically conservative when compared to their Western European colleagues. New kinds of cultural history, such as those that emphasised gender as an artificial construct, had relatively little influence in the East (Funk and Mueller 1993). Political history, on the other hand, continued to have an importance in Communist countries. Questions about the struggles between Trotsky and Stalin were much more relevant in the East than questions about struggles between Lloyd George and Baldwin could ever have been in the West. Historians from Eastern Europe were still concerned with uncovering facts rather than revealing different 'narratives' about the past. The uses of oral history in the two parts of the Continent presented a revealing contrast. In the West, oral history was used to examine the world view of subordinate social groups. In the East, by contrast, oral history was used – for example, by the Polish Solidarity activist Teresa Toranska (1987) – to challenge people who had held positions of power and to make up for the inaccessibility of written sources.

If professional historians in Eastern Europe were more concerned than their counterparts in the West to exercise a 'duty of memory', other groups were more concerned than their counterparts in the West to forget. Few formerly Communist states could afford to do without the expertise of those individuals who had risen to power under the previous regime or the support of everyone who had believed in that regime. Leaders of anti-Communist movements such as Lech Walesa and Václav Havel explicitly called for their compatriots not to scratch at the scabs of the Communist period. Havel himself refused to examine his own secret police file. Sometimes those now in power had an interest in covering up what had happened under Communism. In Bulgaria, the 'reformed Communists' who led the country during the first few years of democracy were said to have caused 130,000 of the 280,000 secret police files to disappear (Châtelot 1997).

The country most reluctant to confront its past was Romania. The Communist Party had been outlawed, and in theory the break with the past was complete. Yet in practice, the old Communist rulers, with the exception of President Nicolae Ceausescu, who had been executed, remained in power. Not surprisingly, the authorities had little appetite for openness about the past. Between 1989 and 1996, 100,000 secret police files are said to have been destroyed. Constantin Ticu Dumitrescu, a former leader of the National Peasants' Party, became a senator in post-Communist Romania. The Senate building had formerly housed the Ministry of the Interior, and it was in the cellars of this building that Dumitrescu had been imprisoned in 1947. When he applied for permission to visit those cellars, he was told that they were 'military property' and therefore out of bounds to parliamentarians (Lieven 1998). Dumitrescu's questions about the past were unwelcome even to the victims of the Communist regime. He was expelled from an association of former political prisoners, many of whom had been forced to become Securitate informers after their release.

The former German Democratic Republic (GDR), by contrast, was the one part of the formerly Communist Europe to look at its past with a more or less unflinching gaze. In this part of Eastern Europe, former Communist functionaries were most dispensable because so much of the country was integrated into West German institutions. Here the parliamentarians who legislated about matters relating to the Communist period, being drawn mainly from the West, were able to confront the past without fear of embarrassing themselves or their political allies. The East German state did not possess the kind of national legitimacy that had been claimed by Communist Poland or Czechoslovakia. The GDR had been the denial of a nation rather than its expression, and its leaders, unlike those of Poland and Hungary, were not able to claim that they had initiated a process of gradual reform before 1989. German attitudes to the Communist past were also influenced by the habits of mind that had developed as a consequence of facing up to a previous dictatorship. The result of all this was that everyone in East Germany was given the right to consult his or her secret police files and a number of officials, particularly those held responsible for the shooting of would-be escapees, were put on trial.

The ways in which, as well as the extent to which, post-Communist countries looked back on their Communist past varied considerably. In Poland, nationalism had provided a certain amount of common ground between the Communist leadership and its opponents. In retrospect, General Jaruzelski's rule came to be seen as a period of nationalist military rule rather than Communist repression. This contributed to the comparative serenity with which Poles recalled their history: in 1997 a round table brought together participants from both the Communist Party and Solidarity to discuss the period of martial law. In Hungary, the relative liberalism of the Communist rule during its final stages meant that some were able to look back on this period with a mixture of nostalgia and irony. Budapest had a museum of statues of Stalin and Marxist 'theme restaurants'. An album containing the 'greatest hits of real socialism' was issued so that the elderly could recall the songs they had sung in the Communist youth movement. Nostalgia of this kind would have been inconceivable in Romania or East Germany.

In Czechoslovakia, matters were complicated by the different memories that existed in Prague and in Bratislava. The Czechs remembered the period of 'normalisation' that followed the repression of the Prague Spring (itself a mainly Czech experience) as a period of extreme intolerance. In Slovakia, memories of Communist rule were rather different. The Slovaks looked back on 'normalisation' as a time of rising prosperity when their part of the country was given a greater degree of autonomy. Czechs were shocked by the fact that many Slovak dignitaries attended the funeral of Gustav Husak, the former Communist leader, in 1991 (Prihoda 1995: 137).

Russians had the strangest attitude of all to their recent past. The Communist period was recalled as one of stability and national pride that sometimes contrasted favourably with the painful confusion that came after, or at the end of, Communist rule. One survey in the late 1990s asked under which ruler life was/is good. The results were as follows:

TABLE 2.1 Survey on Russians' Quality of Life in the Late 1990s

Ruler	Approval Rating
Leonid Brezhnev	41%
Boris Yeltsin	14%
Yuri Andropov	7%
Tsar Nicholas II	6%
Josef Stalin	6%
Nikita Kruschev	4%
Mikhail Gorbachev	3%
Vladimir Lenin	1%
Do not know	17%

Source: VTs/IOM cited in 'Russia's Part-Time President', *The Economist*, 14–20 February 1998.

These statistics reveal disenchantment with official Communist historiography. This is reflected in the low score of Lenin (whose cult had been the basis of all Soviet culture for 70 years), the comparatively high score of the last tsar (who had been killed on Lenin's order) and the equally high score of Stalin (who had been treated as an embarrassment by official Soviet spokesmen since 1956). They also reveal disenchantment with post-Communist leaders and Communist reformers who distinguished Russia from the West and from the former Communist states of Eastern Europe. Brezhnev's association with the defence of Soviet power, which contributed to his popularity in Russia, made him hated elsewhere: the campaign in favour of Czech membership in NATO distributed posters showing Brezhnev's photograph. By contrast Gorbachev, who was still widely admired elsewhere, was very unpopular in Russia.

The general divergence between attitudes to the past in Eastern and Western Europe after 1989 was most marked with regard to the Second World War and the right-wing authoritarian regimes of the inter-war period. In the former Communist countries, war had laid the basis for Communist rule, and a certain view of the war continued to provide a justification for that rule. Challenging Communism or Soviet power meant challenging a certain vision of the war, and this in turn sometimes meant rehabilitating the very right-wing regimes that were most denounced in Western Europe.

This process occurred under many different guises. In Romania, historians underwrote the diplomatic independence of their country by emphasising the actions of local partisans rather than those of the Red Army. In Bratislava, historians from the 1960s onwards began to explore the role of the Slovak uprising of 1944, which conflicted with orthodoxies that emphasised both the Red Army and the Czech resistance. In Belgrade, Veselin Djuretic published a book in 1985 that questioned the Titoist monopoly on anti-German resistance (Rupnik 1993: 114).

The fall of Communism speeded up such reassessments. This was most dramatic in Poland, the country mauled at the hands of both Hitler and Stalin during the war. Official recognition that the Katyn massacre of Polish officers had been carried out by Soviet, not German, forces came in March 1989. Most important of all was the rehabilitation of the non-Communist resistance in Poland, which had been condemned to exile or repression during Communist rule. In December 1990, this group secured the recognition of the newly elected president of Poland, Lech Walesa, who insisted on taking office from them and not from the outgoing Communist leader (Rothschild 1993: 234).

Public debate in Western Europe often emphasised a 'duty of memory' that involved denouncing those right-wing authoritarian regimes that had worked under the aegis of – and had collaborated with – Nazi Germany. Public debate in post-Communist Europe, by contrast, sometimes involved a partial rehabilitation of such regimes. Two states in post-Communist Europe – Slovakia and Croatia – had previously existed only under the aegis of the Nazis. In both countries, some nationalists recalled the wartime regime with nostalgia. A plaque to Josef Tiso, the wartime prime minister of Slovakia, was unveiled in July 1990 (Glenny 1993: 137). In Slovakia, school textbooks in the late 1990s stressed the 'humane' character of Slovak concentration camps (Plichta 1997). Memories of the Second World War became associated with the violent disintegration of Yugoslavia. Serbs demanded compensation for Croat wartime atrocities and used the memory of this brutality to justify further bouts of racial attacks (Glenny 1993: 138). In Hungary, the attempt to resurrect a pre-Communist national identity led back to the dictatorship of Admiral Miklos Horthy, whose rule had included a period of alliance with Hitler and Hungarian participation in the extermination of Jews. Horthy's ashes were brought back to Hungary in 1993.

Reassessment of the Second World War was the most extreme in Romania. Parallels were often drawn between the crimes of Nazism and those committed during the 'Red holocaust'. Many members of the Romanian political establishment found it convenient to rehabilitate those who had committed crimes during the Nazi period rather than punish those who had committed crimes under Communism. In 1991, the Romanian parliament observed a minute's silence in memory of Ion Antonescu, the right-wing dictator who had been allied with Nazi Germany. The Romanian chief prosecutor called for the posthumous pardoning of eight of Antonescu's ministers (Ioanid and Laignel-Lavastine 1998).

Sometimes the fall of Communism was connected with renewed anti-Semitism, something which attracted the most attention in Poland. Here the whole history of Jewish-Gentile relations diverged sharply from that seen in the West. The Jewish community, which had been large in 1939, was small in 1945 and was diminished even more by the exit of Jews to Palestine. In the late 1960s, the Jewish population was further reduced by emigration to Israel in the face of state-sponsored anti-Semitism. Poland did not participate in the new interest in Jewish suffering that marked Western European countries during the early 1970s. The contrast with France, where the Jewish population had increased in the aftermath of the Algerian war, was especially marked. Poland was influenced both by anti-Communist anti-Semitism, exacerbated by the fact that many leaders of the Communist Party during the early years of its rule had been Jews, and by Communist anti-Semitism, which was tied in with the breech between Communist states and Israel and by the efforts of the party to construct a popular nationalist basis of support. Polish anti-Semitism became widely known as a result of arguments about the location of a Carmelite convent in Auschwitz.

History a Family Affair?

The recent past has always been, in one sense, a family matter. Much of what people know about that past has traditionally been imparted by their own relatives. Two things were special about the late twentieth century, however. First, rapid social and economic change after 1945 meant that inter-generational relations changed. French historian Fernand Braudel, raised by his peasant grandmother in the early twentieth century, suggested that the conservatism of peasant societies came from the fact that children were so often looked after by grandparents while their parents worked in the fields. After 1945, fewer children in Western Europe were looked after by their grandparents (although, curiously, it may have increased in Communist countries). A child whose father had migrated to find work in the Belgian coalfields might not even speak the same language as his Sicilian grandmother. At the same time, the idea of generational conflict became increasingly projected onto the public sphere (particularly during the student protests of 1968) and was often likely to involve reference to past political conflict. Students in Germany were particularly prone to reproach their parents for what they had supposedly done under Nazism.

In spite of all this, certain kinds of history continued to be discussed primarily in the family. This was true, for example, of the French army's experience in Algeria, and particularly the extent to which it had used torture. After the French departure from Algeria in 1962, this matter was rarely discussed in public. Gillo Pontecorvo's 1966 film, *The Battle of Algiers*, was banned for many years; Pierre Vidal-Naquet's book, *Torture: Cancer of Democracy*, had to be published in English because at first no French publisher was interested in it. However, when history teachers began to address the issue during the 1990s, they found that most French people did know about the army's use of torture and that many of them had found out about it from a close relative, presumably a father, uncle or brother who had served in Algeria (Coulon 1993). Significantly, the first popular film to deal with the Algerian war was Gérard Mordillat's *Cher Frangin* (Dear Brother) in 1989.

The passing down of memory in families was particularly important in the Communist states, where discussion outside the family was strictly controlled. In the summer of 1968, the Hungarian-born journalist Paul Neuburg interviewed a group of Czech workers. All had been born after 1945, but all expressed enthusiasm for the first Czech Republic, which had ended in 1939. When Neuburg (1972: 133) asked them how they knew about this era, which had been expunged from official memory, they replied simply: '[W]e have parents.' Sometimes family memories intersected with the more formal recollection of academia and the law courts. Consider, for example, two key figures in the trial of Maurice Papon in 1998: Arno Klarsfeld, one of the lawyers representing the *parties civiles*, and Jean-Pierre Azéma, a professor of history at the Institut d'Etudes Politiques who had been called as an expert witness. Both men were highly trained specialists but both were also obviously influenced by personal experience. Klarsfeld's father was a Jew whose parents had been deported, and his mother was the daughter of an SS officer. Azéma's father had been sentenced to death in absentia for collaboration in 1945.

The recollection of historical events in families was also closely linked to changing relations between the sexes. History has, until recently, been seen as the province of men. Male politicians and soldiers were the historical actors, and male historians were the historical narrators. Sometimes the division between fact and fiction was seen as a division between men and women. Leslie Stephen, who produced Great Britain's first *Dictionary of National Biography*, was the quintessential master of fact; his daughter, the novelist Virginia Woolf, was the quintessential exponent of a subjective view of the world.

Some obvious changes affected this neat division of labour in the last part of the twentieth century. Women were recruited to the historical profession in large numbers and acquired positions of power (or at least prestige) within it: Joan Scott and Joyce Appleby, both historians of France, were two recent presidents of the American Historical Association. Notions of what constituted legitimate history changed so that the focus on the primarily male leaders in political and military affairs diminished. The difference between history and literature, which had seemed so clear and so significant in the nineteenth century, began to blur as historians moved from the search for facts about events to the search for myths and memories.

The changing balance of power between the sexes also had an impact on a more intimate level. The recounting of certain experiences that were often seen as quintessentially male (violence or revolutionary activism) ceased to be a monologue in which men addressed passive and admiring women; instead, it became a dialogue in which women questioned, challenged and pressed for new revelations. Two recent and interesting publications – French journalist Olivier Rolin's (2002) autobiographical novel, *Tigre en papier*, and Italian philosopher Antonio Negri's (2002) collection of autobiographical interviews, *Du retour* – illustrate different ways in which the recollection of history was influenced by relations between the sexes. Both Negri and Rolin had been Maoists linked to underground revolutionary action in the early 1970s. Both men recounted their experiences to a younger women: Negri was interviewed by the French philosopher Anne Dufourmantelle, while the hero of Rolin's novel recounts his experiences to the daughter of 'Treize', his dead comrade-in-arms. However, the two pasts are described in very different ways. Negri's interviewer is respectful and allows him to present his story as that of a great revolutionary project. Rolin, born 14 years after Negri, gives his hero a very irreverent female interlocutor, who continually forces his hero into admitting the absurdity of his revolutionary career.

Recollection of the French role in the Algerian war illustrates how historical memory was intertwined with changing relations between the sexes. In the 1960s, writers on the Algerian war had stressed the strongly masculine character of the French army. War had been associated with virility, seduction and promiscuity. The return of the Algerian war to the centre of French public discussion was linked to a new assertiveness on the part of women. The historians and journalists who did the most to resurrect the subject – Florence Beaugé,[5] Raphaëlle Branche (2001), Claire Mauss-Copeaux (1998) – were all women. Their research often took the form of interviewing veterans, and these interviews, in which young, determined, articulate women confronted old, confused, guilty men, illustrate perfectly the way in which oral history some-times moves power from the historical actor to the historian.

More importantly, men's recollections (or at least the manner in which they expressed those recollections) were often influenced by the women in their own household. Mauss-Copeaux interviewed many veterans with their wives, and it was often the wives who pushed the men to talk about their participation in torture during the war. General Jacques Massu, who later apologised for his actions during the war, seemed to have come to terms with his actions largely through the mediation of his second wife. Hélie St Marc, who also recalled his role in Algeria with certain serenity, dedicated his autobiography to his wife and three daughters. By contrast, General Aussaresses, who boasted of his activities as a torturer and murderer, admitted that he had never been able to talk about his actions with his three daughters and that his wife had warned him that he would be 'shot in the street' if he published his account. One of his daughters subsequently wrote to the newspaper *Le Monde*, asking readers to remember that her father was a 'very diminished man' and that his account could not be trusted.

European History Recalled outside Europe

The Algerian war raises another important aspect of the ways in which Europe related to its past. For the French, recollection of the Algerian war (the French state finally recognised the conflict as a 'war' in 1999) crystallised around certain precise dates. The war was seen to have a clear beginning (the Algerian attacks on European settlers on 1 November 1954) and a clear end (the cease-fire of 20 March 1962). Algerians, by contrast, saw the conflict as something much more open-ended. For them it began with the Sétif massacres of 8 May 1945 (a date with a very different significance on the European mainland) and ended not with the ceasefire (which many nationalist fighters regarded as a betrayal) but with final French withdrawal. Furthermore, French official agencies spent 27 years denying that the conflict had been a war at all, while Algerian agencies always presented it as such. French memory after 1962 concentrated increasingly on the French army's use of torture, a subject that official circles in Algeria (mindful of allegations about the Algerian army's behaviour in the 1990s) were not keen to evoke.

More generally, the past of the European imperial powers intersected with those of the colonised countries in complicated ways. The contributions that the colonial forces made to British and French efforts in the two world wars was recognised rather grudgingly both by the imperial governments (reluctant to say anything that might imply obligation to those who had fought on their behalf) and by the governments of newly independent countries (reluctant to celebrate men who had fought for what they saw as a foreign power). Anniversaries were celebrated in uneven ways: the left-wing municipal government of London in the 1980s was keen to celebrate the anniversary of Indian independence but appeared to forget that the same day was also the anniversary of the creation of Pakistan (a pro-American and authoritarian country). Most of all, it must be remembered that substantial groups of people who lived in Europe from the 1960s onwards came from outside its frontiers – largely, from what had been the British and French empires. For many of these people, references to the commemoration of national history meant very little. Indeed, those who grew up in the anarchic schools of the Paris *banlieue* in the 1980s probably found French history more alien than their grandfathers (who had learned about 'our ancestors the Gauls' in the schools of the empire of the Third Republic) would have done. A group of North African football supporters notoriously enraged the president of the Republic in 2002 by booing that supreme French historical symbol, 'La Marseillaise'.

It was not just the former colonies whose histories intersected with those of Europe. Certain kinds of Americans looked to certain kinds of Europeans as the incarnation of the values they admired. Winston Churchill, who had an American mother, was certainly more celebrated in the United States than in his homeland (Ramsden 2002). The migration of Europeans to America meant that certain kinds of European national identity were cultivated outside of Europe. Italian and Irish migrants had a huge influence on the public perceptions of European history in the United States. Central European Jews had taken a particular conception of European history to both America and Israel. Indeed, the extermination of the European Jews eventually became central to the sense of Jewish identity in both countries, and was probably evoked more often there than in any of the European countries where the murders had been carried out (Novick 1999).

The United States came to play a particularly important role in mediating Europe's relationship to its past because there was a shift of power in the historical profession across the Atlantic during the late twentieth century. American universities were bigger and richer than their European counterparts. The flight of European Jews from Nazism in the 1930s meant that a generation of historians who had been born in Europe (Felix Gilbert, Raul Hilberg, Eugen Weber) or were the children of Europeans (Charles Maier, Daniel Jonah Goldhagen) gave new energy to the study of European history in the United States. The prestige of American universities drew the most talented and ambitious European historians to spend at least part of their time in the United States. Thus, Stanley Hoffman (a refugee from Nazi Austria who had been educated in France) co-founded the Harvard Center for European Studies in 1968. Hoffmann subsequently subscribed to the work of the American historian Robert Paxton, which revolutionised the French approach to the Vichy period. By the 1980s, Harvard had become so important that even the major francophone historians of Vichy (Henry Rousso and Philippe Burrin) spent long periods there. Rousso was not being entirely flippant when he remarked (in Robert Paxton's festschrift) 'we are all American historians' (Rousso 2000).

Notes

1. For a briskly sceptical view of Anglo-American neurosis about recent developments in historiography, see Noiriel (1996).
2. Nora (1984–91) returns to de Gaulle several times in *Les lieux de mémoire*, particularly in his essay on statesmen's memoirs.
3. On the role of *énarques* (graduates of the ENA) in the composition of de Gaulle's memoirs, see Blanc (1990).
4. For the interest in 'great historians' of the nineteenth century, see Nora (1984–91). See also Steedman (2001) and Grafton (1997).
5. Journalist Florence Beaugé is the special correspondent of *Le Monde* who conducted the notorious interview in which General Aussaresses admitted to having tortured and murdered Algerian prisoners.

References

Annan, N. 1990. *Our Age: The Generation That Made Post-War Britain*. New York: Random House.

Arendt, H. 1963. *Eichmann in Jerusalem: A Report on the Banality of Evil*. London: Faber.

Blanc, P. 1990. *De Gaulle au soir de sa vie*. Paris: Fayard.

Branche, R. 2001. *La torture et l'armée pendant la guerre d'Algérie, 1954–1962*. Paris: Gallimard.

Châtelot, C. 1997. 'Une page d'histoire qui doit être lue avant d'être tournée'. *Le Monde*, 27 October.

Cordier, D. 1989–9. *Jean Moulin: L'inconnu du Panthéon*. 4 vols. Paris: J.-C. Lattès.

Coulon, A. 1993. *Connaissance de la guerre d'Algérie. Trente ans après: Enquête auprès des jeunes de France de 17 à 30 ans*. Paris: Laboratoire de Recherche Ethno-méthodologique Université de Paris.

Debray, R. 1990. *A demain de Gaulle*. Paris: Gallimard.

De Gaulle, C. 1989–99. *Capitale de la Résistance, Novembre 1940–Décembre 1941* and *La République des Catacombes*. Paris: First three volumes published by J.-C. Lattès, 1989–93. Fourth volume published by Gallimard, 1999.

Dupláa, C. 2000. 'Memoria colectiva y lieux de mémoire en la España de la Transición'. In *Disremembering the Dictatorship: The Politics of Memory in the Spanish Transition to Democracy*, ed. J. Ramon Resina, 29–42. Amsterdam: Rodophi.

Evans, R. 2000. *In Defence of History*. Cambridge: Granta.

_____. 2002. *Telling Lies about Hitler: The Holocaust, History and the David Irving Trial*. London: Verso.

Funk, N. and Mueller, M., eds. 1993. *Gender, Politics and Post-Communism: Reflections from Eastern Europe and the Former Soviet Union*. London: Routledge.

Glenny, M. 1993. *The Rebirth of History: Eastern Europe in the Age of Democracy*. London: Penguin.

Goubert, P. 1996. *Un parcours d'historien: Souvenirs 1915–1995*. Paris: Librairie Arthème Fayard.

Grafton, A. 1997. *The Footnote*. Cambridge, MA: Harvard University Press.

Heseltine, M. 2000. *Life in the Jungle: My Autobiography*. London: Hodder and Stoughton.

Hobsbawm, E. 2002. *Interesting Times: A Twentieth-Century Life*. London: Penguin.

Ioanid, R. and Laignel-Lavastine, A. 1998. 'Nouvel accès révisionniste en Roumanie'. *Le Monde*, 27 January.

Jackson, J. 1994. 'De Gaulle and May 1968'. In *De Gaulle and the Twentieth Century*, ed. H. Gough and J. Horne, 125–46. London: Edward Arnold.

Kriegel, A. 1991. *Ce que j'ai cru comprendre*. Paris: Robert Laffont.

Le Goff, J.-P. 1996. *Une vie pour l'histoire: Entretiens avec Marc Heugeon*. Paris: La Découverte.

_____. 1998. *Mai 68: L'héritage impossible*. Paris: La Découverte.

Le Roy Ladurie, E. 1982. *Paris-Montpellier: PC–PSU*. Paris: Gallimard.

Lieven, A. 1998. 'Revealing Romania's Shameful Past'. *Financial Times*, 2 January.

Mauss-Copeaux, C. 1998. *Appelés en Algérie: La parole confisquée*. Paris: Hachette.

Negri, A. 2002. *Du retour, abécédaire biopolitique: Entretiens avec Anne Dufourmantelle*. Paris: Calmann-Lévy.

Neuburg, P. 1972. *The Hero's Children: The Post-War Generation in Eastern Europe*. London: Constable.

Noiriel, G. 1996. *Sur la 'crise' de l'histoire*. Paris: Belin.

Nora, P., ed. 1984–91. *Les lieux de mémoire*. 7 vols. Paris: Gallimard.

_____, ed. 1987. *Essais d'ego-histoire*. Paris: Gallimard.

Novick, P. 1999. *The Holocaust in American Life*. New York: Houghton Mifflin.

Passerini, L. 1987. *Fascism in Popular Memory: The Cultural Experience of the Turin Working Class*. Trans. R. Lumley and J. Bloomfield. Cambridge: Cambridge University Press.

_____. 1996. *Autobiography of a Generation: Italy, 1968*. Trans. Lisa Erdberg. Hanover, NH: University Press of New England.

Plichta, M. 1997. 'En Slovaquie, le révisionisme retourne sur les bancs de l'école'. *Le Monde,* 10 May.

Prihoda, P. 1995. 'Mutual Perceptions in Czech-Slovak Relationships'. In *The End of Czechoslovakia*, ed. J. Musil, 128–38. Budapest: Central European University Press.

Ramsden, J. 2002. *Man of the Century: Winston Churchill and His Legend since 1945.* London: HarperCollins.

Ridley, N. 1991. *My Style of Government: The Thatcher Years*. London: Hutchinson.

Rolin, O. 2002. *Tigre en papier*. Paris: Seuil.

Rothschild, J. 1993. *Return to Diversity: A Political History of East Central Europe since World War II*. Oxford: Oxford University Press.

Rousso, H. 1987. *Le syndrome de Vichy de 1944 à nos jours*. Paris: Seuil.

_____. 2000. "The Historian, a Site of Memory." In *France at War: Vichy and the Historians*, ed. Sarah Fishman, Laura Lee Downs, Ioannis Sinanoglu, Leonard V. Smith and Robert Zaretsky, 283–302. Oxford: Berg.

Rousso, H. and Conan, E. 1994. *Vichy, un passé qui ne passe pas*. Paris: Gallimard.

Rupnik, J. 1993. *L'autre Europe: Crise et fin du communisme*. Paris: Odile Jacob.

Samuel, R., ed. 1989. *Patriotism: The Making and Unmaking of British National Identity*. London: Routledge.

Sellar, W. and Yeatman, R. 1930. *1066 and All That*. London: Methuen.

Steedman, C. 2001. *Dust*. Manchester: Manchester University Press.

Taylor, A. J. P. 1983. *A Personal History*. New York: Atheneum.

Toranska, T. 1987. *Oni: Stalin's Polish Puppets*. Collins: Havrill.

Wieviorka, O. 1994. *Nous entrerons dans la carrière: De la Résistance à l'exercice du pouvoir*. Paris: Seuil.

Chapter 3

THE POLITICAL STRUCTURING OF CULTURAL IDENTITIES IN THE EUROPEAN UNION

Marion Demossier

> Our dependencies are now truly global; our actions however are still local.
> (Bauman 2001: 127)

Today, Europe offers a challenging and complex terrain for any study of concepts such as politics, identity and culture.[1] Yet despite its great potential as a field of research, there have been few serious attempts to investigate it from an interdisciplinary perspective.[2] If we consider the academic works on European integration produced over the last 30 years, it is clear that each discipline has been content to conduct its debates within the limits of its own boundaries. It is, for example, very rare to see political scientists treading on the dangerous ground of the social scientists, and the opposite is also true for social and cultural scientists, as 'cultural contributions to political analysis are relatively rare and far less developed' (Ross 2000: 40).

It is also clear that, in general, the issue of culture has been treated as secondary to any discussion of the process of European integration, and it is not a subject that has been addressed by the majority of scholars. Instead, they have given priority to economic, institutional and political integration, and have neglected or even dismissed the relevance of a 'people's Europe'. The European population has been envisaged as a group of voters and/or consumers who will adapt to the new political and economic space offered to them, and as such, they have been largely underestimated as a group of citizens.

Yet concepts of culture and identity have become politically charged, shifting significantly from the discourse of 'identity politics' that helped to define

---

Notes for this chapter are located on page 64.

the 1970s towards a discourse of 'fragmented identities' that is symbolic of the 1990s. Thus, questions of identities (in the plural) have recently mushroomed at the national level, and there has been a growing interest in national, regional and local issues that tend to emerge as a counter-reaction to wider economic, social and cultural processes attached to globalisation and Europeanisation (Borneman and Fowler 1997). Such diverse groups as Muslims in France or the English residents of North East London, for instance, have proclaimed their right to a specific identity in cultural, economic and social terms. In this context, culture has come to the fore as a political tool,[3] and its definition has become problematic. It might be said that nowadays everything has become a matter of culture,[4] from the issue of the veil in Republican France to the proclaimed differential treatment of English residents in deprived areas of London. While culture has become part of everyday discourse, it has also started to lose its original meanings.

Identity and culture have also become an important part of the ideological battlefield between supporters and opponents of the European project. In this conflict, various groups have tried to dominate the political arena, especially the pro-European political elites based in Brussels and Strasbourg, political leaders in the main core nations and the advocates of various forms of Euro-scepticism. From 'we are true Europeans' to 'we will never be Europeans', a wide range of discourses, meanings, symbols and representations confront the actual reality – if there is one – of being a European. The political realm is no longer constituted simply around ideological or political cleavages that have been orchestrated and operationalised by political parties and institutions; rather, it has acquired a cultural and social content which challenges the very project of European integration. This debate leaves few people impartial, and almost everybody has something to say about it. Problems of definition, schools of thought, political engagement, ideologies and legitimatisation have complicated this new political process and are likely to continue to do so.[5] The place and definition of culture in the European political project is by the same token under debate. At a European level, several attempts have been made by the European Union to foster a political allegiance in relation to this new transnational political space. For example, the European Union has, over the years, put increasing emphasis on the cultural construction of the mythical figure of the European (Shore 2000) through a range of cultural policies, but it has largely failed in its attempt to construct a shared sense of Europeanness.

Nonetheless, while a generally recognised sense of European identity remains elusive, Europeanisation has created new sets of cultural identities or at least has enabled the expression of new collective identities, be they political or social in nature. At the national level, from the Northern League in Italy to the fight for Corsican independence in France, identity and culture have been repackaged by groups and political actors as part of their strategies of empowerment in the new space offered by the European political arena (see Peter Wagstaff's chapter on regional identities in this volume). Moreover, at the local level, the often drastic economic changes that have accompanied the end of the industrial era have threatened many traditional communities with the loss of their livelihood and even their existence. These communities have tried to redefine their identity by embracing new cultural opportunities – very often emanating from European institutions – such as heritage, local development or cultural uniqueness.[6] The fragmentation of identities and the quest for difference and cultural uniqueness have become part of the process of defining Europeans and the 'Other' in the European sphere. Culture has come to the fore in this process. However, what is meant by culture varies greatly from one situation to another.

In his analysis of comparative national politics, Ross (2000: 40) has argued that culture is the basis of social and political identity that affects how people line up and act on a wide range of matters. Culture is a framework for organising the world, for locating the self and others in it, for making sense of actions and interpreting the motives of others, for grounding an analysis of interest, for linking collective identities to political action and for motivating people and groups towards some actions and away from others. The relationship between culture, identity and politics therefore offers a fruitful way to examine the effects of attempts to create a transnational or multicultural sense of belonging to shared institutions and to foster it at a European level. The formation of a new Europe challenges many of our cultural constructions by raising questions about the nature of our societies and their cultural uniqueness. Yet cultural divides tell us a lot about the current and shifting meanings of culture in the context of a new political sphere.

This chapter aims to shed some new light on the various debates at the core of the process of European integration and the rise of a so-called European identity. By examining the various aspects of the dynamics of this new political construction and the areas where it creates tensions and uncertainties, this chapter suggests that the only clear way forward for Europe is to propose a new political arena in which active citizenship and engaged political activity at both the European and national levels will complement each other. By combining both levels of allegiance, Europe could offer a possible space to express specific interests that are no longer addressed by the nation. It could also be argued that with the emergence of a European identity, we are in a transitional or formative phase of political identity, and in this respect any attempt to define it is going to fail. The time is ripe for a review.

Debates over European Identity

Since the 1990s, psychologists,[7] anthropologists,[8] sociologists,[9] political scientists[10] and cultural theorists have all contributed to the dialogue on European identity and have offered different scenarios of its possible future development. The debate has opened the door on a European level to issues such as citizenship, multiculturalism and national identity that were already being debated at the national level. At the end of the day, it could be argued that European identity can have a viable future only if it refers to a political process which takes into account cultural diversity and social issues that are at the core of Europe. Its cultural content is largely shaped by – and at the same time shapes – the current political transformations of the Union. The background of the economic and political changes that have shaped the European project plays a major role in determining cultural identities at both the European and national levels. The issue of 'interpenetration' between national, regional and local sentiments is also crucial, especially the idea that the local can fill a dual void between the weakness of national identity and the haziness of European identity.[11]

The majority of political scientists have been concerned with studying the process of European integration from an institutional perspective and have assumed that it will either replicate or produce a hybrid form of the nation-state. There has been much discussion about the possible future shape it could adopt, with references to, for example, the German federal model or a United States of Europe. Political scientists have therefore tended to consider the question of European identity as part of the process of European integration and to do so from a political and historical perspective. One of the weaknesses of this approach, which concentrates almost exclusively upon a functional or institutional type of allegiance, is that it neglects the mass of the population that will form the basis of the new European polity. The cultural dimension is also overlooked, with the citizen frequently presented as a peripheral or passive actor in the construction of the European state at a time when individual identities have come to the fore.

More recently, sociologists have joined the debate about European integration and have placed an emphasis upon the relationship between society, identity and politics. Issues such as multiculturalism and social fragmentation have been examined in the context of a postmodern state. Since the 1970s, claims for new cultural identities have proliferated from women, gays, and ethnic and regional movements, and their content has become politicised as these groups have adapted and initiated political change. A complex process of negotiation between the social groups composing each nation and the political class has taken place within the political sphere. In short, they have acted as 'motive forces' of history (Macdonald 1993: 7). For sociologists, these identities that are no longer determined by national, economic, social or family ties are being examined and redefined, as individuals, cities, regions and states come to terms with the dynamics of the 'new Europe' (Laffan 1996: 83). In their description of European societies, the individual is a free agent responsible for his or her actions. However, in their studies of European integration, sociologists have tended to downplay the importance of political constraints and historical factors, emphasising the role of the actor as a consumer.

A third area of inquiry into the nature and importance of a European identity is provided by the work of social anthropologists. They have been at the forefront in investigating issues such as Europeanisation, the cultural construction of citizenship and the various cultural representations attached to the project of European integration. What is particularly innovative about this approach to European identity is that it aims to address the link between politics and culture.[12] Most of the research conducted in this field seeks to understand to what extent Europe could become a new political object by examining the representations and practices associated with the movement of European integration and the various groups at the core of the process. It also underlines the tensions in the making of Europe, which could provide areas where culture and politics interact. The main interest of this approach is that it addresses the question of Europe from the perspective of the individual and places culture at the centre of the discussion.

European Identity and Europeanisation

Before going further, it is necessary to distinguish European identity from Europeanisation. The concept of a European identity can be easily dismissed as an elusive and contradictory creature; it can even be regarded as utopian. However, European identity can also be defined as a political tool operationalised by various policies, decrees and programmes created by European institutions with the aim of developing a new sense of collective and political identity among the peoples of Europe (with a strict definition of belonging to a new political space, i.e. the European Union). It could also be defined as a new, hybrid form of transnational and cultural identity that is evolving progressively and might become the platform for future political allegiance. At this stage, only a minority of people – the elites, national expatriates within Europe and students educated in a European context – would belong to this category. However, with regard to the development of a European identity, we are referring to at least two things: the development of a sense of belonging to Europe (with difficulties concerning its definition) and the development of a collective sense of what it means to be European (Medrano and Gutierrez 2001).

When dealing with this idea of constructing European identity, traditional values of national belonging to a political 'imagined community' clash with the postmodern character of our societies. By necessity, any attempt to discuss what is meant by European identity requires us to take into account traditional and contemporary ways of self-identification, such as national or local sense of belonging. It is also necessary to consider the effects of economic transition, which are experienced at different speeds by various European countries and by the diverse social groups within them. To be British or to be French is to be conscious of different historical, cultural, economic and political processes in which the concept 'European' has become increasingly relevant and also problematic, as national and political contexts shape the nature of the debate. For several commentators, such as Jean Baudrillard, European identity can be perceived when desired and wanted, as was the case in parts of Eastern Europe before 1989 or in Turkey today, whereas Western Europeans have heretofore evinced little interest. Indeed, it could be argued that in Western Europe the desire to become European varies greatly from one country to the next and from one social group or generation to another.

Europeanisation, on the other hand, defined by Borneman and Fowler (1997: 488) as an accelerated process and a set of effects that are redefining forms of identification with territory and people, has challenged traditional cultural concepts and has given rise to a new type of participation in which identity is manifested actively through individual identification and consumption of specific products. For Bauman (2001: 129), instead of talking about inherited or acquired identities, it would be more in keeping with the realities of the globalising world to speak of identification as a never-ending, always incomplete and open-ended activity in which we are all, by necessity or choice, engaged. If this process has indeed taken place in modern European societies, it has not affected people in the same way. Factors such as the rural-urban divide, class, ethnicity, political affiliation, generational cultures, lifestyles and nationality help to explain the wide variations in the way in which culture is perceived and experienced. Farmers in France and British academics have radically different ways of defining Europe and of thinking about their own identity. These aspects need to be taken into consideration when discussing the future of European identity and of Europe as a new political space. Only by addressing this diversity can the new political entity have a future.

European Identity: A Complex Cultural Concept with a Political Content

In the debate over the political structuring of cultural identities, European identity can be defined from either an external or internal point of view. For Lars-Erik Cederman (2001: 3), the external dimension is defined by boundaries that emerge out of specific interactions with the European Union's external environment. Inclusionary and exclusionary mechanisms regulate these interactions and provide a trade-off for the construction of an external European identity. For instance, several speeches delivered by Jean Monnet, one of the founding fathers of the European project, defined Europe in relation to American and international global forces. It is clear that since its inception, the European Union has been envisaged as a new political order that was designed, in part, to counterbalance the global economic and military dominance of the United States and, until 1989, the Soviet Union.

Recent political processes, such as the introduction of the euro and the enlargement of the European Union to 27 members, have challenged the Union's traditional boundaries and have confirmed the exceptional transnational character of this new political object. These new partners have different conceptions of politics and culture, of the nation and of their place in a new global order. The notion of boundaries is central to the process of identity building. As recent events have shown, even this external dimension appears as fluid, divided and negotiated by the various partners. 'Old' and 'new Europe' are categories, for example, which have been invented in the international arena to make sense of the diversity of positions adopted by European Union members in relation to the Iraq war. If these three factors play a major role in the definition of European identity as a concept defined by external forces, the internal dimension of European identity remains more difficult to grasp. The tribal nature of European societies has also been evoked to describe the challenging nature of the composite nations of Europe. It refers to a more complex process which we need to analyse further, as it is defined partly by its external dimension and partly by its internal dynamics. To sum up, the concept of European identity is arguably very flexible and changing, but what defines its core is mainly the 'Other' and the context in which Europe takes shape and defines itself.

For progress to be made in analysing and defining a European identity, the debate has to go beyond the external-internal dimension. Since the Maastricht Treaty and the various referenda threatening its legitimacy, the question of the emergence of a European identity has come to the fore and has been seized upon by a European political elite anxious to legitimise its actions before an increasingly critical public. Institutions such as the European Union as an economic, cultural and social space have given prominence to issues of convergence, but at the same time to issues of divergence and differentiation. Several processes have been part of the changes accompanying the creation and development of this newborn political community and its imaginary realm.

Bo Stråth (2002) has argued that European identity can be defined by the construction of multiple identities confronting each other and intersecting with national or other levels. Any definition of identity has to take into account the various levels at which such ideas of self-identification function, be they local, national or transnational. According to Ifversen (2002), when the geometry of identification is examined, it can be seen either as a larger container encapsulating other forms of identity or as an alternative type of identity because of the possible exclusion of national identity. At the core of European identity remains the question of European culture as the 'cultural raw material', and the content given to it illustrates the extent to which politics is about the control of culture.

From the European Project to European Uncertainties

The historical background to the European Union is vital for an understanding of how groups are socially constructed through social institutions and the everyday practices that shape the sense of belonging to a political community. When summarising the ideas behind the evolution of the European Union, it is important to keep in mind that it has become a complex political entity defined by a set of treaties, laws and institutions which have altered the political, economic, social and cultural landscape of Western Europe.[13] If the idea of Europe has prevailed for many centuries and has itself been the subject of intense disputes,[14] the concept of a European political entity is more recent, dating back institutionally to 1952 with the European Coal and Steel Community, which provided the impetus for the European Economic Community in 1958. The post-war economic reconstruction was accompanied by the understandable desire to combat German nationalism, and it was quickly followed by the need for security in the context of the Cold War. These factors supplied the background to the European project, and during this period, the external dimension of European identity was largely secured by the notion of the West. Yet if it is clear that the European project was, in many ways, a product of the Cold War, created in part by the integrative stimulus of the Marshall Plan and hatched under the military wings of the United States and NATO, that is not the whole story. It has also been a voluntarist and collective project based on the power of ideas generated by a handful of politicians and intellectuals in Europe, mainly from France, Italy and Germany, who have argued in favour of unity and federalism.

However, at the institutional level, other values have been at the core of the political model. According to Laffan (1996: 81), 'the Union has moved from issues of instrumental problem-solving to fundamental questions about its nature as a part-formed polity', and in this context, the question of its identity has surfaced. Several anthropologists, among them Maryon McDonald (1996), have argued that the European Commission was constructed upon the methods and strategy of the neo-functionalist Jean Monnet, and it is interesting that the culture of management, at least in some of the Directorate-Generals, has been portrayed as moving from a neo-functional to a more pragmatic Anglo-Saxon approach in recent years. Cris Shore (2000: 18), for example, has argued that until the 1980s, public support was not a high priority for European Union political elites and that the dirigiste approach of the period was influenced by traditional neo-functionalist theories of integration directly inspired by the bureaucratic and elitist French republican tradition. These elites assumed that political and social integration would follow automatically from economic integration, almost as a by-product of the measures required for building the European Economic Community and the single market.

Somewhat contradictorily, models of national identity building were thought to be the ideal tools to construct the new Europeans, and they have inspired a variety of initiatives including European Day,[15] which most people have never heard of, and the European flag and European anthem, which are still only partially recognised. The euro was also seen as the cornerstone of further political integration. It cannot be denied that the goal of 'ever-closer union' of the 'people's Europe' was already in the political background of the 1957 treaty. However, even if the European project was founded on possible further political and cultural integration, it was still the case that most of the political leaders of that time could not foresee its scope. A new generation has now taken over the leadership of the European movement and assumed responsibility for an increasingly complex and powerful political entity. However, some of the traditional and founding values of the European project are still at the core of the European Union. As Shore (2000) has demonstrated, nationalism is a subject which is largely avoided among European commissioners, who have a strong tendency to look forward rather than reflect on the past. Yet building Europe remains an authoritarian and elite-driven programme that has developed in relation to the changing political and economic context.

European Identity from the European Union's Perspective

The concept of European identity and the cultural content given to it have attracted growing interest amongst scholars, resulting in a proliferation of works on European culture and identity. The role of identity in European Union cultural policies has also become more important. However, these attempts to generate a European identity have been largely unsuccessful.[16] The Commission's approach has also been chiefly dominated by the views of policy makers and public relations companies. Despite a wide range of measures, people living in Europe do not think of themselves as Europeans and do not articulate a growing sense of belonging to Europe. For its most convinced proponents, Europe has been transformed into a new superpower which ensures a sense of stability and peace (excluding the violent episode of ex-Yugoslavia and the divisions over the Iraq question) and which has altered the way Europeans relate to each other. For those of a more sceptical persuasion, Europe has become a monstrous bureaucratic machine that is dominated by a corrupt, privileged class of politicians and is incapable of responding to the growing concerns of the majority of Europeans. These two extreme positions mark the limits of a broader debate over Europe and reflect the diversity of European public opinion.

Thus, one of the major obstacles to the construction of a European identity is the absence of a consensus amongst the political class, policy makers and experts about the nature, content and purpose of this new instrument of political identification. To illustrate the degree of confusion over – and the lack of a coherent vision of – European identity, it is interesting to look at the way that the various bodies of the European Union conceptualise it. According to Enrique Banús (2002: 164), the institutional discourse varies from the diversity of cultures in Europe to the idea of a single European culture: 'It is noteworthy that the highest level documents talk, as does Article 151 of the Treaty, about cultural cooperation on the Community level and about cultures, in the plural, although they are located within the framework of common European civilisation. But other documents do in fact talk about European culture.' The author cites the European Parliament, the Economic and Social Committee, the Committee of the Regions and the Commission, emphasising that representatives of the member states take great care not to talk about European 'culture' and instead use the 'politically correct' plural form. Drawing upon this lack of a unified conception of culture, the European Commission itself seems to accept that a cultural policy does not exist – or at least not in a sense that would be acceptable to the Council.

Since 1973, the European Commission has put in place various resources that have enabled the sharing of quantitative data within the European Union. As Shore has argued (2000: 31–2), these new Eurobarometer and Eurostat statistics, which were first used in the 1990s, are not only powerful instruments for creating a knowable, quantifiable and hence more tangible and governable 'European population' and 'European space'; they are also powerful moulders of consciousness that furnish the meta-classifications within which identities and subjectivities are formed. For the Commission, Eurobarometers are believed to be the most efficient way to measure the degree to which members of the European nation-states are increasingly identifying with Europe (ibid.). They have also become a useful instrument to test public support for European integration, and many texts at the national level refer to them.

For some theorists, measuring European identity through questionnaires is essentially an elusive process, since personal, educational and economic factors are likely to have an impact on attitudes towards European identity. However, it could be argued that it is, first and foremost, an instrumental approach to assessing European identity, and it could be said that support for European integration does not tell us a lot about the identity-related facets of support for the European Union (Duchesne and Frognier 1995: 202). There is no direct contradiction between declaring pride in one's nationality and considering oneself to have a European identity. Data spanning almost 30 years provide strong evidence of a general weakening of the strength of national identities in Europe, even though the level of national pride varies strongly from one country to another and this shift is not matched by one in favour of Europe (Dupoirier, Roy and Lecerf 2000: 51). Another important feature illustrated by the various studies of Eurobarometers is the fact that attachment to the locality, whether a village or a town, remains very strong. The 'return of the local' has been linked with anxieties about the rise of neo-liberalism and the inroads of multiculturalism (Gerson 2003: 541).

A Bottom-Up Process: European Identity in Perspective

Most of the works published on European integration have been dominated by 'the view from above' in which European identity is analysed as a possible supra-national type of allegiance requiring a unified and culturally homogeneous community of Europeans who will be actively involved in political participation at the European level. For Duchesne and Frognier (1995: 202), we are facing a vanguard phenomenon that views European identity as a new type of political allegiance which is emerging in the context of the decline of national identities. We therefore need to turn our attention to the definition of identity in the European context to find plausible scenarios concerning its likely future development. This view, drawn largely from the construction of national identity, poses the question of political institutionalisation and that of the existence of a civil society, both of which, it could be argued, are lacking on a European level. Moreover, for the advocates of this position, the main elements traditionally defining national identities (Laffan 1996: 81) – historic territory or homeland, shared myths and historical memories, a mass political culture, common legal rights and duties for all members, a unified economy with free movement of workers and capital – are still lacking. For Anthony Smith (1995: 128), for example, a genuine European identity cannot be achieved without a common set of myths and shared memories that are the basis for a durable collective identity. The nation-state, according to Smith, will continue to be the bedrock of world politics, and the nation provides the only realistic socio-cultural framework in today's world order. Scholars sharing a similar approach to the concept of European identity have raised the issue of the ambiguous relationship between national and European identity, which they have described as potentially problematic and necessarily exclusive.

At the core of the discussion lies the link between culture and politics and the theoretical position adopted by these scholars. Two broad schools of thought – essentialists and constructivists – dominate the debate on European identity. While the essentialist approach to identity formation is driven primarily by cultural background variables (Cederman 2001: 10) – also referred to as 'ethnic core', which is composed of roots, heritage, language and religion – the constructivists place more emphasis on politics seen as an active process of identity formation entailing the manipulation of cultural symbols. Their discussions refer to the wider debate concerning the question as to whether there is some biological or other deep 'essence' to any particular identity or whether identities are socially constructed. Corresponding to this broad classification, essentialist views dominate the conception of the nation-state as a territory defined by specific, stable borders and by a historical dimension which provides a collective, durable, homogeneous sense of identity. For the constructivists, universalism, identification and fabrication define the new world order, and participation in the political process refers to identity politics and negotiation within the social arena. The essentialists, on the other hand, argue that there is no future for European identity in this context unless it becomes a replica of the nation-state. For Craig Calhoun (1994), both essentialist and constructivist positions tend to emphasise the creation of identities by external processes, whether that of biology or society, and accordingly downplay the idea of choice. However, European societies and the individuals composing them have experienced, to different degrees, radical changes to the nature of their identities, which have become in most cases less constrained by structural forces and more self-reflexive.

If we take as a starting point the notion of core identity being defined by various attributes such as sex, race, place of birth and affiliation, it could be argued that they constitute in most cases the core elements of our sense of identity. However, they can be downplayed, emphasised, or politicised depending on the context in which they are expressed. Experiences and contexts will then be the major constraints on the way that individuals define who they are, and it could be argued that the process of identity building should be seen as an evolving and constructive one. The relationship between social and political identities could be theorised as dependent upon the way people interpret actions and the motives of others in relation to the conception of culture (seen as essential or constructed). On that basis, individuals will view culture as fluid, deterritorialised, created or negotiated, and it will form the basis of their political involvement. For others, culture will be seen as anchored, bounded, nested and unchanged. This dichotomy is in reality more complex and fragmented, as individuals will adopt different positions in relation to the issues that they have to face and the context in which their identity is expressed (see figure 3.1).

It is clear that the idea of choice has become an integral part of the process, but it is also clear that identities are contextual and evolving. At one end of this scale, it could be argued that specific political movements such as extreme right-wing parties or nationalist supporters endorse the sense of belonging; the uniqueness of their own culture, which they define as under threat in cultural, economic and social terms; and the traditional, unchanged values defining their identity. This type of political ideology can be found at the European and national levels. At the other end of the scale, modernity, consumerism and cosmopolitanism define the opposing group of individuals who, in broad terms, feel more in tune with transnational, cosmopolitan and postmodern types of identity. Another variation of this set of ideas could be illustrated by the opposition between universalism and particularism (Ifversen 2002: 7–8). Essentialist approaches tend to be particularistic when European culture is configured in national terms, but they can also go along with a universalist approach when referring to European civilisation. Constructivists tend to transgress boundaries through the operation of universalism (ibid.). These different conceptions articulate the idea of Europe and the way people feel towards it.

By acknowledging the wide range of positions in relation to political identities, the possible emergence of a European identity can be seen in a different light. First, in order for European integration to develop, the need for a European identity has to be taken into account. Secondly, the political sphere needs to be reconciled with the social and cultural issues affecting the everyday life of Europeans. In this respect, Europe could provide a new political arena based on social needs and designed to compensate for the weaknesses of the nation-state at the political level. To achieve these aims, Europe would have to be a stronger political space – in terms of democratic elections, political institutions and its civil community – than it currently is. Finally, not only do European policies have to be developed to facilitate or foster a sense of

Figure 3.1 Concepts of Identity: Practices and Representations in Europe

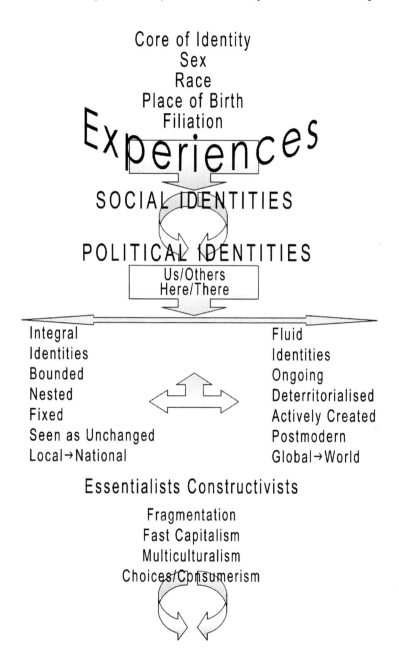

Note: This graph has been conceptualised on the basis of a series of questionnaires circulated during four years (1999, 2000, 2001, 2004) to the Euromasters students of the University of Bath. I want to thank all of them for their contributions to the debate on European identity.

allegiance to this new virtual and transnational object, but the political nature of Europe needs to be further strengthened. The democratic character of the process of decision making is at the core of such methods of identification at a time when the European Commission has been accused of corruption and a lack of accountability.

Constructing Europe: The Jigsaw of Modernity

A growing number of scholars argue that progress towards European integration will be impeded by the lack of such an identity. At present, it could be said that a European identity is not vital to the functioning of the European Union. However, further integration is likely to require a common political identity to ensure economic, social and political stability. In the debate over European identity, the concept of citizenship and the notion of a European constitution are presented as central to its future and require further discussion. For some authors, such as Jürgen Habermas (1992), the process of immigration at the European level has exacerbated the conflict between the universalistic principles of constitutional democracies and the particularistic claims of communities seeking to preserve the integrity of their habitual way of life. The expansion and consolidation of the European Union as a transnational political body cannot take place without the political support of its members, and scholars advocating a more inclusive and participatory process of identification have put various scenarios forward.

Anthony Smith, an ardent defender of the nation-state, does not see a future in European identity unless a clear common memory can be established which could then create a sense of identity. Smith is certainly correct to emphasise the incomplete and fragmented nature of European identity, but he does not take fully into consideration the decline of the nation-state and the post-national character of the European Union. For instance, the 'crisis of memories' experienced by France (Blowen, Demossier and Picard 2000) and Germany in relation to the Second World War illustrates the breakdown of a national memory in favour of recently developed social and fragmented memories. Pierre Nora's acclaimed work, *Les lieux de mémoires*, is an excellent example of this interpretation (Gerson 2003). According to Nora, contemporary France has lost the collective memory, the underlying social consensus that, under the aegis of the state, integrated all citizens within the nation.

The idea of citizenship that has emerged from the official European Union discourse has mainly come to serve as an intermediary between a neo-liberal and an exclusive ethno-culturalism (Hansen 2000: 20). With the ratification of the Maastricht Treaty in 1993, the concept of citizen of the Union was formally defined, and there were several references to the notion of citizenship and its various corollaries: community citizens or citizens of the Union. Some authors, such as Po Hansen (2000), have argued that in conjunction with the community's adoption of a neo-liberal-leaning agenda in the 1980s, the European Union has been moving towards a desocialised and increasingly ethno-cultural understanding of citizenship and identity. The term 'Fortress Europe' does illustrate to some extent the debate surrounding the question of citizenship for non–European Union members.

By contrast, another group of scholars has defined European identity as a sense of belonging with regard to the institutions of personhood themselves, such as citizenship and the rights and duties that go with it. Martin Kohli (2000), for example, argues that the development of a European identity depends on the long-standing social question of funding a viable social contract, whereby the old agenda of inclusion and welfare remains critical. In the same vein, both Etienne Tassin (1992) and Gerard Delanty (1995), who have provided a critique of cultural essentialism, have appealed to Habermas's (1996: 287) concept of a constitutional patriotism as a new type of post-national citizenship founded on the existence of a shared political culture. In this view of a patriotism based upon an interpretation of democratic citizenship with a republican flavour, political culture must be emptied of cultural meaning. For Delanty (1995: 31) too, the identity of the self is defined not by culture but by law. He advocates active participation by citizens and anti-racism as the key elements in the creation of the 'substantive dimension'. A civil society based on these notions of citizenship will offer a new forum for the expression of political identities at the European level.

Despite their divergent approaches, all of these interpretations are dominated by theoretical debates. According to Neveu (2000: 123), the idea of citizenship has to be defined in political and not cultural terms in order to avoid racism and xenophobia. She has offered the most convincing variant of the European citizenship scenario by arguing that it should take into account both its vertical and horizontal dimensions, i.e. where the polity is conceived as the set of relationships both of the individual citizens with the state and amongst citizens themselves (the notion of civil society). However, such definitions of citizenship rely upon a strong political involvement, which is largely lacking today. Various initiatives and policies implemented by the European Union at the local and regional level do, however, seem to be encouraging a sense of citizenship through collective mobilisation and political participation. Perhaps such initiatives offer a means of fostering new types of allegiance that could promote both a national and a European sense of belonging.

It is still too early to reach any firm conclusions. The most likely scenario for the future of European citizenship is that it will function alongside existing levels of citizenship and that it will compensate for those areas where the nation-state is no longer sufficient or effective in regulating social relations and economic change. Thus, these different forms of identity and citizenship are likely to remain inextricably linked and dependent upon each other.

Notes

1. By Europe, I mean the ongoing political construct as it could be defined at the time of writing, which includes the European Union with its 27 member states (Belgium, France, Germany, Italy, Luxembourg, the Netherlands, Denmark, Ireland, the United Kingdom, Spain, Portugal, Greece, Austria, Finland, Sweden; after 2004, Cyprus, the Czech Republic, Estonia, Hungary, Latvia, Lithuania, Malta, Poland, Slovakia and Slovenia; and in January 2007, Bulgaria and Romania) and the various elements forming the European political space, such as the European Commission, the European Parliament and the Council of Europe.

2. By interdisciplinary, I mean a standpoint which combines the social, political and cultural perspectives in relation to Europe as an object of study.

3. For a key contribution to the politicisation of culture, see Wright (1998).

4. The anthropological definition of culture in the Geertzien sense has become widely used by the press, the political class and international organisations. Geertz (1973: 89) defines culture as 'an historically transmitted pattern of meaning embodied in symbols, a system of inherited conceptions, expressed in symbolic forms by means of which men communicate, perpetuate, and develop their knowledge about and attitudes towards life'.

5. When discussing European integration, it is essential to take into account the successive generations which have been at the heart of the political project. The social reproduction of this political elite helps one understand the nature of the political project and its evolution. The French model dominated at the outset, while the Anglo-Saxon model is now the norm.

6. A strong emphasis has been placed on locality. See, for example, Gravari-Barbas and Violier (2003).

7. For more details on the works of psychologists in the area of European identity, see, for example, Breakwell and Lyons (1996) and Cinnirella (1997).

8. For a serious introduction to the research on the anthropology of Europe, the following three books are very useful: Macdonald (1993), Bellier and Wilson (2000) and Shore (2000).

9. See the special issue, 'Europe and the Search for Identity', of the *European Journal of Social Theory* 5, no. 4 (2002).

10. The following publications by political scientists have been selected as the most relevant to our discussion concerning the concept of European identity and the relationship between culture and politics: Laffan (1996) and Cederman (2001).

11. This is an important point, and several works have been devoted to the rise of the local in France and Europe. For a review of the French debate, see Gerson (2003). His article includes a very helpful bibliography.

12. See, in particular, the excellent anthology edited by Bellier and Wilson (2000).

13. For a useful and solid introduction to the European Union, see Gilbert (2003) and McCormick (1999: xi).

14. For an introduction to the historical origin of the notion of Europe, see Lowenthal (2000).

15. There is also a European Day of Disabled People, a European Day of Languages, etc.

16. Most studies of European cultural policy share similar conclusions about the failure of the European Union to promote a European identity at the national level.

References

Banús, E. 2002. 'Cultural Policy in the EU and the European Identity'. In *European Integration in the 21st Century: Unity in Diversity?* ed. M. Farrell, S. Fella and M. Newman, 158–81. London: Sage.

Bauman, Z. 2001. 'Identity in the Globalising World'. *Social Anthropology* 9, no. 2: 121–9.

Bellier, I. and Wilson, T. M., eds. 2000. *An Anthropology of the European Union.* Oxford and New York: Berg.

Blowen, S., Demossier, M. and Picard, J., eds. 2000. *Recollections of France: Memories, Identities and Heritage in Contemporary France.* Oxford and New York: Berghahn.

Borneman, J. and Fowler, N. 1997. 'Europeanization'. *Annual Review of Anthropology* 26: 487–514.

Breakwell, G. M. and Lyons, E, eds. 1996. *Changing European Identities: Social Psychological Analyses of Social Change.* Oxford: Butterworth-Heinemann.

Calhoun, C. 1994. *Social Theory and the Politics of Identity.* Oxford: Basil Blackwell.

Cederman, L.-E., ed. 2001. *Constructing European Identity: The External Dimension.* London: Lynne Rienner.

Cinnirella, M. 1997. 'Towards a European Identity? Interactions between the National and European Social Identities Manifested by University Students in Britain and Italy'. *British Journal of Social Psychology* 36: 19–31.

Delanty, G. 1995. 'The Limits and Possibilities of a European Identity: A Critique of Cultural Essentialism'. *Philosophy and Social Criticism* 21, no. 4: 15–36.

Duchesne, S. and Frognier, A.-P. 1995. 'Is There a European Identity?' In *Public Opinion and Internationalized Governance*, ed. O. Niedermayer and R. Sinnott, 193–226. Oxford: Oxford University Press.

Dupoirier, E., Roy, B. and Lecerf, M. 2000. 'The Development of National, Sub-national and European Identities in European Countries'. *Cahiers Européens de Sciences Po*, no. 4: 4–51.

Geertz, C. 1973. 'Religion as a Cultural System'. In *The Interpretation of Culture*, ed. C. Geertz, 87–125. New York: Basic Books.

Gerson, S. 2003. 'Une France locale: The Local Past in Recent French Scholarship'. *French Historical Studies* 26, no. 3: 539–59.

Gilbert, M. 2003. *Surpassing Realism: The Politics of European Integration since 1945.* Lanham: Rowman & Littlefield Publishers.

Gravari-Barbas, M. and Violier, P. 2003. *Lieux de culture, cultures de lieux: Production(s) culturelle(s) locale(s) et émergence de lieux.* Rennes: Presses Universitaires de Rennes.

Habermas, J. 1992. 'Citizenship and National Identity: Some Reflections on the Future of Europe'. *Praxis International* 12, no. 1: 1–19.

———. 1996. 'The European Nation-State – Its Achievement and Its Limits: On the Past and Future of Sovereignty and Citizenship'. In *Mapping the Nation*, ed. G. Balakrishnan, 281–94. London: Verso.

Hansen, P. 2000. '"European Citizenship", or Where Neoliberalism Meets Ethno-Culturalism: Analysing the European Union's Citizenship Discourse'. *European Societies* 2, no. 2: 139–66.

Ifversen, J. 2002. 'Europe and European Culture: A Conceptual Analysis'. *European Societies* 4, no. 1: 1–26.

Kohli, M. 2000. 'The Battlegrounds of European Identity'. *European Societies* 2, no. 2: 113–37.

Laffan, B. 1996. 'The Politics of Identity and Political Order in Europe'. *Journal of Common Market Studies* 34, no. 1: 81–102.

Lowenthal, D. 2000. 'European Identity: An Emerging Concept'. *Australian Journal of Politics and History* 46, no. 3: 314–21.

Macdonald, S., ed. 1993. *Inside European Identities*. Oxford: Berg.

McCormick, J. 1999. *Understanding the European Union: A Concise Introduction*. London: Palgrave.

McDonald, M. 1996. 'Unity in Diversities: Some Tensions in the Construction of Europe'. *Social Anthropology* 4, no. 1: 47–60.

Medrano, J. D. and Gutierrez, P. 2001. 'Nested Identities: National and European Identity in Spain'. *Ethnic and Racial Studies* 24, no. 5: 753–78.

Neveu, C. 2000. 'European Citizenship, Citizens of Europe and European Citizens'. In Bellier and Wilson 2000, 119–35.

Ross, M. H. 2000. 'Culture and Identity in Comparative Political Analysis'. In *Culture and Politics: A Reader*, ed. L. Crothers and C. Lockhart, 39–70. New York: St. Martin's Press.

Shore, C. 2000. *Building Europe: The Cultural Politics of European Integration*. London: Routledge.

Smith, A. D. 1995. *Nations and Nationalism in a Global Era*. Cambridge: Polity Press.

Stråth, B. 2002. 'A European Identity: To the Historical Limits of a Concept'. *European Journal of Social Theory* 5, no. 4: 387–401.

Tassin, E. 1992. 'Europe: A Political Community?' In *Dimensions of Radical Democracy*, ed. C. Mouffe, 169–93. London: Verso.

Wright, S. 1998. 'The Politicization of Culture'. *Anthropology Today* 14, no. 1: 7–15.

Chapter 4

European Identity in a Transnational Era

Ralph Grillo

There is only one Europe, of course in all its diversity – national, regional, linguistic, cultural, religious. This diversity is a precious common heritage, and we must defend and protect it, so that citizens may continue to feel at home in their town, their region, their nation, in the larger European entity … Diversity is part of the European identity … We have different nationalities. We speak different languages, are attached to different towns and regions, to different traditions, to different symbols, legends and myths. But we are all the inheritors of a European culture which is profoundly marked by an enigmatic and fascinating amalgam of diversity and unity. In the spirit of such unity, we are committed to the same fundamental values and principles. They are at the very heart of our European identity.[1]

'It's odd to think of Linford Christie as a "European"', remarked a British academic participating in an Economic and Social Research Council (ESRC) workshop held in London in the early 1990s to discuss a research programme on European integration. Linford Christie, the most eminent British athlete of the period, is of Afro-Caribbean origin. He is black. In a similar vein, Jacqueline Andall (2002: 400) reports the following exchange that had occurred between an Italian official and an Italian of African extraction in Milan: 'I brought along my CV where everything is written down – where I was born, how old I am, what I have done. He looked at me and said, "but were you born here"? And I said, yes, it's written there. Then he said, "but are you an Italian citizen"? and I said, again, yes, it's written there, I was born here. Then he said, "so you speak Italian"? At that point I just looked at him and said no and left.'

Notes for this chapter begin on page 80.

That the idea of a black European seems anomalous – 'mutually exclusive categories' (Andall 2002: 400) – to a British academic and an Italian bureaucrat should not surprise us. The concept of a Frenchman named Ahmed seemed equally puzzling to a policeman in the 1995 film *La haine*. Elsewhere, Gullestad (2001: 51) draws attention to the Norwegian writer Mah-Ruk Ali. Born in Norway of parents from Pakistan, 'she has passed all her childhood in Norway, she is a Norwegian citizen, she speaks Norwegian perfectly, and she celebrates the 17th May ... she is Norwegian, an ordinary Norwegian girl with a Pakistani background and Muslim religion', but she is not accepted as such. Wikan (1999), also writing about Norway, observes that in contemporary accounts of 'minority' cultures in Europe, i.e. regional minorities and minorities of immigrant origin, 'they' are ethnics. These and other examples oblige us to examine assumptions about what Walter Schwimmer, then secretary general of the Council of Europe, speaking at a colloquium in 2002, called the 'spirit of unity' underlying conceptions of European (or British, French, Italian or Norwegian) identity. If Ahmed cannot be a Frenchman, Mah-Ruk Ali a Norwegian, and Linford Christie a European, what does this say? The answer, of course, is not difficult.

Since the 1960s, European identity has been much debated in academic circles and in institutions such as the Council of Europe (CoE), and the European Union (EU), notably in the context of European expansion and integration. The European Commission (the EU civil service), says Cris Shore (1998: 12), firmly believes that a project of European identity will 'forge a new kind of European ... subjectivity, a distinctly "European" consciousness capable of transcending nationalism and mobilising Europe's 370 million citizens towards a new image of themselves as "Europeans"'. For anthropologists, this project is of concern in the light of two related phenomena: first, transformations in the theoretical understanding of culture and its relationship with identity, which have brought into question the essentialist character of culture and its availability as the basis for community; and, second, processes such as globalisation and migration, which have brought into Europe populations from other parts of the world who consider themselves to be living lives across borders, i.e. transnationally. Transnationalism is one vector through which (in theory) the essentialism integral to the prevailing system of nation-states breaks down and is potentially replaced by more complex networks and identities of a diasporic, crossover character. Analysis of these networks and identities has played a large part in changing our understanding of culture. Thus, contemporary theory and contemporary social and cultural processes apparently work to undermine previously accepted ideas of an easy congruence of identity and polity.

Drawing extensively on the anthropological work of Shore, Marc Abélès, Irène Bellier, Maryon McDonald, and others, especially their detailed ethnographic studies of the European Commission, and incorporating material from colloquia organised by the CoE, this chapter summarises findings on how European identity has been conceptualised within European institutions. It asks whether – and if so, how – those conceptualisations address contemporary paradigms of non-essentialised, transnational identities. Do they in fact transcend nationalism and provide an alternative to ethnic and national rootedness?

Making Europeans

In December 1973, the nine, as they were at the time, members of the European Community issued a declaration on European identity. They wished, they said, in phrases later echoed in the Maastricht Treaty (Delgado-Moreira 1997), 'to ensure that the cherished values of their legal, political and moral order are respected, and to preserve the rich variety of their national cultures. Sharing as they do the same attitudes to life, based on a determination to build a society which measures up to the needs of the individual, they are determined to defend the principles of representative democracy, of the rule of law, of social justice – which is the ultimate goal of economic progress – and of respect for human rights. All of these are fundamental elements of the European identity'.[2]

This was said in anticipation of application for membership from Greece, Portugal and Spain, which were then still under fascist rule. The nine, later expanding to 12, 15 and more, needed to define their identity, metaphorically marking out their territory, by adherence to common political and social values. Such a project was important in respect of both the future and the past. After the Second World War, numerous institutions sought to draw a line under the preceding era of aggressive nationalism and construct a new world order. In Europe, the two most important and enduring were what eventually became the EU and the CoE, the latter being a much larger organisation, based in Strasbourg, with a broader and looser remit. Peter Schieder, then president of the Parliamentary Assembly of the CoE, speaking in April 2002, defined it as an 'international multilateral organisation dealing with human rights, democracy and the rule of law, in the same way as the World Trade Organization is an international multilateral organisation dealing with trade'. Democracy, rights, the rule of law, the individual – the continuity between the classic liberal language of the Copenhagen Declaration of 1973 and that of Schieder 30 years later is readily apparent.

The EU and the CoE have often debated European identity. Schieder's remark was made at a CoE colloquium in 2002,[3] one of a series organised at Strasbourg with the intention of producing a new Declaration on European Identity to supplement or replace the Copenhagen and subsequent EU statements. At the time of writing, such a declaration has not appeared,[4] and perhaps, like the long-sought European Cultural Charter, will always be pending (Garcia 1993b: 27).[5] Nonetheless, a 2002 report, 'Prospects for a Third Summit of the Council of Europe', argued that the agenda for such a summit might include 'solemn recognition of a European "community of values" (incarnated by the Council of Europe and the European Union and enshrined in a declaration on European identity)'.[6] These discussions usually coincide with periods of enlargement and debates about who should be admitted and on what basis. Thus, at a Federal Trust seminar titled 'Regional, National and European Identities' in Berlin in November 2001, Fritz Groothues, former head of strategy at the BBC World Service, reflecting on enlargement, concluded that 'even something as basic as a fundamental declaration on European identity could serve as an icon and strengthen cohesion within Europe'.[7] In the new millennium, the EU has grown from 15 to 27 members (as of January 2007), and since 1989, the CoE, a much bigger organisation, has expanded to 46 (Serbia and Montenegro joined in April 2003). Hence, defining who and what 'we' are becomes imperative.

In that connection, a contribution by the French journalist and historian, Alexandre Adler, to the second Strasbourg colloquium, seems significant. In an interesting exercise in realpolitik, also concerned with boundary drawing – literally and metaphorically – Adler defines Europe through a series of negative geopolitical contrasts. It is:

- *Not a continuation of the Roman Empire.* But it accepts a 'plurality of states and forces'.
- *Not the Catholic faith.* '[I]t is fundamentally Christian, but accepts different versions of Christianity'; it is open to other religions (he mentions Islam and Buddhism), but 'Europe has no public religious space'.
- *Not 'the will to power'.* The lessons of the twentieth century (especially of 1945) have been learned.
- *Not the whole West.* In fact, it is decidedly *Not America.*
- *Not a continent.* In fact, regretfully, it does *Not include Russia.* On the other hand, it does include Turkey (or at least it should).
- *Not a state or state-like entity.* And it should not aspire to be one.

For Walter Schwimmer, however, '"Europe" clearly means all of Europe, including the three Transcaucasus States … Armenia, Azerbaijan and Georgia are part of Europe'. Peter Schieder agrees: 'When it comes to human rights, democracy, and the rule of law, there should be only one Europe. A Europe based on one set of values, embodied in one set of rules, protected by one mechanism. A Europe from Moscow to Brussels, from Ankara to Luxembourg, and from Sarajevo to Strasbourg.'

Thus, one agenda for European identity is concerned with political definitions: what kind of political project is Europe, and what are its boundaries? Another agenda is concerned less with boundary questions than with what it means to be European, which, although it overlaps with the definition of Europe as a political project (based on, for example, common democratic values), moves on to other terrain. Schwimmer's remarks cited earlier provide an indication of what this second agenda is about: defining Europe and European in social and cultural terms, accepting diversities, but also stressing commonalities – a 'shared but multiple identity' (the CoE version of the EU slogan,

'Unity in Diversity', adopted in the 1990s)[8] – and seeking a so-called political architecture to reflect this.

There is a third, overlapping agenda. The European Commission has long sought more than economic integration. It has been conscious of the need to give the EU wider popular appeal (Bellier and Wilson 2000; McDonald 1996), transforming their 'technocrats' Europe' into a 'people's Europe' (Shore 1998), the title of the 1980s campaign to popularise the notion of a European identity. As Václav Havel's 1994 speech to the European Parliament argued, 'Reading the Maastricht Treaty, for all its historical importance, will hardly win enthusiastic supporters for the European Union. Nor will it win over patriots, people who will genuinely experience this complex organism as their native land or their home, or as one aspect of their home. If this great administrative work, which should obviously simplify life for all Europeans, is to hold together and stand the tests of time, then it must be visibly bonded by more than a set of rules and regulations.'[9]

As is well known, during nineteenth- and early-twentieth-century modernisation, many nation-states (certainly in Northern and Western Europe) sought to engage their populations in processes of national integration, what the French call *nationalisation* (see Thiesse's chapter, this volume). Paradoxically, European nationalism both affirmed and denied difference, demanding recognition for 'national' differences (as French, German, Italian), but requiring suppression of difference within national territories. In France, everyone had to become French. As D'Azeglio remarked in 1861, 'Now we have made Italy, we need to make Italians' (cited in Pratt (2002: 26); see also Shore (1995: 221). Cultural homogeneity, absent from the old regimes, was a key feature of modernity, but as Eugen Weber's (1976) book, *Peasants into Frenchmen*, recorded, it was a long, drawn-out process. Not until the First World War would the French nation be 'One and Indivisible'. In this process, the role of the school was crucial. If, as Gramscians say, ideology is the cement holding society together, then the school is the cement mixer. When Rousseau (1964) advised Poles of the importance of creating in the minds of their citizens a sense of the difference between Poland and other nations, he sought the means above all in education: 'At the age of twenty a Pole must be nothing but a Pole. In learning to read he should read nothing but material about his country. At ten, he should know everything about its products; at twelve, he should know all about its regions, its roads and its towns; at fifteen he should know all about its history; at sixteen all its laws. There should be no fine deed, no hero which he does not know about and has taken to heart' (ibid.: 966). Similarly, Jacobin projects, such as the Abbé Grégoire's proposal, in 1794, to eradicate the patois and universalise the use of French, sought to ensure that in school all children would learn the language of the state (Grillo 1989).

The contemporary continuity is well illustrated by Shore, who discusses how the European Commission has sought to inculcate a sense of Europeanness among the EU's diverse citizenry. The project of a European identity is,

Shore observes (2000: 207), 'the last and possibly the greatest of the Enlightenment grand narratives' (see also Abélès 1996: 39; 2000: 38). Analysing how and why the European Commission gives substance to what Borneman and Fowler (1997: 492) call the 'empty sign' of European identity, Shore (ibid.: 200) shows that the officials have 'translated into policy … elite conceptions of culture and identity', employing them as 'mobilising metaphors'. Applying behaviourist models of social action which 'reify culture into a static, object-like entity to be intervened upon and managed', they have assumed the existence of a 'European' culture that 'can be developed to underpin the more technical, legal and economic aspects of the integration process' (ibid.: 40). Emphasis is placed on 'symbols, history and invented traditions' (the title of one of the book's chapters), with a 'symbolic ordering of time, space, information, education and the media in order to reflect the "European dimension"' (ibid.: 50). National icons (Beethoven, Comenius, Erasmus, Shakespeare, Socrates, etc.) have been recuperated and incorporated into EU iconography as representatives of European culture, and a 'community history' has been invented. Schemes such as educational exchanges and Women of Europe Awards, along with the euro, are all thought to contribute to Europeanisation.

In this process, Europe's cultural heritage is portrayed as a 'well-established and static "object": an organic phenomenon arising naturally from Europe's rich diversity and centuries of shared history', a 'moral success story' (Shore 2000: 57), but 'fragile and vulnerable' (ibid.: 63) and in need of protection (e.g. from Americanisation). This essentialist, elitist and ethnocentric vision of European culture reflects a 'stereotyped "Occidentalism"' (Shore 1993: 792). There is widespread enthusiasm for European 'core values', as they are called, 'invariably located in the Graeco-Roman tradition, in Judaeo-Christian ethics, Renaissance humanism and individualism, Enlightenment rationalism and science, traditions of civil rights, democracy, the rule of law' (Shore 2000: 225). This constant litany is covered in a single paragraph on 'core European traditions' in Soledad Garcia's (1993b: 5–6) contribution to a volume on European identity.

There is thus an 'essential Europe' of enlightenment, democracy, liberalism and individualism, which in some widely distributed European textbooks is 'equated unequivocally as Christendom defending itself against the resurgent forces of Islam' (Shore 2000: 59). This echoes older accounts of a European 'culture-area', of Europe as a 'distinctive, bounded region set apart from others by race, religion, language and habitat … conceived as a "civilisation" set apart from (and above) others by Christianity, science, the Caucasian race and the Indo-European family of languages' (ibid.: 57). Shore cites extracts from a paper by Hélène Ahrweiler (1993: 32), which is a paean to Greek humanism (and the Byzantine Empire), quoting Valéry for support: 'All peoples and all lands which were in turn Romanized, Christianized and subjected – at least mentally – to Greek discipline are thoroughly European.' In a passage cited by Shore (2000: 58), Ahrweiler herself notes that in the original Valéry said 'races'. She adds, in Renanesque fashion: 'What this means in effect is that Europe is a world of historical references and memories shared by all Europeans who draw sustenance from these [Greek and Roman] teachings.' But what might this say about those who cannot claim such memories? Is not Renan's definition of a nation ('Great things done together') an exclusive conception if you cannot say that you and yours participated?

The CoE's Strasbourg Colloquia

As a coda to this discussion, I refer briefly to the CoE's Strasbourg colloquia organised under the auspices of the 'L' countries (Latvia, Liechtenstein, Lithuania and Luxembourg), illustrating the role of small nations in this venture. The purpose was to ask whether there is a European identity, and if there is, to discuss how it expresses itself and how it can be encouraged. Walter Schwimmer, introducing the first colloquium, declared: 'By launching campaigns on such issues as cultural heritage, language learning and landscape protection, we have made Europeans more aware of the things which unite them in spite of their diversity: we now want to go further, determine what the concept of a European identity means for Europeans in an everyday sense, and adjust our policy, so that it can promote and consolidate that concept.'

An overview of the proceedings commented: 'European identity is rooted in national diversity, and emerges at the point where countries realise that they share a common future. Fundamental rights and parliamentary democracy, which are a reality in the CoE's 43 member states, are unquestionably the basis of this identity today. But they, though indispensable, are not enough to make every individual feel fully a part of a country and of Europe too. European identity will achieve its full potential through a freely accepted "community of values", and connect with national and regional identities to form a varied, many-faceted concept, which will also be the source of its strength and special features.'

The colloquia were attended by a distinguished group of invited academics, diplomats, journalists, officials and theologians. Some of them, notably the academics, prepared substantial papers that dealt with theories of ethnicity, identity, culture and nation, but also addressed the practical implications of those theories. The first colloquium had several papers exploring the meaning of identity from a variety of theoretical perspectives. Marc Crépon (CNRS, Paris), for example, interrogated the whole concept. Others took a less deconstructionist position, emphasising that identities are multiple and often complementary (family, town, region, country), and that the basis of these admittedly constructed identities is often solid. Such institutional identities are 'building blocks', and Rasma Karklins (University of Illinois, Chicago) argued that they should be used to create unity rather than destroyed for unity's sake. The objective, however, is not just to add another identity to those that exist. Franz-Lothar Altmann (German Institute for International Politics and Security, Berlin) stated: 'European identity is a reality, but it's still not obvious enough, and it's hard to say, "I feel European first" … [W]hen you feel European, you are saying: "I'm a Bavarian and a German, but I'm also part of something bigger and more complex" … To be genuinely real, European identity has to transcend all frontiers. After all, identity does not stop at customs posts!' Thus, not just 'first Latvian, then European', an example discussed by Karklins, but as Peteris Elferts (Latvian Ministry of Foreign Affairs), put it: 'We are now searching for a vision of a European community which is capable of creating its own "mystique". After all, even "national states" are imagined communities built on powerful myths, besides foundations such as language and common historical experience.'

It is necessary, Altmann argued, to attempt to alter the priority and give this identity 'emotional content', adding: 'The question is whether this emotional content is constructed by political will or can develop just by itself in the course of history.' For the Reverend Father Laurent Mazas (Pontifical Council of Culture, Holy See), the answer lies in education. Asking whether it is possible 'to integrate certain peoples whose identity characteristics are so very different from the majority culture', he expressed the view that a political authority capable of having an educating influence – and keen to do all that it can to ensure that the values at the heart of European civilisation remain the stable foundation for our modern changing societies – will be rewarded with confident support. Thus, any policy that aims to develop a European identity must include an education policy. Mazas advised that the participants must 'try to outline an identity that is common to all the different peoples of Europe and then to come up with ideas for promoting – or preserving? – this common identity'. For him, the source of that identity is in culture: 'The identity of a given people comes from its culture, which is rooted in creative skills and in a capacity to adapt to both other human beings and natural surroundings.' Hence, 'care must be taken not to reduce Europe's identity to its mere political identity'.

Denis Driscoll (an Irish political scientist), summarising the first colloquium, concluded: 'The construction of identity uses building blocks from history, from myth or mythology, from religion, from language, from law and … from psychology which gives us … a profound sense of belonging … For me the question then is: do these building blocks construct an edifice, a building, that is quintessentially European?' For Driscoll, the essence was 'probably rights', and his insight provided the keynote for the remaining colloquia. Thus, by the time of the third colloquium, with Schwimmer admitting that 'European identity may be difficult to define, and its component parts not easy to make out, as the earlier colloquies have shown', although 'it certainly does exist', the debate had moved out of the arenas of identity and culture and more towards those of politics, law and international relations. So the agenda returned to that of the Copenhagen Declaration, where it started. Thus, if, as Schwimmer proposed at the second colloquium, Europe is 'a community of shared values in a given geographical area', those shared values are quintessentially political. It is Europe's 'political culture', its shared liberal values, which define Europe.

Transcending National Boundaries and Identities?

If the nation-state is 'historically obsolete', as many politicians and social scientists argue, most Europeans nevertheless remain stubbornly wedded to their national identities, against which the notion of a 'European identity' pales into insignificance (Shore 2000: 224). There are numerous objections to these conceptions of European identity which assume a close connection between identity and culture, and we must be concerned about their problematic theoretical assumptions. Culture in these accounts is usually seen as the property of an identifiable collectivity, i.e. peoples who are carriers of that culture. As I have argued elsewhere (Grillo 2003), there are three conceptions of culture in this sense:

1. *A dynamic, anti-essentialist conception.* Cultures, communities and identities are constructed (dialectically from above and below) and are in constant flux. Creolisation is the norm; there are multiple identities whose form and content are continuously negotiated.
2. *An essentialist conception.* 'My' culture, a static, finite and bounded ethno-linguistic bloc labelled 'French', 'German', etc., defines my essence and determines my place in social and political schemas.
3. *A socio-historical–political conception.* National identities are not natural, and the process of constructing them is long and difficult. Once constructed, they carry a great deal of emotional and other weight and are therefore difficult to dislodge. The best policy is to recognise this and to use national identities, and the regional identities of which they are often composed, as building blocks. Nonetheless, we all have multiple identities, and there is no reason why these should not be complementary: region *and* nation; region *and* nation *and* Europe. Similarly, national cultures are seen by EU officials as 'smaller units in a greater European design' (Shore 2000: 54).

There is an obvious disjunction between these visions, with their different social and political agendas, and between their protagonists and the constituencies they represent. The first conception is a postmodernist, intellectual and academic version of culture and identity, although its advocates might claim to find it in popular culture among young people. There are few full-blown postmodernists in EU and CoE debates, and they get short shrift. The second conception is also notable for its limited appeal. There are hardly any essentialist, ethno-nationalist voices in the EU Commission (by contrast with the Assembly). However, this conception represents a popular (not to say populist) 'common sense' notion of culture and identity. It is present in a great deal of contemporary political and social rhetoric and is highly persuasive. The third conception is a modernist-realist notion of culture and identity, although it may combine with other, more solidaristic doctrines (Holmes 2000). In many respects, it is mainstream social science thinking and is relatively easy to translate into technical, bureaucratic terms. In the EU and the Council of Europe, it is the predominant view.

Although in public discussions about European identity this third vision tends to prevail, it sometimes drifts from its constructionist moorings into essentialist water. This happens when, instead of defining Europe in terms of a political architecture in which historic identities and loyalties are recognised and in which 'European' represents a commitment to 'human rights, democracy and the rule of law', this conception moves to wider questions of identity, culture, roots and the 'core values' of a historic European heritage. It thus readily becomes elitist and ethnocentric (see Delanty 1996; Rex 1996; Shore 2000). This, of course, raises the question about who should define such values. It also obliges us to consider the degree to which elitism, essentialism and Eurocentrism are relevant in an age of globalisation and transnationalism. In many ways, it seems a curiously old-fashioned project. The EU seeks modernity of a classic kind, 'while the postmodernist critique of the Enlightenment legacy has largely been overlooked' (Shore 1995: 221). Moreover, although what I have called the contemporary 'Sciences Po' version of European identity (Grillo 2003: 161)[10] is not of and in itself racist, it may have 'systematic, largely unspoken, racial connotations', to quote a phrase from the controversial report of the Commission on the Future of Multi-Ethnic Britain (2000), perhaps reflecting an underlying and widespread 'common sense' racism, as revealed in the comment, 'It's odd to think of Linford Christie as a "European"'.

The project of a European identity, then, seems oblivious to processes and ideas that undermine classic notions of Europeanness or at least put a huge question mark over them. But it also fails to confront an older threat to a European idea, the national rootedness of things, and it is this last to which I now turn.

Bellier (2000: 64) draws attention to Jean Monnet's reference to the European Commission as 'a new breed of people'. Picking up this theme, Picht (1993: 87) says of the 'new European', that he or she must be 'as sophisticated as the merchants and courtiers of the Renaissance or the multicultural and multilingual inhabitants of Central and Eastern Europe … [and] know foreign languages beyond the superficial and unreliable koiné'. What a challenge! It is not easy being cosmopolitan and/or transnational, and there are multiple reasons why it is hard to escape contextual and institutional constraints and to shrug off nationalism.

Back, Crabbe and Solomos (2001: 247), reflecting on football, refer to new forms of interaction constructed 'around the notion of distinct national cultures' which provide a 'new context for the celebration and affirmation of previously defined versions of national identity and "ethnic absolutism"'. Any follower of international sport would confirm the truth of this, but their observation is equally relevant to the working environment of Brussels, which Abélès (1996: 36) sees as a sort of laboratory for observing the construction of a European identity. Is this indeed a milieu in which a 'supranational, multicultural and post-national political system' is likely to flourish (Shore 2000: 172)? Are European Commission officials a 'new class of deterritorialised, transnational political actors' (ibid.: 34) who 'embody the "Europeanist" vision proclaimed in official texts' (ibid.: 3) and who will 'play a similar role for Europe as Oxbridge … did for the British Empire, or the Komsomol Pioneers did for the Soviet Union' (ibid.: 153)?

The officials do indeed see themselves as a 'European vanguard' and frequently describe themselves as 'cosmopolitan' (Shore 2000: 140, 153). In their daily lives they are a breed apart, living literally and metaphorically in an administrative enclave or ghetto; for the most part, who they are and how they work 'remain distant and opaque' for EU citizens (Abélès 1996: 37). For them, what happens in the bureaucracy 'is the reality of European integration', like Ottoman officials who believed that the institutions they created on paper actually existed. To an extent, though, the European civil service is indeed a kind of melting pot (Shore 2000: 172). Many officials come from a similar educational background in economics and law, share a commitment to a European ideal and speak the same administrative language, with a penchant for legalistic jargon and esoteric vocabulary (e.g. 'subsidiarity'). They are also multilingual and adept at language switching, 'flitting between languages, depending on who has just joined or left the group' (ibid.: 188). Engaged in 'mixing' and 'blending', the European Commission sees itself as a 'mosaic of different nationalities whose "unity" is contained within, and expressed through, its cultural "diversity"'. However, the institutional practices of the Commission are dominated by French and, to a lesser extent, German models (ibid.: 179ff.). There are difficulties 'reconciling "southern and northern European" styles of management' (ibid.: 198), and, says Abélès (1996: 38) there is frequent resort to age-old national stereotypes and simplified versions of reality. Moreover, 'in the context of the Commission', notes Shore (2000: 192), '"cosmopolitan" means "multinational" rather than multiracial'. Few officials are of non-white background.

Abélès and McDonald emphasise the extent to which difference in fact undermines the claims of 'unity in diversity', an idea of Europe described by Borneman and Fowler (1997: 495) as a 'saccharin concept'. The lack of a common language and the subsequent need for interpreters and simultaneous translation make dialogue in a multilingual assembly extremely difficult. Indeed, multilingualism and diversity of traditions are disorienting (Abélès 1996: 37), and 'the very use of some languages inevitably seems to portend chaos' (McDonald 1996: 58). Thus, whereas the European Parliament and Commission are, 'in their public face at least, structured to promote supranational identities', diversity and difference make this extremely difficult. When issues such as bullfighting or the colour of marmalade are debated in the Parliament, 'cultures are … talked and written into existence' in that very 'encounter of differences' (ibid.: 56). In the Parliament and the Commission, therefore, 'intercultural contact may actually reinforce national barriers instead of generating a common identity' (Abélès 2000: 42). Significantly, too, individuals retain strong links with their co-nationals in the Commission and in their own countries: clout (*piston*), operating through national networks, remains fundamental and, at worst, leads to nepotism and deep-seated corruption, as emerged in the scandals of 1999.

If the EU is a multicultural world, it is one with 'a very light symbolic structure' (Bellier and Wilson 2000). Certainly, there is a kind of emergent syncretism, including 'Eurospeak', a common language arising from 'working daily in multicultural practices'. But Eurospeak, 'emblem of the multicultural job demanded in European institutions' (Abélès 2000: 44), is pick and mix, and Abélès concludes that what we are witnessing is not the emergence of a European identity but rather 'a vast multicultural bricolage', consisting of common practices seeking to combine ways of knowing and speaking, of doing administration and politics, which may be very hard to reconcile (ibid.: 42).

Conclusion

Perhaps thankfully, the effectiveness of measures to construct a 'people's Europe' is unclear. Abélès (1996: 38) notes the sparse and jejune character of the symbols that have been produced, sometimes after many years of deliberation. Shore (2000: 227) acknowledges the increasing importance of 'bottom-up Europeanisation', as a growing list of European icons and symbols from the Eurostar high-speed rail service to the Eurovision Song Contest (and the euro) would seem to testify. But Shore wonders whether these reflect wider processes of globalisation, rather than processes of Europeanisation, and points to the risk of confusing consumption with identity formation.

Certainly, the concept of European identity is full of pitfalls. First, as Bellier and Wilson (2000: 6) observe, EU leaders 'borrow heavily from the models of nation and state building, precisely because many do not know how to escape intellectually and linguistically from the dominant model of the nation state'. As they see it, European identity is likely to be as essentialist, ethnocentric, racist and exclusionary as the national identities on which it is modelled.

Secondly, although the hope is that 'European' might become, as did nationality, 'a self-evident reality ... to be taken for granted ... an almost "natural" quality of the person ... imprinted in our hearts and minds' (Stolcke 1997), national rootedness and cultural embeddedness are extremely difficult to shift, as Jenkins's (2000) account of Denmark's referendum on Maastricht testifies. Writing about Northern Ireland, Wilson (2000: 149) comments 'national identities so dominate the cultural identifications of border people, of all people ... that, to the extent that it is acknowledged as a possible alternative, European identity is often scoffed at as little more than a tactic to get funding, or to support the European stance of a local political party'.

Thirdly, despite attempting to transcend existing ethnic and racial categories, the idea of European identity reinforces them, undoubtedly inadvertently.

It certainly runs against the grain of 'common sense' popular racism. Timera (1996: 123), in his study of the Soninké people in Paris, quotes these reflections of a young woman of African origin: 'Someone French, for me they've been French for generations. When a foreigner comes into the picture, they're not French. Therefore I am not French ... my origins, my colour, my blood. They're not from Paris.'[11] Likewise, Gullestad (2002: 52) observes of Mah-Ruk Ali: 'That [her] Norwegian identity is not confirmed indicates that metaphoric blood relations, and indirectly "race", is the bottom line of national identity.' 'A passport', says Melhuus (1999: 69) is 'not enough to make a Norwegian', and this lack of what Back, Crabbe and Solomos (2001: 279) call a 'cultural passport' (which 'equips and facilitates belonging and identity') means that many of Europe's citizens, who cannot lay claim to the European heritage as defined, experience the idea of European identity (a term that is redolent of colonial systems of racial classification) as exclusionary in theory as it is in practice.

Fourthly, therefore, the idea of European identity fails to address the reality of a transnational, globalised, multicultural Europe. Transnationalism, however, is double-edged. It brings the 'Other' within and increasingly blurs the boundary between 'here' and 'there', disrupting historic ideas about European identity and what constitutes a European community. It also undermines long-standing essentialist ideas and gives rise to new understandings of culture and identity. These, however, are not received positively in popular and political discourse; on the contrary, they are experienced as highly threatening. We are thus witnessing across Europe an increasing upsurge of 'cultural anxiety' (Grillo 2003) – exploited by political parties of both the mainstream and the fringe – together with a 'backlash against difference' (Grillo 2002: 15) and a reassertion of 'core values'. As Gullestad (2001: 34) observes: 'Globalization and migration bring out and even exacerbate the ethnic subtext in nation states.'

Finally, anxiety can be a powerful unifying force. Thus, Garcia (1993b: 14) wrote: '[T]he increasing consensus on what is considered dangerous in Western Europe (terrorism, pollution, drugs consumption, urban crime, on one side, and Islamic fundamentalism, uncontrolled immigration from certain parts of the world, on the other) constitutes a substantial common ground for sharing perceptions of what we need to be protected from, not only as individuals but also as Europeans.' As this comment reveals, already by the early 1990s, fundamentalism had become 'Europe's latest "Other"'. Now, post-9/11, it is firmly established as 'the new Bolshevism' (Margaret Thatcher in the *Guardian*, 12 February 2002). Islamism is constructed as what Europe is not, and an exclusionary European identity is projected as its opposite.

Consequently, it is hard to be positive. Picht (1993: 87) optimistically calls for 'a new humanism', with 'intercultural training' to foster the 'ability to relativize and to promote a fruitful confrontation with others – the opposite of self-protective aggression'. Writers such as Touraine (1997) and Nowicki (2001) in France and Parekh (2000) in Britain converge on the idea of 'intercultural dialogue' as the way forward. Parekh (ibid.: 221), for example, recognising that multicultural societies require some common ground, seeks to go beyond a simple, shared, pragmatic commitment to a political and economic association of mutual benefit, or a static, historical identity, rooted in supposed 'common values'. Instead, he envisages commonality as an emergent phenomenon, what he calls an 'interculturally created and multiculturally constituted common culture'. But we should not deceive ourselves that a 'dialogically constituted' (ibid.: 222) multicultural society is easily achieved. As members of the European Commission have discovered, the grip of national interests and of national cultural embeddedness remains extremely strong.

Notes

This chapter originally formed part of a presentation to a symposium, 'Creating a European Identity', held in Krakow on September 2002. I thank the Jagiellonian University (Krakow) and the Forum International des Sciences Humaines (Paris) for their hospitality, and Jeff Pratt for his comments.

1. Secretary General Walter Schwimmer of the Council of Europe, April 2002. See http://www.coe.int/T/E/Com/Files/Themes/Identity/Col3_SG%20-%20RZ_One%20Europe.asp.
2. European Community, Copenhagen Declaration, December 1973.
3. In 2001–2, the Council of Europe organised three colloquia: 'The Concept of European Identity' (April 2001), 'From Cultural Identities to a European Political Identity' (September 2001), and 'European Identity Now and in the Future' (April 2002). Extracts from the proceedings may be accessed from http://www.coe.int/T/E/Com/Files/Themes/Identity/default.asp/.
4. The relevant page of the Council of Europe web site (http://www.coe.int/T/E/Com/Files/Themes/Identity/), reporting on the 2002 colloquium, was still saying, in mid-2006: 'In the next few months, the Council of Europe will be looking more closely at the various ideas put forward on this question, which will feed into a future "Declaration on European identity". This text will be much more than a mere statement of principle, since it will allow the Council to forge instruments to strengthen cohesion and the sense of belonging to Europe. These instruments will be used to evaluate, expand and enrich the work of the Organisation which, through political, cultural and legal co-operation, has already been helping for fifty years to build a "Europe united in its diversity".'
5. See also H. Lueders, 'Federalism! What Federalism? Questions about European Cultural Governance', background note of an oral statement at the governance hearing of the European Commission, Brussels, 16 March 2001.
6. See https://wcd.coe.int/ViewDoc.jsp?id=264727&BackColorInternet=DBDCF2&BackColorIntranet=FDC864&BackColorLogged=FDC864.
7. See http://www.fedtrust.co.uk/berlin_summary.htm/ (accessed February 2003).
8. See McDonald (1996) and Shore (1998) for a discussion on unity in diversity.
9. See http://old.hrad.cz/president/Havel/speeches/1994/0803_uk.html/.

10. The term 'Sciences Po' is the colloquial and conventional way of referring to the Fondation Nationale des Sciences Politiques in Paris and to the values with which it is associated (see http://www.sciences-po.fr/).

11. 'Un Français pour moi, il est français depuis des générations. Dès l'instant qu'il y aura un étranger qui se mettra dans la filière, ce n'est plus un Français. Donc je ne suis pas française … mes origines, ma couleur, mon sang. Ça vient pas de Paris.'

References

Abélès, M. 1996. 'La communauté européenne: Une perspective anthropologique'. *Social Anthropology* 4, no. 1: 33–46.

———. 2000. 'Virtual Europe'. In Bellier and Wilson 2000, 31–52.

Ahrweiler, H. 1993. 'Roots and Trends in European Culture'. In Garcia 1993a, 30–45.

Andall, J. 2002. 'Second-Generation Attitude? African-Italians in Milan'. *Journal of Ethnic and Migration Studies* 28, no. 3: 389–407.

Back, L., Crabbe, T. and Solomos, J. 2001. *The Changing Face of Football: Racism, Identity and Multiculture in the English Game*. Oxford: Berg.

Bellier, I. 2000. 'The European Union: Identity, Politics and the Logic of Interests' Representation'. In Bellier and Wilson 2000, 53–74.

Bellier, I. and Wilson, T. M., eds. 2000. *An Anthropology of the European Union*. Oxford: Berg.

Borneman, J. and Fowler, N. 1997. 'Europeanization'. *Annual Review of Anthropology* 26: 487–514.

Commission on the Future of Multi-Ethnic Britain. 2000. *The Future of Multi-Ethnic Britain: The Parekh Report*. London: Profile Books for the Runnymede Trust.

Delanty, G. 1996. 'Beyond the Nation-State: National Identity and Citizenship in a Multicultural Society – A Response to Rex'. *Sociological Research Online* 1, no. 3. http://www.socresonline.org.uk/1/3/1.html.

Delgado-Moreira, J. 1997. 'Cultural Citizenship and the Creation of European Identity'. *Electronic Journal of Sociology* 2, no. 3. http://www.sociology.org/content/vol002.003/delgado.html.

Garcia, S., ed. 1993a. *European Identity and the Search for Legitimacy*. London: Pinter.

———. 1993b. 'Europe's Fragmented Identities and the Frontiers of Citizenship'. In Garcia 1993a, 1–29.

Grillo, R. D. 1989. *Dominant Languages*. Cambridge: Cambridge University Press.

———. 2002. 'Towards a Multicultural Europe?' *Slovak Foreign Policy Affairs* 3, no. 2: 12–22.

———. 2003. 'Cultural Essentialism and Cultural Anxiety'. *Anthropological Theory* 3, no. 2: 157–73.

Gullestad, M. 2001. 'Imagined Sameness: Shifting Notions of "Us" and "Them" in Norway'. In *Forestillinger om den andre: Images of Otherness*, ed. L.-A. Ytrehus, 32–58. Kristiansand: Høyskoleforlaget.

———. 2002. 'Invisible Fences: Egalitarianism, Nationalism and Racism'. *Journal of the Royal Anthropological Institute* 8, no. 1: 45–63.

Holmes, D. 2000. 'Surrogate Discourses of Power: The European Union and the Problem of Society'. In Bellier and Wilson 2000, 93–118.

Jenkins, R. 2000. 'Not Simple at All: Danish Identity and the European Union'. In Bellier and Wilson 2000, 159–78.

McDonald, M. 1996. 'Unity in Diversity: Some Tensions in the Construction of Europe'. *Social Anthropology* 4, no. 1: 47–60.

Melhuus, M. 1999. 'Insisting on Culture?' *Social Anthropology* 7, no. 1: 65–80.

Nowicki, J. 2001. 'L'homme des confins: Pour une anthropologie interculturelle'. In *Actes du XIIe Congrès National des Sciences de l'Information et de la Communication*, ed. Société Française des Sciences de l'Information et de la Communication (SFSIC), 95–102. Paris: UNESCO.

Parekh, B. 2000. *Rethinking Multiculturalism: Cultural Diversity and Political Theory*. Basingstoke: Macmillan.

Picht, R. 1993. 'Disturbed Identities: Social and Cultural Mutations in Contemporary Europe'. In Garcia 1993a, 81–94.

Pratt, J. C. 2002. 'Italy: Political Unity and Cultural Diversity'. In *The Politics of Recognizing Difference: Multiculturalism Italian-Style*, ed. R. Grillo and J. Pratt, 25–40. Basingstoke: Ashgate.

Rex, J. 1996. 'National Identity in the Democratic Multi-Cultural State'. *Sociological Research Online* 1, no. 2. http://www.socresonline.org.uk/1/2/1.html.

Rousseau, J.-J. 1964. 'Considérations sur le gouvernement de Pologne'. In *Oeuvres complètes*, vol. 3, ed. B. Gagnebin and M. Raymond, 951–1041. Paris: Gallimard.

Shore, C. 1993. 'Inventing the "People's Europe": Critical Approaches to European Community "Cultural Policy"'. *Man* 28, no. 4: 779–800.

_____. 1995. 'Usurpers or Pioneers? EC Bureaucrats and the Question of European Consciousness'. In *Questions of Consciousness*, ed. A. P. Cohen and N. Rapport, 217–36. London: Routledge.

_____. 1997. 'Governing Europe: European Union Audiovisual Policy and the Politics of Identity'. In *Anthropology of Policy: Critical Perspectives on Governance and Power*, ed. C. Shore and S. Wright, 165–92. London: Routledge.

_____. 1998. 'Creating Europeans: The Politicization of "Culture" in the European Union'. *Anthropology in Action* 5, no. 1/2: 11–16.

_____. 2000. *Building Europe: The Cultural Politics of European Integration*. London: Routledge.

Stolcke, V. 1997. 'The "Nature" of Nationality'. In *Citizenship and Exclusion*, ed. V. Bader, 61–80. London: Macmillan.

Timera, M. 1996. *Les Soninké en France: D'une histoire à l'autre*. Paris: Karthala.

Touraine, A. 1997. 'Faux et vrais problèmes'. In *Une société fragmentée? Le multiculturalisme en débat*, ed. M. Wieviorka, 293–319. Paris: La Découverte.

Weber, E. 1976. *Peasants into Frenchmen: The Modernization of Rural France 1870–1914*. London: Chatto and Windus.

Wikan, U. 1999. 'Culture: A New Concept of Race'. *Social Anthropology* 7, no. 1: 57–64.

Wilson, T. M. 2000. 'Agendas in Conflict: Nation, State and Europe in the Northern Ireland Borderlands'. In Bellier and Wilson 2000, 137–58.

PART II

Cultural and Political Identities in Transition

Chapter 5

HERITAGE VERSUS TRADITION

Cultural Resources for a New Europe?

Ullrich Kockel

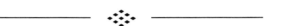

Attempts by the European Union (EU) to create a common European identity have attracted much cynicism. Corresponding to the increasing politicisation of culture, there is now in European policy an extraordinary range of initiatives promoting the exploitation of cultural resources as a key to enhancing the social and economic conditions of local areas. These initiatives include long-term programmes such as 'Culture 2000' or 'City of Culture' and limited-life ones such as PACTE or Pleiades,[1] and it has been suggested that the 'objectification of culture at national, regional, and local levels', while 'not wholly unprecedented', has 'become singularly powerful over the last twenty years' (Thomas 1997: 336). Markers of local culture include food and crafts, fine art, language, folklore, drama, literature, landscapes, and buildings and sites of historical interest (Ray 1998: 3).

Alongside established administrative regions, there are a growing number of cultural regions trying to utilise aspects of their cultural identity for the purpose of developing their socio-economic vitality. There is a certain schizophrenia at play in this process, as regions try to overcome disadvantages such as peripherality by integrating into the EU and the wider global economy whilst, at the same time, looking 'inwards into the cultural system in order to redefine the meaning of development according to values within the local culture' (Ray 1998: 5). To what extent this process contributes to the widely – if somewhat prematurely – proclaimed decline of the nation-state is a moot point that cannot be pursued here. However, it may be noted that the institutional characteristics of the nation-state are indeed – if only partially and to varying degrees in different parts of Europe – transferred to both larger and smaller territorial entities than the presently constituted nation-states. A 'Europe of the Regions' thus represents a metamorphosis of the nation-state rather than its outright decline.[2]

In the new rhetoric – which became fashionable at about the same time as neo-liberal politicians began to dismantle the welfare state across much of Western Europe – giving a boost to local culture is regarded as providing foundations for social and economic growth. For most regions across Europe, and not only the peripheral ones, that has meant promoting local and regional 'culture' and 'heritage' (whatever that may be in each case), especially as a resource for tourism development. However, the reappraisal of local and regional resources may also revive an ailing primary sector, in particular, agriculture and fishing, which can supply raw materials for the production of 'cultural' goods, including culinary specialities. Moreover, a growing emphasis on sustainability has meant that the utilisation of regional culture is increasingly expected to enhance rather than diminish a region's cultural resource base. As an element of cultural identity typically perceived as threatened by social and economic development, language may be a case in point here. There is an increasing number of local and regional initiatives, such as *Menter A Busnes* in Wales or *Gaillimh le Gaeilge* in Ireland, that are using language as a resource to generate development which, in turn, enhances the language by spreading its use not only to an increased population of speakers but also to new areas of application, such as information technology and the media industries.

In this chapter, I consider examples of how culture and identity are utilised, under the banner of 'heritage', to promote development. The underlying purpose of such development is, arguably, the fostering of social cohesion in an expanding Europe that is seeking 'unity in diversity'. In pursuit of this goal, the EU has invested in what I will call 'public identities', that is, cultural identities that are projected into the public sphere (as opposed to 'home identities', which are held in the domestic sphere). The EU sees these 'public identities' as holding the potential for inclusion in the widest sense. If one accepts that perceptions and stereotypes are culturally conditioned, it makes a certain sense to initiate policy moves towards inclusion and cohesion by 'working on' people's identities. But identities tend to be more complex and less mechanical than these policies seem to assume, and the strategy may not pay off.

This essay does not aim to present a critique of EU policy in relation to heritage and identity, nor does it attempt to review the heritage debate of the past two decades. Rather more humbly, it seeks to interpret some aspects of the relationship between identity, heritage and tradition in a contemporary European development context. I begin with a brief categorisation of identities, which will provide a framework for the evaluation of the examples that follow. In conclusion, I consider whether the utilisation of heritage and identity in Europe today leaves any scope for tradition as a progressive force (Kockel 2002).

Home Identities and Public Identities

In her chapter in this volume, Marion Demossier – following Ifversen (2002: 8) – points out that 'the essentialist approach to identity formation is driven primarily by cultural background variables' such as heritage, while 'constructivists place more emphasis on politics seen as an active process ... entailing the manipulation of cultural symbols'. From an essentialist perspective, these background variables produce identities more or less directly, restricting agency to 'articulation of a given cultural heritage' (Cederman 2001: 10). The concept of a European identity, on the other hand, may imply a more constructivist viewpoint. 'Whereas culture relates to forces that actually shape and have shaped Europe, identity points directly to the discursive level where peoples – consciously or unconsciously – create Europes with which to identify', argues Ifversen (2002: 13ff.), who suggests that '[a] culture projected back in time is normally conceptualized as tradition, whereas history is the grand narrative which orders the past' (ibid.: 8). Heritage can be regarded as an aspect of tradition that has become 'fixated'[3] – a parameter rather than a variable. For the purpose of historiographic identities, 'heritage' has to be immutable and, ideally, indisputable. In other words, the constructivist project needs an essentialised ethnic core as its foundation. Perhaps this is why constructivists find it difficult to explain humans' intuitive essentialisation of culture (ibid.: 6).

Identity has many facets. For the present purpose, I want to distinguish two levels of identity, which I refer to as 'home identities' and 'public identities'. Both are relational (as identities always are, despite what some social theorists may say), but their orientation is different. Whereas home identities are directed 'inward', public identities are directed 'outward' – the former define the individual vis-à-vis him- or herself, the latter project this individual in relation to the outside world. Each level, again, has an 'inward' and an 'outward' aspect. Taking the level of home identities first, these aspects can be described as 'autological' and 'xenological' – conveying knowledge about the 'Self' and the 'Other', respectively. With regard to public identities, I distinguish between a 'performance' aspect and a 'heritage' aspect. Following the discussion in the previous paragraph, the distinction could also be cast in terms of constructivist and essentialist. Since the objectives of EU policy with regard to heritage and identity are inclusion and cohesion, it may be instructive to consider these different identity aspects in that light. This can be represented as a grid (figure 5.1).

Speaking Gaelic in Northern Ireland may illustrate these four fields: autologically, the performance of Gaelic speech affirms one's identity for oneself, while the same act connects one with a specific shared heritage. Xenologically, the performance includes an audience who may not speak the language but who understands its significance to the actor, while excluding all – speakers and non-speakers alike – who do not share that specific heritage.

When the EU promotes culture and identity under the heritage banner, it targets the 'identity fields' AH and XP. Identity is performed (constructed)

FIGURE 5.1 Grid of Identities at Home

		Public Identities	
		Performance Identities (P)	Heritage Identities (H)
Home Identities	Autological Identities (A)	AP exclusive (the acting Self excludes any audience – the Others)	AH inclusive (the acting Self identifies with certain Others)
	Xenological Identities (X)	XP inclusive (an audience of Others is needed for the performance of the acting Self)	XH exclusive (the acting Self does not identify with certain Others)

before an audience of Others who are an essential part of 'the theatre', whether as accession countries to be brought under the EU umbrella, the friendly rival across the Atlantic or the perceived barbarian threat closer to home. This performance is essentially founded on what is assumed to be a common European heritage, constituted by individuals, groups and regions identifying themselves with certain Others who are also, as it were, part of 'the cast'.

From a public policy perspective, treating identities as merely public identities in this way makes sense, and it works up to a point. However, the ultimate arbiter of identities is the individual, and the decision over whether or not identity politics works is made at home, where the emphasis tends to be on the reverse constellation – AP and XH – which favours exclusion. This need not be confrontational; it is simply an expression of the prevalent spirit of individualism that stresses distinction over sameness and therefore focuses more on what differentiates the individual from other individuals (even if postmodern individuals, on a quest for distinctiveness, tend to become increasingly indifferent in practice).

Before I move on to some examples, a note of caution may be in order. Although 'performance' has been a fashionable concept in ethnology and other social science disciplines for some time, one needs to be careful in applying it in this context, as it carries an implication of virtuality. In a performance of *Macbeth*, we do not see the Scottish king and political reformer, but someone who is pretending to be him, playing out a rather propagandistic horror story. If we consider identity as performance, are we thereby attributing to it a similar 'as if' quality – identity as something that we do not really have but merely pretend to have? The answer will depend on how we regard historicity, heritage and tradition in this context.

Musical Traditions and Heritage

Tourism has been widely perceived as a remedy for the problems of peripheral regions. The overseas market in particular has been targeted as a growth sector in the development strategies of many such regions. Treating heritage – widely regarded as an essential aspect of identity – as a commodity has implications for the cultural framework that forms the backdrop for any development, leading potentially to the alienation of local people from their (supposed) heritage. Musical heritage has been used in many different regional contexts to attract tourists and thus provides a good starting point for a broader exploration.

A sparsely populated, remote region, Karelia has been slow to open up to the wider world. Like many other cultural regions in Europe, it has been divided by a state boundary imposed by political interests external to the region itself. Finnish North Karelia has benefited from significant regional development initiatives for many decades, and the vitality of Karelian regional identity has remained undiminished. However, exploitation of culture as a resource for the development of tourism has created a situation whereby the stereotyping of the region's identity for marketing purposes has to be conserved in order to sustain the commercialisation of its culture (Rizzardo 1987: 48).

This stereotyping of regional culture is not a uniquely Karelian problem, nor is it limited to the cultural tourism context. In the 1930s, Scandinavian ethnologists developed the concept of 'cultural fixation' to explain how, under certain historical socio-economic circumstances, cultural forms are conserved, with their meaning reduced to merely a stereotypical badge of identity. In popular perception, Karelia has had a long association with traditional music, and the Singer's House at Ilomantsi, near the border that divides Karelia into a Finnish province and an autonomous republic of the Russian Federation, is an important site of Finnish national heritage. This provides a reference point for a historical narrative that portrays Karelia as a region disposed towards music and song more generally and thus constructs music as a heritage resource. At the contemporary end of this semi-fabricated continuity, there are three major international events in the cultural calendar hosted annually by North Karelia – a chamber music festival in February, the Joensuu Song Festival in June, and the Lieksa Brass Week in August.

Like Karelia, Estonia has a history of being subjected to conquest and colonisation stretching back for centuries. In 1992, the newly independent Estonian government prioritised tourism as part of a strategy to overcome the country's economic problems. Planners recognised history and culture as key factors in international tourism. Like South Karelia, Estonia had suffered severe repression under Soviet rule. Although publicly paraded at an annual internationalist festival in Moscow, traditional cultures were persecuted at home in the republics that made up the USSR (Panteļējevs 1991). Tourists from the West have long regarded Estonia as a window on a 'European culture' of the past. History and heritage are acknowledged as major resources for tourist development, but it is observed that '[i]n addition to our rich historical and cultural heritage we also have our everyday activities to carry out' (Ehrlich and Luup 1993: 10). This echoes concerns that in cultural tourism, where local people themselves may be the primary tourist attraction of a place or region, these people should decide how much of their culture they actually wish to share with tourists. Moreover, it reflects a strategy for the promotion of cultural tourism that has been pursued with some success in North Karelia, where the repertoire of regional musical events is based not on a celebration of the Karelian cultural past itself but on a concept of music as tradition. This approach is characterised by a specific creativity and the originality of its material, or, to turn a famous phrase on its head, a 'tradition of invention' in which the emphasis is on the continual development of 'traditional' skills rather than on the conservation of some unadulterated 'heritage'.

An overwhelming majority of tourists visiting Estonia tend to stay in or around its capital city, Tallinn. In the process of opening up other parts of the country and developing them for tourism, attractions such the Estonian

National Song Festival are playing a significant role. With its origins dating to the 'national awakening' in the nineteenth century, the first song festival was held in 1869. Although Latvia, in 1873, and Lithuania, in 1924, followed Estonia's lead in establishing national song festivals, the link between song and cultural identity has remained particularly strong in Estonia, where the struggle for national independence from the Soviet Union came to be known as 'the singing revolution'. Estonia's recent success in the Eurovision Song Contest is viewed as a continuation of this musical tradition, and the event in 2002 provided a valuable injection of tourist revenue between two national song festivals. These song festivals offer potential for a skilful blend of traditional culture and modern originality, a strategy that appears to be working well in North Karelia, where a strong musical tradition has also given a boost to tourism (Rizzardo 1987: 49).

As in North Karelia and Estonia, the tourist season in Ireland is relatively short by international standards. The nature of Irish tourism has shifted significantly from a North American market primarily in search of its 'Irish roots' towards European markets where family links with Ireland are of minor relevance. Although continuing migration to European destinations may in time create a 'roots-seeking' market there, the current shift has obvious implications for the tourism product. According to Fáilte Ireland, the Irish tourist authority, the key characteristics of Ireland are practically the same as for North Karelia and Estonia: scenic landscapes, a quiet and relaxed pace of life, a distinctive heritage and culture, and the absence of mass tourism.

In the 1970s and 1980s, and supported by an international folk music revival, the Republic of Ireland also utilised its musical heritage as a resource for tourism, extending the season and attracting large numbers of visitors to ecologically vulnerable areas by staging a range of international folk festivals, mainly along its western coast.[4] Music has played a crucial role in the development of Ireland as a tourist destination beyond this, not least through the country's success in the Eurovision Song Contest, which incidentally produced one of the most fascinating examples of 'glocalised' musical heritage – the *Riverdance* show and its various imitations. An extended version of this musical/dance performance, which had appeared as an interlude to a Eurovision Song Contest, went on to tour the globe, becoming Ireland's key cultural export in the 1990s. But it also had a significant impact back home, radically changing the styles of performance in 'traditional' Irish dancing and, consequently, raising issues of authenticity.

The importance of musical heritage for regional identity has been asserted since the 1990s in new ways and from an unexpected direction, which, like the popular impact of *Riverdance*, has brought issues of authenticity and legitimacy to the fore. In Northern Ireland, there has been a growing movement demanding the recognition of an Ulster-Scots heritage, involving language, literature and music. This heritage is seen by its advocates as in contrast to, but not necessarily in conflict with, the Irish-Gaelic heritage perceived as the dominant, if not hegemonic, heritage discourse in the region. At the same time, this newly discovered heritage is also in contrast with the more 'traditional' emphasis on a British heritage linked to the Union with Great Britain as a whole, aligning itself more with a devolved – and perhaps aspiring to be independent – Scotland than with the United Kingdom of the past three centuries. The growth of this movement has been augmented to a degree by the Good Friday Agreement of 1998, with its provision for parity of esteem between the different cultures in Northern Ireland (Nic Craith 2002). This has enabled an Ulster-Scots non-material heritage to be performed publicly and with government support – a level of support that, in the face of tight budgets, has been a major bone of contention (Vallely 2004). In 2004, *On Eagle's Wing*, an Ulster-Scots epic musical intended to match the cultural impact and international success of *Riverdance*, was launched, targeted primarily at the North American heritage tourist market. The television screening of extracts during Burns' Night celebrations on BBC Northern Ireland raised the temperature of the political debate in the region, and at the time of writing, the controversy continues.

Heritage Centres

While musical heritage has been an important element in the Irish case, heritage tourism is linked to broader historical themes presented with an expanded temporal horizon. Local people commenting on new heritage projects often express the hope that they would 'bring tourists in', and this is generally looked upon as a good thing, almost as if the tourists' readiness to travel huge distances to a remote corner of the world is regarded as vindicating the region's way of life. Historically, tourism has tended to create mainly low-paying jobs for local women (Breathnach 1994). During the 1990s, the heritage centre – a postmodern version of the local museum, displaying some aspects of local, regional and even national archaeology, history and culture – was seen as offering better-quality jobs with higher pay. From a planner's perspective, heritage centres have several advantages. 'Heritage' is an omnipresent resource, in the sense that anyone anywhere, regardless of social, political or economic position, can claim some kind of cultural heritage. As a postmodern product, heritage is highly flexible and can be readily adapted to changing market requirements. If it then transpires that a heritage centre is not viable in the long term, the building is usually more attractive and less depressing than an empty factory. This attitude is even found among people involved in the promotion of tourism.[5]

From an ethnological perspective, the economic benefits of such developments are only one aspect of the wider context. At the applied level, community involvement is a far more important concern, as it indicates the degree to which the version of heritage represented at a particular heritage centre is actually grounded in everyday cultural experience. Heritage centres may offer more dynamic forms of display than orthodox museums, but the danger of 'musealisation' – the detachment of material objects and everyday experiences from their real-life context – remains. In the conventional local museum, the focus has been on actual cultural objects of the past, whereas in the heritage centre the dynamics of the display, facilitated by modern technology and know-how, takes centre stage. When tourists remember the stunning special effects rather than the story line, the success of a heritage centre becomes questionable. Heritage as entertainment does not require any basis in historical facts or a real-life geographical frame of reference. Just like conventional museums, heritage centres by their very nature tend to accelerate the process of cultural fixation.

While sharing certain structural characteristics and being very much on the periphery of Europe, the three cases considered so far have had diverse experiences with the development of heritage, indicating both challenges and opportunities for EU policy. That an expanding EU will find it increasingly difficult to engineer a coherent 'European' heritage identity – perceived as based on a common past – in all but the most abstract terms is a truism that needs no elaboration. However, the Karelian experience suggests that identity may be based on excellence in a field of contemporary international culture, such as music, and need not be based – at least not exclusively nor strongly – on a glorious past. Present policy in Estonia reminds us that although history and folk culture do hold significant potential as resources for development, the fixation of some aspects of cultural heritage for purposes outside the sphere of everyday life, for example, through EU-funded regional development projects promoting cultural tourism, may ultimately have alienating effects. The exploitation of heritage makes sense only if it is grounded in the everyday concerns of contemporary people who continue to engage with it. In a Europe that is becoming increasingly polycultural – through both immigration and the indigenous cultural differentiation celebrated by the EU's 'unity in diversity' rhetoric – Ireland not only demonstrates the need to devise complex narratives of culture and history that remain, in spite of their complexity, widely intelligible across different groups in society. It also illustrates rich examples of how this task may be attempted, thus affording opportunities to analyse why and under what conditions such narratives may work or fail.

Heritage on the Plate

Predominantly rural, the French region marketed as Pays Cathare (Land of the Cathars, a mediaeval heretic movement) has suffered population decline through emigration, bringing with it all the usual problems of a downward spiral in the provision of local services and infrastructure. In the aftermath of the events of May 1968 – the student and general strikes which led to the collapse of the de Gaulle government – the region experienced inward migration, both from urban centres in France and from abroad. As in Ireland, immigration contributed to a change in attitude among the local people, many of them no longer regarding emigration as the best option.

In response to the growth in beach tourism, promoted by the French government since the 1970s, activists in the department of Aude began to see the region as a destination for sustainable tourism. Being at the same time a regional identity and a marketing brand, the Pays Cathare label is governed by quality criteria defined for each of the main economic sectors by the relevant professional organisations in conjunction with Aude's Conseil Général. The three main sectors are tourism, which includes accommodation and restaurants; professions and providers of services, including mainly artisans and heritage guides; and agriculture and food. The last is particularly prominent in the new self-image of the region. Traditionally associated with the production of wine, the region is presented as home to a broad palette of distinctive food products. The tourist is invited to sample these at so-called *étape terroir*, places that have been especially designated for the demonstration of how local produce is made. Claiming culinary distinction within a country that itself claims such distinction on a global scale is no mean ambition for a peripheral region with few resources. In doing so, the region has been able to capitalise on the changing preferences of an increasingly affluent society: the rise in tourism, combined with a growing interest in traditional foods and craft products and the quest for encounters with 'authentic' local people and practices. In late-industrial urban society, the local and authentic is once again becoming synonymous with the rural.

The elevation of food as a key ingredient for a new style of comprehensive regional identity has been observed in other European regions as well. Jonas Frykman (1999: 16) notes that food from his home region of Skåne in Sweden has become 'a more loaded concept than it ever was in the days to which the tradition refers'. The label 'Skåne' is used 'as a seal of quality' for food produced in the region, and the area 'has become something far more than a region, it has become a site, a place charged with meaning that does not necessarily have a geographical foundation'. Here Frykman indicates two characteristics of this identity badge: it is more comprehensive and coherent than the fractured identities favoured by late postmodernity; yet at the same time, this comprehensiveness and coherence is built on constructed meaning independent of any actual place and its history, in a way that appears rather postmodern. Globalisation has brought 'ethnic' foods from around the world into most European regions and, in some cases, has rehabilitated domestic cuisines. At the same time, the growth of the organic movement and farmers' markets indicates an increasing significance of food and its preparation as markers of locally rooted identities. Subtly, the shopping for and cooking of a Sunday dinner is becoming something of a public statement and political act.

Talking Heritage

The food one eats is a key signifier of one's cultural belonging. For German migrants in the British Isles, for instance, bread has long been at the top of a list of items distinguishing German from British culture. Another important cultural marker passing through the mouth, in the opposite direction, is language. Nowadays, we no longer have simply languages but rather categories of language: official and non-official, national and regional, major and minor, high and low, more widely and less widely used, standardised and non-standardised, less widely taught and used languages, disputed language varieties, ethnolects and so forth (Nic Craith 2000). This multiplicity of terms has reinforced the social implication that speaking a major language empowers the individual. It has given a false validity to the notion of a social hierarchy of languages, which implies that certain languages not only are socially more useful and economically more viable than others, but also are inherently superior vehicles for communication. With very few exceptions, European nation-states have adopted a single national language, thus marginalising all other languages within their respective territory.

Many of the so-called minority languages are located on the periphery of modern nation-states. 'Minority' languages are often a consequence of boundary changes or migration. By speaking a minority tongue, a group deviates from the norm and could be seen as placing itself on the margins. As the *Euromosaic* report points out, the term 'minority', when used with reference to a language group, refers primarily to power relationships rather than to any specific statistical measure (Nelde, Strubell and Williams 1996). From the 1980s onwards, 'the regional revival throughout Europe has been accompanied by initiatives to bolster minority languages as a component of regional development strategies' (Ray 1998: 12). One reason for this has been that in their search for markers of cultural distinctiveness, European regions have found that language is 'a powerful means by which one culture can display its difference from all others' (ibid.). Many regions, even those where there has been a positive attitude to linguistic diversity, have treated regional languages as a liability, as something that costs money, rather than as a resource. Policies have been implemented in order to maintain and protect the linguistic heritage. In Ireland, for example, the government has created language-protection areas called 'Gaeltacht'. Protectionist policies like this have often served to reinforce stereotypes of lesser-used languages in terms of a rural-urban, agrarian-industrial, archaic-modern dichotomy, which has led people to disengage from their regional language.

Government support for viewing language as a 'heritage' can be interpreted in different ways. The French government, a long-time champion of cultural centralisation, has recently recognised regional languages as part of the national heritage and has begun to support some 'minority' languages such as Alsatian.[6] The designation of a language as 'heritage' may be a giveaway, however. Culture becomes 'heritage' only when it is no longer current, that is, when it is no longer actively used. In other words, 'heritage' is culture that has dropped out of the process of tradition. The term 'tradition' literally refers to cultural patterns, practices and objects that are 'handed down' to a later generation, for use according to their purposes, as appropriate to their context. By contrast, 'heritage' refers to cultural patterns, practices and objects that either are no longer handed down in everyday life (and therefore left to the curators) or are handed down for a use significantly removed from their historical purpose and appropriate context – such as to attract tourism.

The undeniable cost factor associated with the protection of such 'heritage languages' is frequently resented by majority-language speakers. Against this view, it could be argued that language, unlike many other resources, is enhanced rather than diminished by its use. Moreover, as the language environment increases, the capacity to generate economies within that environment is also amplified. At an individual as well as an organisational level, many entrepreneurs have recognised that where a social and cultural infrastructure has been created that fosters language use and promotes a particular language environment, the economic pay-off has been considerable and has facilitated further strengthening of the language. Many diverse projects aiming to increase the use of less widely spoken languages in the commercial sector have been initiated across Europe (Nic Craith 1996). In a situation where most of these languages have few or indeed no native speakers, their use becomes very much a deliberate and pointed performance. However, the same can be said for ethnolects whose status as language is disputed. For example, Ulster-Scots may or may not have thousands of native speakers, depending on your political perspective. If it does, then speaking (and writing) it in a form that emphasises distinction from English is arguably the legitimate practice of a living language; if it does not, then such practice constitutes a performance act that – as performance – differs little from the use of undisputed languages such as Gaelic or Welsh.

Authenticity, Tradition and Mimetic Heritage

When we are dealing with culture, identity and heritage, the question, is it authentic? frequently arises and is hotly debated – 'on the ground' as much as in academic discourse (e.g. Bendix 1997). The Frankfurt School initiated a critique of 'the jargon of authenticity' (Adorno 1973), especially with regard to culture, contesting the implication that there is 'something immanent in local culture systems' because the assumption of such immanence would 'deny any agency of human subjectivity' (Ray 1998: 15). Rather than being an expression of the 'false' or 'distorted' consciousness of people who do not quite know how to live their lives unless instructed by a social theorist, the recent resurgence of popular concern with cultural identity and the authenticity of cultural products can be interpreted in several ways. Nowadays, 'few cultural regions in Europe can claim to be homogeneous entities', and in each locality there are people from whose personal perspective what is called 'indigenous culture' may appear 'alien' (ibid.: 16). The power of definition is where Ray looks for a solution to the problem of authenticity, which he suggests 'might more usefully be reformulated as a question of legitimacy, i.e., who confers legitimacy on what form of cultural activity?' (ibid.). He argues that the analysis should ask not so much whether or not an identity is 'authentic', but to what extent a locality or region has control over its identity and whether 'the cultural identity [can] be tied to the particular territory so as to meet local needs'. Ray then postulates a research agenda that sends social scientists, and European ethnologists in particular, back to basics: 'We need to look more closely at the processes whereby territorial/cultural identities are constructed, promoted and protected … We need to know more about the specific relationships between place, history and the on-going process of symbolic construction' (ibid.: 17). Indeed, we do.

If we acknowledge that 'authenticity' is less a matter of true or false consciousness than a matter of the historical legitimacy of any associated identity claim, we can revisit the 'invention of tradition' debate and recognise 'heritage' as a fixation of 'tradition', conceived as process. This enables us to grasp that it is not so much tradition that has been invented but rather heritage. Tradition as a process involving cultural actors always includes the possibility of modifying what is being handed down between generations in order to adapt it to a changed historical context. Only if it becomes fixated as heritage does tradition cease to imply process and change. From this perspective, the use of the label 'traditional' no longer implies something immutable and eternal; it refers to legitimacy derived from everyday historicity. The alternative would be the postmodern view of identity in the age of globalisation. Following that view, doing anything at all becomes hard identity graft, and identity is no longer self-evidently grounded in the everyday. Identity becomes 'mimesis' (Kockel 1999: 68), and peer group pressure to conform to the mass-produced individualism of the identity warehouse replaces old-style paternalism and imperialism as the force colonising our life worlds.

Globalised Heritage and the Destruction of Traditions

The period of fieldwork reflected in this chapter happened to coincide more or less with the flowering of postmodernism and its distinctly anti-historical attitude. During this time, the original interior of many historical local pubs was ripped out and replaced by off-the-peg 'heritage pub' designs. A similar fate afflicted many other aspects of both material and non-material culture. Could the postmodern disdain for history (and tradition), with its concomitant 'knock down-build new' attitude, be a reflection of the globally dominant culture in the second half of the twentieth century – that of 'white'

US-America, industrially creating surrogate heritage to compensate for its often alleged shortage of history? If Ernest Gellner (1983: 34) is right in arguing that '[t]he monopoly of legitimate education is now more important ... than the monopoly of legitimate violence', then what are the implications of progressive privatisation and commercialisation of education, as envisaged in the proposals for a General Agreement on Trade in Services (GATS), driven by the United States' world-trade agenda and fended off provisionally by the EU? The GATS vision implies a transfer of power over the social order from political (state) to economic (business) interests. Cultural traditions are endangered through a commercial takeover by the economically most powerful player; even after its eastward expansion in 2004, the EU, while more populous, has a smaller economy than the US.

The heritage boom of recent decades may have camouflaged an erosion of European cultural traditions, hiding it behind the smokescreen of 'culture as a resource', a strategy that uses cultural fixation to commodify identity as heritage. Earlier, I proposed to conceptualise 'tradition' as a process that is at its heart about sustainability – about the 'handing on' of knowledge and practices for appropriate future use – and 'heritage' as objects and practices that have become fixated and have thereby seemingly fallen out of this process – or have been deliberately removed from it. The distinction is important. If the two are confused, tradition can be represented as static and branded 'bad for progress', as it has been for some time. This raises the question of in whose interest the maligning of tradition – especially European traditions – might have been.

Most of the examples cited in this chapter fit with the identity fields promoted by the EU, wherein individuals define themselves via the constructive performance of essentialised heritages, the latter forming a basis for the regional identity that the former presents to an audience of Others. Both identity fields are selectively inclusive in their own way – autological heritage identities define the 'in-group', as it were, while xenological performance identities need an audience of Others before whom they are played out. In some cases, these practices go back a long time. The association of Karelia with musical tradition dates at least to the 1830s, when Elias Lönnrot gathered folklore and turned it into the Finnish national epic about the magic power of song. Likewise in Estonia, the emphasis on music played a key role in the 'national awakening' during the nineteenth century. The same can be said for many other European countries and regions. What makes these two cases different is that in the contemporary utilisation of culture as a resource, music is not fixated as heritage but retains its historicity as a creative tradition. The celebration of 'pristine' folk dances and other heritage is marginal compared to a strong emphasis on creativity and evolving practice. In other words, the regions' cultural traditions are characterised by an enthusiasm for innovation. Even though music is essentialised as a root of identity, agency is by no means limited to expressing a *given* heritage (Cederman 2001: 10) but is free to progress tradition.

The same is basically true for more recent examples, such as the Pays Cathare branding that essentialised 'resistance' and 'unruliness' as roots of an autological heritage identity and developed from this a xenological performance identity celebrating 'difference' – not just from foreign tourists but also from the rest of France. However, many of the cultural traditions displayed in the Pays Cathare could easily become fixations if they are presented as time-honoured ways of doing things that must not be changed. The historical frame of reference of this 'rebellious' identity is at its core a backward-oriented, conservative one, whereas the orientation in Karelia and Estonia appears much more forward-looking.

The case of Ulster-Scots, featured here both in relation to music and in the context of language, is interesting for its 'split' perspective. While its proponents have been charged with inventing a tradition, all tradition has been initiated by someone somewhere and therefore is invented. Thus, the charge of invention points to something else – the question of legitimacy. If we accept that all tradition is invented, then legitimacy cannot be derived from any primordially grounded authenticity. As a musician in Galway once said to me, a tradition is authentic if it works. A working tradition is one that is 'handed on' continuously, both across space and through time. In this regard, the jury is still out on Ulster-Scots.

However, this 'tradition' highlights one critical aspect of public identities more clearly than any of the other cases (to which it applies nonetheless, if to a lesser degree). At the level of home identities, autological performance identity is directed at defining the Self to the exclusion of Others, as is the xenological heritage identity. This is inherent and, in itself, not necessarily problematic. All identity is about affirming what we are and, thereby, what we are not. This is often seen as the crucial issue for multiculturalism, and some analysts (e.g. Day 2000) seem to regard a specifically European discourse of diversity as the root of all evil, as if only Europeans knew how to construct Others. Conversely, the construction of and emphasis on differences has been proposed as 'the only way to oppose the hegemony of Euro-American thought' (Schiffauer 1996: 62). That other cultures may have other ways of doing this is an issue that cannot be followed up here. The important point is the use to which such differentiation is put. In the 1970s, the right to difference was heralded as part of an emancipatory agenda. Emancipation is, not least, an autological performance rejecting hetero-stereotypes in favour of auto-stereotypes, thereby denying ascribed inferiority and breaking down hierarchies. When such differences are used to assert essential superiority over Others, however, the ethos of diversity becomes a major political and ethical problem.

At the same time as culture became a political issue, the study of culture in the social sciences and humanities ironically turned its attention to textual analysis. Contemporary theories of modernity overstate the 'reflexive and subject-oriented nature' of culture and identity, and, consequently, cultural analysis 'has found it difficult to incorporate the perspective of action' (Frykman 1999: 22). Focusing on action 'gives room for curiosity about the many reworkings that take place locally, their conditions and constantly occurring transcendences'. After a period when the desk, the library and the Internet seemed to become the primary tools of studying culture, we may now find it appropriate to make 'the local' once again a crucial element in our ethnological fieldwork (ibid.). Such fieldwork can demonstrate the progressiveness of many cultural traditions and challenge the interests behind the fixation of certain heritages – not least those interests who would like to write off 'Old Europe' politically, turning it into a heritage theme park for roots-searching global tourists. Whether or not this fieldwork would affirm any 'unity in diversity' from below is quite another matter. Either way, we should not allow an irrational 'fear of difference' (Schiffauer 1996: 62), however politically correct it might be, to determine our research agendas.

Notes

1. See, for example, Johler (2002). Details of PACTE can be found in Kilday (1998). For the Pleiades programme, see Åhlström (1999).
2. A key debate in this context revolves around the issue of citizenship, in contrast to nationality and identity (see Kockel 1999).
3. For a more detailed discussion, see Kockel (2002: chap. 6).
4. The International Musical Eisteddfod, held annually at Llangollen in North Wales for more than half a century, while much smaller in scale, is another example of how a particular tradition associated with the identity of a region, as choir music is with Wales, may be utilised as a resource for attracting thousands of tourists each year.
5. In the early years of the twenty-first century, many heritage centres – including the Ulster History Park and Navan Fort, representing major investment – have had to close down due to a drop in visitor numbers, adding more than a grain of salt to this sarcastic view voiced by a tourism planner interviewed in the 1990s.
6. At the time of writing, France has signed but not yet ratified the European Charter for Regional and Minority Languages. Unlike his prime minister, President Chirac opposed the completion of the process because he viewed it as going against the French written constitution, which stipulates that French citizens must speak French.

References

Adorno, T. 1973. *The Jargon of Authenticity*. Evanston: Northwestern University Press.
Åhlström, E., ed. 1999. *Cultural Itineraries in Rural Areas: Go Cultural with Pleiades!* Llangollen: ECTARC.
Bendix, R. 1997. *In Search of Authenticity: The Formation of Folklore Studies*. Madison: University of Wisconsin Press.

Breathnach, P. 1994. 'Gender and Employment in Irish Tourism'. In *Culture, Heritage and Development: The Case of Ireland*, ed. U. Kockel, 47–60. Liverpool: Liverpool University Press.

Cederman, L. 2001. *Constructing Europe's Identity: The External Dimension*. London: Lynne Rienner.

Day, R. 2000. *Multiculturalism and the History of Canadian Diversity*. Toronto: University of Toronto Press.

Ehrlich, R. and Luup, L., eds. 1993. *Estonia: The New Tourist Destination*. Tallinn: Department of Tourism.

Frykman, J. 1999. 'Belonging in Europe: Modern Identities in Minds and Places'. *Ethnologia Europaea* 29, no. 2: 13–24.

Gellner, E. 1983. *Nations and Nationalism*. Ithaca: Cornell University Press.

Ifversen, J. 2002. 'Europe and European Culture: A Conceptual Analysis'. *European Societies* 4, no. 1: 1–26.

Johler, R. 2002. 'The EU as Manufacturer of Tradition and Cultural Heritage'. In *Culture and Economy: Contemporary Perspectives*, ed. U. Kockel, 221–30. Aldershot: Ashgate.

Kilday, A., ed. 1998. *Culture and Economic Development in the Regions of Europe*. Llangollen: European Centre for Traditional and Regional Cultures.

Kockel, U. 1999. *Borderline Cases: The Ethnic Frontiers of European Integration*. Liverpool: Liverpool University Press.

_____. 2002. *Regional Culture and Economic Development: Explorations in European Ethnology*. Aldershot: Ashgate.

Nelde, P., Strubell, M. and Williams, G. 1996. *Euromosaic: The Production and Reproduction of the Minority Language Groups of the EU*. Luxembourg: Office for Official Publications of the European Communities.

Nic Craith, M., ed. 1996. *Watching One's Tongue: Issues in Language Planning*. Liverpool: Liverpool University Press.

_____. 2000. 'Contested Identities and the Quest for Legitimacy'. *Journal of Multilingual and Multicultural Development* 21, no. 5: 399–413.

_____. 2002. 'Politicised Linguistic Consciousness: The Case of Ulster-Scots'. *Nations and Nationalism* 7, no. 1: 21–37.

Panteļējevs, A. 1991. 'Die scharfe Waffe der Dialektik: Der sowjetische Internationalismus in Theorie und Praxis'. In *Das Ende des Sowjetkolonialismus: Der baltische Weg*, ed. A. Urdze, 65–75. Reinbek bei Hamburg: Rowohlt.

Ray, C. 1998. 'Culture, Intellectual Property and Territorial Rural Development'. *Sociologia Ruralis* 38, no. 1: 3–20.

Rizzardo, R. 1987. *Cultural Policy and Regional Identity in Finland: North Karelia between Tradition and Modernity*. Strasbourg: Council for Cultural Co-operation.

Schiffauer, W. 1996. 'The Fear of Difference: New Trends in Cultural Anthropology'. *Anthropological Journal on European Cultures* 5, no. 1: 49–62.

Thomas, N. 1997. 'Anthropological Epistemologies'. *International Social Science Journal* 153: 333–43.

Vallely, F. 2004. 'Singing the Boundaries: Music and Identity Politics in Northern Ireland'. In *Communicating Cultures*, ed. U. Kockel and M. Nic Craith, 129–48. Münster: LIT Verlag.

Chapter 6

DINOSAUR, SHIPWRECK OR MUSEUM PIECE?
The Unstable Identity of European Cinema

Wendy Everett

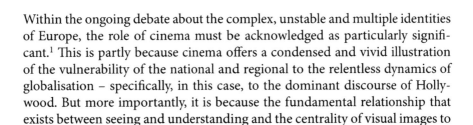

Within the ongoing debate about the complex, unstable and multiple identities of Europe, the role of cinema must be acknowledged as particularly significant.[1] This is partly because cinema offers a condensed and vivid illustration of the vulnerability of the national and regional to the relentless dynamics of globalisation – specifically, in this case, to the dominant discourse of Hollywood. But more importantly, it is because the fundamental relationship that exists between seeing and understanding and the centrality of visual images to the formation of identity place the cinema in a uniquely powerful position.

While cinema can be situated within the context of other forms of cultural expression, such as literature, theatre, painting and music, it differs from them, to varying degrees, by virtue of the vast sums required for its basic production processes and the problems involved in its distribution and exhibition. However, the main difference is perhaps one of perception, for the very status of cinema is contradictory and uncertain. Unlike theatre and music, which may encounter similar practical and financial problems, cinema is as likely to be viewed as an industrial product and to be judged by strictly economic criteria as it is to be considered an expression of cultural identity, arguably requiring financial support and protection, and certainly calling for a very different form of critical evaluation. The fundamental dichotomy that destabilises the identity of film itself – as artistic or cultural articulation or/and industrial product, as challenging, idiosyncratic discourse or/and popular entertainment for a mass audience – inevitably influences and even polarises dominant critical debate. Moreover, the problems of fragmentation and difference that lie at the heart of any assessment

---

of European identity are perhaps nowhere more deeply and uncompromisingly etched than in its cinema(s). Before assessing its role and significance within the articulation of European identity/identities, it is thus necessary to explore both the problematic identity of European cinema as a 'volatile meeting place of art and commerce' (Finney 1996: 1) and the major economic and political difficulties that confront its present and future existence.

Defining European Cinema

The problems inherent in defining the fragmented and divergent identities of Europe lie at the heart of this volume, where they emerge in an exciting range of critical and theoretical approaches. Such definitions therefore are not the concern of this chapter. But, interestingly, applying the already problematic notion of 'European' to cinema serves, if anything, to complicate issues still further. If Europe presents an uneasy and fragile allegiance of diversities shaped by unstable and problematic borders and by linguistic and philosophical differences, its cultures too remain distinctive, even idiosyncratic: 'a patchwork, a juxtaposition of various conceptions and practices of entertainment, a collection of individual ways of singing, dancing, telling stories' (Sorlin 1991: 3). For a long time, the notion of Europe as a collection of differences both reflected and perpetuated the privileging of the nation-state as creator of culture and identity. Still today, it is the case that many discussions of European culture, not least its filmic culture, focus upon individual national productions rather than attempting any transnational, pan-European perspective.

It is, of course, the case that adopting a more flexible and inclusive approach is equally problematic, and if countless studies in the field begin by asking what European cinema is, far fewer attempt an answer, however provisional. At one extreme, one might argue that, like Europe itself, European cinema is a mirage, a concept that has no reality outside the critical discourse that frames it (Fowler 2002). It is certainly true that we cannot speak of European cinema in terms of a cultural monolith, a static unitary identity – but then any such intention must surely be rare within postmodern discourse. And despite Fowler's hesitation, she, along with increasing numbers of other critics and scholars (Everett 1996; Forbes and Street 2000; Petrie 1992; Vincendeau 1998; Wayne 2002), feels able to identify and assess key trends and concerns visible across different national and regional cinemas that enable us to identify certain key characteristics of European cinema. These include cultural and historical traditions, of course, often cited by those who equate European cinema with art cinema or high culture. But increasingly they have to do with new and complex notions of identity and voice; with gender, sexuality and marginalisation; and with the shifting dynamics of centre and periphery within a social and political context shaped by exile, immigration, conflict and change. Such an approach, whilst rejecting the attempt to supply a closed definition of European cinema, does allow for fruitful exploration of, and new insight into, an idea of European identity which openly acknowledges multiplicity, instability and fragmentation, and clearly reveals the formative role of cinema within the process.

History, Tradition, Identity

Despite the present domination of the film industry by Hollywood, the fact that Europe still feels that it has a privileged affinity with cinema is in no small part due to the seminal role it played in the invention of this art form. There is still a keen awareness of the fundamental and open-ended relationship between the formation and articulation of identity – whether personal, national or European – and the moving image. Moreover, it is undoubtedly the case that much of the talent that helped to develop and sustain the Hollywood system originated in Europe. The majority of the genres that characterise contemporary film (comedy, romance, costume dramas, thrillers and science fiction, for example) were developed in Europe in the first decade of the twentieth century, and in the work of pioneer directors such as Georges Méliès, the precursors of today's camera techniques and special effects can be found.

Until the First World War, European cinema entirely dominated international markets, a position highlighted by the fact that between 1906 and 1913, a single French studio (Pathé) was responsible for one-third of the world's film output, for which it controlled the means of production, distribution and exhibition (Sadoul 1947: 221). Moreover, its closest competitors were other European nations, primarily Italy and Denmark. Ironically, Pathé's largest market at this time was the United States, where only about one-third of the films that were screened in the decade preceding the First World War were American (Nowell-Smith 1996: 24). It is interesting to compare this with the present situation in which the American film industry accounts for 74 per cent of worldwide film production investment (Wayne 2002: 6).

However, by the time that the war had ended, much of Europe lay in ruins, and its film industry had been largely destroyed. In the meantime, Hollywood had set about creating an economically efficient method of film production, based on a highly developed studio system and conceived, from the first, as a profit-making industry; its films would henceforth dominate European screens. A second event, although far less consequential in its wider impact than the war, proved no less fatal for European cinema: the development of sound in the early 1930s by those same American studios derailed fresh European efforts to reclaim something of its earlier position. The expensive new equipment that was needed to screen 'talkies' led to the closure of vast numbers of cinemas and studios across Europe. In addition, the transition of film from a 'universal' visual language to a form of narrative largely dependent upon its linguistic component served to reveal the essential diversity of Europe's languages, while brutally restricting potential audiences outside the country of origin.

European national cinemas reacted to the increasing domination of their screens by foreign (particularly American) products by developing systems of quotas and financial support. Germany was the first to decide on the need to adopt protective measures. In 1917, the Universum-Film-Aktiengesellschaft (UFA) was founded in Berlin, with the government acting alongside financial organisations and the armed forces, all of which recognised the role that film could play as propaganda. Foreign film imports were limited, and the UFA developed a strong production, distribution and exhibition network (Mattelart 1998: 479). This system would have a considerable impact on the European film industry in general, and it enabled Germany to provide the only credible challenge to Hollywood in the aftermath of the First World War (Forbes and Street 2000: 6). In Russia, trade blockades imposed by the West (which were not lifted until 1921) meant that foreign films were simply not available. Lenin, famously recognising in film the most powerful of all forms of propaganda, concentrated on strengthening domestic production and exhibition to establish a strong film industry (Taylor 2000: 225). Other countries, including Austria, Britain, Czechoslovakia, France, Hungary and Italy, devised, with varying degrees of success, their own forms of quotas and limits in an attempt to protect individual domestic markets. Across Europe, in other words, systems were already being developed that would shape the future and, some would argue, the essentially defensive responses of national cinemas to the historical vicissitudes of the twentieth century (Forbes and Street 2000; Nowell-Smith and Ricci 1998; Sadoul 1947).

Thus, the protective and defensive strategies that characterise present-day European concerns for its cinema(s) are far from new. Many of them have been in place for the best part of a century, and the concept of the need for some form of subsidy, however contentious, is frequently referenced in any definition of European cinema. As we shall see, within the European Community framework there have been numerous attempts to establish a more systematic approach to the problems experienced by the film industry, primarily involving multi-national collaborations of various kinds. Nevertheless, attitudes to fundamental issues such as subsidies still vary from country to country, and funding and infrastructures remain inadequate. It thus seems difficult to view the present or future of European cinema in other than pessimistic terms.

However, as I indicated earlier, it would be misleading to posit a 'them-and-us' scenario as the cause of the problems facing the contemporary European film industry. This is not only because of the oversimplification that results from positing identity upon Otherness but, more importantly, because many of the problems currently facing European film are entirely European in their origin. Nevertheless, any assessment of contemporary European film production cannot ignore the problematic domination of Europe by mainstream US cinema – a complex situation which, referenced by the title of this chapter, can be illustrated by the following brief examples.

European Cinema and the Hollywood Empire

Although the American market share in Europe has fluctuated widely since 1945 (peaking in 1950 and the late 1980s), the US has consistently been the leading exporter of films to Western Europe, with its share of the EU film market regularly surpassing the local (Lev 1993: xi–xii). Europe is a lucrative market that by 1992 accounted for almost 50 per cent of the turnover of the major American studios. The corollary is that an average of 72 per cent of all cinema takings in Europe go to American films, whose box office receipts for 2002 showed an increase of 13.2 per cent over the preceding year, the largest increase in 20 years (European Audiovisual Observatory 2003; Mattelart 1998: 482). At the same time, the market share of European films in EU cinemas has fallen steadily from approximately 60 per cent in the mid-1960s, a period now widely characterised as the golden age of European cinema, to a mere 23 per cent in 2000. In the early 1990s, Pierre Sorlin (1991: 1) commented: 'We Europeans create images of the world through Hollywood's lenses.' His words are perhaps even more apt today.

It is important not to underestimate the power of the American film industry. In striking contrast with the fragmented, struggling national cinemas of Europe, the Hollywood majors have wide-ranging, big-business interests in areas that include property, theme parks, television, video, satellite broadcasting, merchandising, music recording, newspapers, magazines and beyond. Such a position allows them to exercise economies of scale, to spread their risks and to cross-subsidise their various activities (Wayne 2002: 5–7). Hollywood currently owns the majority of the world's distribution networks and cinema chains, and thus controls what is shown on European screens and when and where it is shown. (A walk around the centre of almost any European city will reveal the extent to which this is true.) Exports in film and media are second in value only to aerospace technologies and agricultural products for the American market (De Grazia 1998: 30). Furthermore, amongst other industries, the status of cinema is particularly privileged because of its political and ideological power, so that although 'the cinema on its own is no longer the economic force it was in the heyday of Hollywood between 1930 and 1960, it remains the central element in a much larger design' (Nowell-Smith and Ricci 1998: 1).

Both the extent to which the American government continues to consider cinema as 'the spearhead of [its] efforts to dominate the media and communications market in general' (De Grazia 1998: 30) and the gulf between American and European attitudes to the identity of film were made particularly clear in 1993, when European film producers and directors, under the leadership of France, fought to exclude film and audiovisual media from the General Agreement on Tariffs and Trade (GATT). American opinion was that film is a commodity just like any other, and that in the name of free trade and consumer choice, subsidies and quotas should not be permitted. The Europeans, however, argued its cultural specificities: 'The film industry is unlike any other. Its products are cultural, public as well as private goods, with a symbolic (historical, national, linguistic, social) significance that cannot be reduced to a mere commodity. No other industry has similar non-economic pretensions' (Hoskins, Mc Fayden and Finn 1997: 3).

A few examples serve to illustrate the repercussions of this situation. In 1993–4, for instance, *Jurassic Park* topped box office charts in Austria, Belgium, Denmark, Finland, Germany, Greece, Hungary, Iceland, Ireland, Italy, Luxembourg, the Netherlands, Norway, Poland, Slovakia, Spain and the UK – that is to say, in all but three of the countries whose statistics I was then able to obtain (Everett 1996: 13). There were, of course, exceptions. France, Switzerland and Sweden relegated *Jurassic Park* to second position, but since it was preceded by other American productions (*Aladdin* in France and Switzerland and *Sister Act* in Sweden), these exceptions offer little consolation. Four years later, *Titanic* became the most financially successful film ever, accounting for some 100 million admissions in the EU and earning more than 500 million euros in box office receipts in 1998.

This trend continues. In 2002, for example, the top 10 films (by number of admissions) in Germany were wholly or partly US funded: *Harry Potter and the Chamber of Secrets* (US); *Ice Age* (US); *Lord of the Rings: The Fellowship of the Ring* (US/NZ); *Lord of the Rings: The Two Towers* (US/NZ); *Star Wars: Episode II* (subtitled, ironically, *Attack of the Clones*) (US); *Spider-Man* (US); *Men in Black* (US); *Ocean's Eleven* (US); *Die Another Day* (UK/US); *Monsters, Inc.* (US) (European Audiovisual Observatory 2003). The situation in Germany was echoed, with slight variations in the films' ranking, right across Europe, and once again exceptions were rare. Spain, for example, placed a domestic production, *El otro lado de la cama/The Other Side of the Bed* (Emilio Martinez-Lazaro), in ninth position. France accorded the top box office position to a French-German co-production (*Astérix & Obélix: Mission Cléopâtre/Asterix & Obelix: Mission Cleopatra*, Alain Chabat), with an entirely French-funded production in eighth position: *8 Femmes/8 Women* (François Ozon). Italy had Italian productions in both first and fourth positions: *Pinocchio* (Roberto Benigni) and *La leggenda di Al, John e Jack* (Aldo Baglio, Giovanni Storti, Giacomo Poretti, Massimo Venier), respectively.

The fact that so few home-produced films make it into the top 10 anywhere illustrates the extent to which US films dominate European screens. However, an even graver problem is revealed by the failure of most European films to cross national borders successfully. The single exception to the above statistics, *Die Another Day*, hardly counts since, despite its 'joint' UK-US production status, it reflects American rather than European production values. As Peter Lev (1993: xi–xii) pointed out more than a decade ago, the inevitable result of American companies investing on a massive scale in European film production since the 1960s is that major decisions about writing, casting, shooting and editing – even in films that are nominally British, French, Italian or whatever – will reflect American, rather than European, values.

Admittedly, the above statistics provide mere snapshots, single frames within a far wider and more complex picture. Nevertheless, they are striking enough to imply that this chapter may be setting itself up as a trailer for yet another disaster movie in which European cinema itself stars as the dinosaur heading for extinction in a new form of Darwinism based upon the survival of the biggest profit makers or, in an alternative scenario, as an ill-fated vessel heading for destruction on an iceberg of Hollywood dimensions. Certainly, the evidence to support such a prognosis is plentiful.

At the heart of the problem is the fact that, on average, in 2000, European films secured only 26 per cent of their already meagre box office takings from sources outside their country of origin. With a few well-known exceptions, therefore, it appears that European films do not travel well. Some of the reasons for this are logistical: national, cultural and linguistic differences continue to complicate the circulation of films within a fragmented internal market, with different strategies (dubbing or subtitles, for example) being demanded by different national audiences. Frustratingly, therefore, although the population of the EU (currently at more than 490 million) constitutes one of the largest markets in the world, European films are not yet able to exploit this potential. An obvious deduction might be that Europeans are not interested in their own films and that, given the choice, European audiences will choose slick American action films with sophisticated special effects over the reputedly slower and more complex European equivalent. If this is the case, it can be argued that there is little point in fighting for European films – that they should simply be allowed to disappear. However, leaving to one side the dubious assumptions underpinning such a response, the equation of small audiences with straightforward consumer choice is disingenuous in the extreme. It echoes the comment made by Robert Shaye (*New York Times*, 12 December 1993), then chair of New Line Pictures: 'Entertainment is one of the purest market places in the world. If people don't like a movie or record they won't see it or buy it. The fact that the American industry has been so successful on a worldwide basis speaks to the quality and attractiveness of what we are creating'.

It is worth scrutinising this idea in light of the situation that has already been described. If European audiences do not have access to European films because distribution networks and exhibition outlets are controlled by the Hollywood majors, then 'choice' simply does not exist. It is difficult to want something that you do not know. Even the dramatic rise of the multiplex across Europe – while undoubtedly contributing to the encouraging phenomenon of growing cinema audiences and their increasingly youthful profile – has served to curtail still further the number of European and non-mainstream films being screened because the multiplexes have not assumed the traditional role of the independent cinemas they replaced. Nor can the severely underfunded European film industry hope to compete with the massive media hype and pre-release merchandising that support mainstream Hollywood. And while cultural and intellectual exchange is extremely important, not least in undermining a 'fortress Europe' mentality, nevertheless, no interpretation of the present situation could present the overwhelming domination by a single nation as fruitful cultural exchange, particularly given the constraints that limit the number of foreign films screened in the US. It could well be that European audiences do not go to European films because they have so little opportunity to do so – that they do not so much 'choose' a Hollywood film as have no choice at all.

The Future of European Cinema

Despite the gloomy evidence and pessimistic prognosis suggested above, it is possible to detect a number of more positive signs. In a recent edition of the American journal *Spectator* (encouragingly, devoted to European cinema), Steven Gaydos (2003), executive editor of *Variety/Daily Variety*, quotes briefly from a speech given by Tom Tykwer, director of *Run Lola Run* (Germany, 1998), in which Tykwer listed the films that he had been watching at the 2001 Netherlands Film Festival – including, for example, *Code inconnu/Code Unknown* (Michael Haneke, 2001), *Harry un ami qui vous veut du bien/With a Friend Like Harry* (Dominik Moll, 2000), *Intimacy* (Patrice Chéreau, 2000), *Die innere Sicherheit/The State I'm In* (Christian Petzold, 2000), *Los amantes del Circulo Polar/Lovers of the Arctic Circle* (Julio Medem, 1998) – before turning to the audience and proclaiming, 'You cannot seriously expect me to speak of a cinematic crisis.' Tykwer surely has a point. The range, number and variety of new films appearing in Europe is little short of astounding. In these terms, it is scarcely surprising that Gaydos (2003: 5) believes that European cinema is 'alive and well' – that rather than being in crisis, it is providing 'a continuing opportunity for both audiences and filmmakers'. It may be that instead of concentrating on the problems, critics should acknowledge the richness, diversity and quality that characterise European film production in general.

For example, 625 films were produced in the European Union in 2002 (European Audiovisual Observatory 2003), an impressive total by any standards. Several countries increased their levels of production, whether through co-productions, as was the case in Britain, France and Germany, or through nationally financed films, as in Austria, Italy and Spain. Broader trends also reveal a number of encouraging developments. Between 1990–2001, for instance, 251 first-time directors made first feature films in Spain, statistics that compare well with the total of 97 first features commercially released in France during the French New Wave era of 1958–62 (Armes 1985: 170). It is recognition of such evidence that led Carlos Heredero (2003: 32), writing in *Cineaste*, to underline the 'rejuvenation' and 'revitalization' of Spanish cinema in the last decade of the twentieth century. Admissions to cinemas across Europe are buoyant: numbers increased by 10 per cent in 2001, so that by 2002, total EU admissions had risen to 933 million. It is thus clear that going to the cinema continues to constitute an important activity across the Continent, despite predictions to the contrary. Even in Britain, numbers are increasing; in 2002, it registered the strongest overall performance, with ticket sales of 176 million making it currently the second-largest market in the EU, after France. And as has already been observed, the average age of cinema audiences throughout Europe is falling. So if the European film industry continues to improve distribution and exhibition structures, the future could very well be positive.

For example, in 2002 the market share for European films in the European Union had risen to 27.6 per cent, a significant gain over the 2000 figure of 22.9 per cent and potentially indicative of a positive longer-term trend (European Audiovisual Observatory 2003). Such developments may reflect European initiatives designed to strengthen the industry, such as the European Union's MEDIA programme in its various incarnations: MEDIA (1987), MEDIA II (1995) and MEDIA Plus (1999). While the programme's responsibilities and levels of success have fluctuated over the years, it has undoubtedly encouraged closer cooperation between various European countries and improved development and distribution strategies. It is largely thanks to the MEDIA initiatives that there has been a steady increase in the number of European films distributed outside their countries of origin and that a range of new and established directors, including Terence Davies, Fridrik Thor Fridriksson, Damien Old, Istvan Szabo and Lars Von Trier, have received financial support. Recent funding trends, however, particularly in Britain, have been designed to promote commercial projects rather than the more traditional low-budget, personal narratives, and that move is problematic in all sorts of ways.

Of the various funding initiatives, Eurimages, the Council of Europe's fund for co-production, which was set up in 1988, is almost unique in prioritising film as a means of expressing cultural identity (Jäckel 2003: 76). Between 1989 and 1992, Eurimages supported a large number of successful films whose cultural importance has been widely recognised, including, by way of example, *Reise der Hoffnung/Journey of Hope* (Xavier Koller, 1990, Switzerland/UK), *Toto le héros/Toto the Hero* (Jaco van Dormael, 1991, France/Belgium/Germany) and *Trois couleurs: Bleu/Three Colours: Blue* (Krzysztof Kieslowski, 1993, France/Poland/Switzerland). By 1996, Eurimages' involvement in European film co-productions reached 46 per cent, and the centrality of its role, particularly for countries with low production capacity, is now widely acknowledged (Bizern and Autissier 1998: 70).[2]

Other positive initiatives and developments include the European Film Promotion Board and the regular provision of accessible data by organisations such as the European Audiovisual Observatory and the Lumière Database. A number of tax incentives have been introduced to assist local film industries without excluding foreign producers, and there is growing recognition of the importance of festivals in creating professional and public awareness, establishing international contacts and launching film careers. While European cinemas continue to experience problems, the broader panorama is encouraging, and in the vast majority of national cinemas there seems to be a sense of guarded optimism. But above all, there is still a conviction that Europe needs to create its own images and to tell its own stories.

What can be deduced from these contradictory viewpoints? In the introduction to *Focus 2003: World Film Market Trends*, published by the European Audiovisual Observatory (2003), André Lange comments: 'The creative wealth of European art house cinema requires no demonstration: it is on display each year at Cannes as at other festivals. But Europe's capacity to produce a significant number of popular films, capable of crossing borders, does remain to be demonstrated.' Quality, in other words, is beyond dispute. What matters, Lange argues, is Europe's ability to sell more popular films – specifically, those designed for the adolescent market. It is interesting to juxtapose this statement with one made by Carolyn Lambert, head of policy for the British Film Council: 'The necessity to take the audience into account is gradually coming to the forefront of the filmmaker's consciousness in Europe. Filmmakers are more aware of the need to satisfy audiences. That is a very important step' (Gaydos 2003: 9).

What is being suggested is that in order to be successful, European directors must learn to 'satisfy' audiences. This idea is worrying, not because of a desire to fight for an elitist, exclusive form of what is known as 'art house' cinema, but because it is misguided to suppose that producing something to satisfy an audience is the solution to European problems. Knowing only too well what effect such a policy has had in the US, there seems little point in aping (in a far less professional manner), the formulaic narratives of mainstream Hollywood. Nevertheless, in many of the arguments currently being put forward by the British Film Council, along with a number of other funding bodies in Europe, we can trace an increasing desire for a predictable, safe product. An obvious example is Sir Alan Parker's infamous speech to the British Academy of Film and Television Arts on 5 November 2002, in which he demanded that British film directors should renounce their 'little England' mentality, should stop squandering lottery money and tax breaks on low-budget domestic films and should embark instead on larger-scale co-productions with the Americans (a policy that is being actively promoted in Britain today). Since 'successful' British films such as *Notting Hill* make 85 per cent of their revenues outside the UK, he maintains, Britain should specifically target this wider (US) market by giving up 'parochial' British films.

His argument is that European films are a failure because they do not produce the profits of their Hollywood equivalents. But low-budget, small-scale films do not, of course, need to achieve so much to recoup their costs. And low-budget, small-scale films are something Europe does very well. Furthermore, one wonders how Parker's notion of the parochial relates to the work of directors such as Ken Loach, Mike Leigh and Lynne Ramsay, given that their low-budget, essentially personal/local (parochial?) films are so widely revered abroad, or to films such as *The Full Monty*, which broke all records in the US even though 'they don't even know where Sheffield is' (Chanan

2003: 3). Indeed, as Alex Cox (2003: 6) points out: 'The most successful films of recent years have been the opposite of the focus-group, sequel-orientated Hollywood model. They are surprises which sprang from the warp and the woof of regional production, low-budget movies whose success could not have been predicted. *Trainspotting, The Full Monty, Billy Elliot* have all been huge international hits. Add to these the international success of *East Is East* and *Bend It Like Beckham* … and it's obvious there's a large market for low-cost specifically British films.'

If it is the case that the differences and fragmentation that characterise the identity of Europe and its cinemas pose manifold problems, they can also be seen as its strength. European films are quirky and unpredictable; deal with personal, regional or national viewpoints; and contain unfamiliar languages, cultural habits and ideas. But they share something far more important: a recognition of the primacy of images in interrogating and creating our individual understanding of ourselves and the world, and the importance of cinema in articulating complex issues of contemporary life and shaping our imaginative and intellectual understanding of these issues. This is not the same as saying that European films are not entertaining, amusing and enjoyable for the spectators – indeed, the contrary is true. But they function in original, individual and essentially unpredictable ways. Far from 'satisfying' us, they are not afraid to challenge, provoke and inspire us.

Reframing European Cinema and Identity

Discussions of the financial and other problems facing European cinema, and of its current position and status, lead us to key questions, such as whether it would matter if European directors were not able to make the sorts of films they think are important, or, more critically, whether we actually need European cinema at all. Does film have a role to play beyond pure entertainment? Would it matter if, as suggested by my chapter title, we simply allowed European cinema to fade gracefully away? In other words, does European cinema continue to play an important role for Europeans, and, if so, what might that role be in a global, postmodern world? The concluding section of this chapter will approach such issues by briefly examining a number of recent filmic trends and ideas.

In highlighting specific trends or individual films, it is not my intention to argue that they are necessarily more significant than any others, nor that they provide some particularly privileged insight into the identity of European cinema, which, as we have seen, is essentially diffuse and multifaceted. Rather, they serve to indicate important aspects of the relationship between film and the changing identities of postmodern European societies.

The first development I shall discuss is the current of autobiographical films, particularly popular in the 1970s and the 1980s, in which directors were looking back at their childhood in an attempt to understand the past. In so doing, of course, their primary concern was to reach a clearer understanding of their present identities, memory and identity being inextricably linked. The phenomenon of filmic autobiography is fascinating in a whole range of ways, not least as the articulation of a new narrative form with its own generic specificities, but also because of its ability to transgress boundaries of public and private discourse. By accessing intensely personal memories, such films were also able to offer new insight into far broader issues of national identity.[3] *Au revoir les enfants/Goodbye Children* (1987), for example, in which the French director Louis Malle probed painful and partly suppressed memories of his childhood experiences at a Catholic boarding school in France during the occupation – specifically touching on his lingering sense of guilt about the arrest of his Jewish friend and schoolmate by the Nazis – also opened up national issues of collaboration, hypocrisy and prejudice that had, in post-war French society, remained hidden beneath a myth of universal resistance. In a similar way, Claire Denis's personal exploration of childhood trauma in her autobiographical film *Chocolat* (1988) was also an assessment of the national guilt of France in relation to its colonial history. One of the earliest German autobiographical films was *Deutschland, bleiche Mutter/Germany, Pale Mother* (1980), in which Helma Sanders-Brahms interweaves her childhood memories of the war with the memories and experiences of her mother. By opposing the notions of fatherland and mother tongue, Sanders-Brahms accesses painful issues of silence, compliance and guilt. Her quest to understand her own identity thus becomes an exploration of the identity of contemporary Germany in relation to its Nazi past. In her autobiographical *Napló gyermekeimnek/Diary for My Children* (1982), the Hungarian director Martá Mészáros searches for her own fragmented identity as a Hungarian child, born in the USSR and repatriated to Hungary after the death of her parents. Essentially, however, she is also trying to understand and articulate the history, memories and identity of Hungary, whose national identity was itself under threat due to the domination of the USSR.

Films such as these were suddenly appearing right across Europe, and if one of their striking characteristics was their ability to cross public and private boundaries, to access universal concerns through their essentially intimate lenses (in vivid contradiction of the comments about parochialism noted earlier), they can also be recognised as successful 'crossover' films, since they appeal to audiences across national, linguistic and temporal borders in a particularly striking way. As part of the postmodern obsession with issues of identity, therefore, they offer a whole range of important new cultural perspectives. But what they also provide, viewed retrospectively, is a powerful insight into the social and political upheavals that were marking Europe at the time. It is as if, on the brink of closer unification, nations and individuals alike felt a need to reassess and re-evaluate historical difference – and to reapportion blame. Given that the sensory immediacy of film images enables spectators to experience, as if at first hand, the divergent viewpoints and angles of the narratives, while thus provoking an essentially creative response, it is clear that such films were able to play a dynamic role in representing and re-evaluating Europe's complex and painful past and, more importantly, in suggesting new routes to future understanding and change.

If this small-scale, intimate genre, flourishing at a moment of historical change and uncertainty, was able to address wider, problematic issues and debates, it is important to recognise that it was equally successful in giving voice to the traditionally marginalised. For example, in the struggle of women to move from the position of object to that of subject or creator of the camera's gaze, autobiographical films played an important part; in the 1990s, a number of young female directors broke into the male-dominated industry with autobiographical first features. Examples include Lynne Ramsay's *Ratcatcher* (1999, Scotland), a film that explores memories of family life in a Glasgow tenement at the time of the refuse collectors' strike, and Sandrine Veysset's *Will It Snow For Christmas?* (1996, France), which deals with memories of equally harsh family life on a farm in Provence. Autobiographical films also continue to give a voice to immigrant directors, both male and female, allowing them to escape their previous marginalisation within European society. Examples include Tevfik Baser in Germany; Mehdi Charef, Yamina Benguigui and Tony Gatlif in France; and Gurinder Chadha in England. To some extent, of course, this is because such films are basically cheap, requiring minimal crew and technical facilities. However, this very feature, along with their intensely personal focus and their open-ended, challenging narrative constructs, also positions autobiographical films centrally within the traditions of European filmmaking.[4]

Another fundamental characteristic of filmic autobiography is its intense self-consciousness and self-referentiality. Films in which the screen doubles as a mirror in all sorts of complex ways – for both director and spectator – are packed with references to cinema as both a source of identity and a means of its articulation. It is to the cinema, for example, that Julie, Mészáros's alter ego in *Diary for My Children*, turns in her desire to recapture a blissful pre-Oedipal existence with her parents and to find the role model that she lacks in their absence. This move is typical of autobiographical films as wide ranging as Guiseppe Tornatore's *Cinema Paradiso* (1988, Italy) and John Boorman's *Hope and Glory* (1987, England). In *The Long Day Closes* (1992, England), Terence Davies not only repeatedly references his childhood passion for the cinema but specifically acknowledges memories of film and popular culture as core components of his personal identity, underlining, in so doing, the centrality of film for us all.

By the 1990s, it was possible to recognise that films dealing with identity, many of which were also autobiographical, were increasingly being framed as journey narratives. Through the mobile camera work and narrative of this genre, we can discern an increasing emphasis upon identity as an open-ended process: the common message of these films is that there is no 'arrival', or that if there is, it is merely the start of a new journey. The journey format enables directors to explore openly central issues of identity – such as changing notions of Self and Other, including linguistic and cultural difference, stereotype and prejudice – and to foreground unstable and shifting notions of centre and periphery (Everett 2003). Fascinatingly, the self-conscious narratives of these films, many of which simultaneously explore and subvert the American road movie genre, also draw attention to film as a construct and thus foreground the shifting identities of European film itself.

From such a wide and complex current of films, it is almost invidious to select a mere handful for discussion, but one striking example that sets the exploration of personal identity alongside the identity of European film is Fridrick Thor Fridriksson's *Á köldum klaka/Cold Fever* (1995, Iceland). During his treacherous journey across Iceland in mid-winter, Hirata Atsushi, the hero of this film, discovers that what matters is not the goal but the journey itself, and that, like a journey, identity cannot be precisely mapped or defined but must be recognised as an ongoing process of change and discovery (Everett 2004b). As part of the journey, Atsushi has to overcome linguistic, gastronomic and cultural differences, and the widening viewpoint that results is signalled by Fridriksson in a move from a tightly restricted screen in the opening sequences to the vast, white spaces of Iceland. In his multi-layered *To vlemma tou Odyssea/Ulysses' Gaze* (1995, Greece/France), Theo Angelopoulos explores the historical and political events that have shaped the violent twentieth-century history of the Balkans by means of a complex journey narrative that transports us backwards and forwards through space and time. In this film, as in his next, *Mia aioniotita kai mia mera/Eternity and a Day* (1998), one of Angelopoulos's particular concerns is the randomness and destructiveness of borders and divisions, whether political, geographical or personal. His films provide a vivid illustration of Rushdie's (2002: 423) comment, 'Give me a line across the world and I'll give you an argument', because they demonstrate the negativity and instability of the markers of difference that we erect between ourselves and the Other. In Angelopoulos's *To meteoro vima tou pelargou/The Suspended Step of the Stork* (1991), we see a village that has been randomly split in two by the repositioning of a national border, so that friends and families are separated and transformed into opposing sides. In both *Ulysses' Gaze* and *Eternity and a Day*, would-be refugees cling desperately to wire fences or stand frozen in a sterile snowy landscape, trapped by such borders within a non-existence of despair (Everett 2004a).

As issues of immigration and exile dominate the media and offer challenges to European preconceptions of place and identity, in a period fittingly characterised by Edward Said (2001: 174) as 'the age of the refugee, the displaced person, mass immigration', so too are these issues increasingly being explored through the films of Europe. These concerns emerge in films as diverse and wide-ranging as *La haine/Hate* (Mathieu Kassovitz, 1995, France), *Raining*

Stones (Ken Loach, 1993, England) and *Trainspotting* (Danny Boyle, 1995, Scotland), for example, and encompass the journey narrative tradition as well as the socio-political treatment of immigration, class and poverty. The films are remarkable for their energy and drive and for the insight they offer into the problems encountered by both immigrants and the societies into which they move, but particularly for their articulation of the experience of exile and homelessness. In *Reise der Hoffnung/Journey of Hope* (Xavier Koller, 1990, Switzerland/Turkey), the exploitation and culture shifts experienced by people on the move are portrayed as a Turkish family embarks upon a doomed journey to Switzerland. Pawel Pawlikowski's powerful *Last Resort* (2000, UK), tracing the nightmare experiences confronting a young Russian woman and her 10-year-old son when they attempt to claim political asylum in Britain, provides a much-needed antidote to the hatred and xenophobia that scream out from the headlines of the popular press.

What is it like to have no home, to live in terror, to attempt to be accepted by a hostile society? Those of us who have not experienced such horrors can perhaps begin to understand, thanks to films such as *Last Resort* and, for example, Michael Winterbottom's powerfully humanitarian *In This World* (2003). These are just two examples of European filmic vision at its best. Along with so many others, these films constitute a key part of Europe's essential process of working through contemporary trauma. The process is made explicit in *De jongen die niet meer praatte/The Boy Who Stopped Talking* (Ben Sombogaart, 1996, Netherlands), in which we see the trauma involved in being forced to leave one's native land for an alien world from the viewpoint of a young Turkish boy. In Holland, a country to which he has no sense of belonging, the child literally stops talking, and the film traces his gradual integration as a process of regaining his voice.

Against the background of the massive changes and upheavals that mark Europe's transition to a multi-ethnic, multicultural society, and in a complex present defined by plurality, diversity and difference, Europeans need, more than ever, their own images to tell their own stories and to explore their own myths and identities. Unlike more commercially orientated films that are designed to 'satisfy' both the audience and the formulaic requirements of the producers by providing their viewers with a clear narrative and an unambiguous conclusion, European films call for a plurality of readings and are perpetually transformative in the open-ended personal journeys they offer. In this way, they are able to celebrate change, variety and difference, and to question dominant attitudes in disturbing and provocative ways. Without its own cinema, Europe would unquestionably be the poorer, for in a world shaped by terror and violence, and increasingly slipping out of control, cinema makes us look afresh at ourselves and the Other, and in so doing becomes an integral and vital part of our mobile and unstable identities.

Notes

1. In terms of cinema, 'Europe' is used to refer to the geographical space which includes, but is not limited to, the European Union. Funding and other initiatives, however, relate in general to the EU member states, as will be made clear in this chapter.
2. In fact, approximately one-third of all UK films made in 1994 and 1995 received funding from Eurimages. Yet despite this, and ignoring considerable protest by British producers and directors, the UK withdrew from the programme in 1996 in a move that seemed calculated to isolate British filmmakers from their European colleagues.
3. For a more detailed account of the theory and practice of filmic autobiography and a lengthier list of such films, see Everett (1995).
4. It is significant that more recently the same phenomenon can be observed in countries such as Iran and Turkey, as women directors – for example, Iranian director Marzieh Meshkini (*Roozi ke zan shodam/The Day I Became a Woman*, 2000) – establish their voice through the first-person narratives of autobiography.

References

Armes, R. 1985. *French Cinema*. London: Secker & Warburg.

Bizern, C. and Autissier, A.-M. 1998. *Public Aid Mechanisms for the Film and Audiovisual Industry in Europe: Comparative Analysis of National Aid Mechanisms*. Vol. 1. Paris and Strasbourg: Centre National de la Cinématographie/European Audiovisual Observatory.

Chanan, M. 2003. 'Cultural Exception, OK?' *Vertigo* 2, no. 4: 3–4.

Cox, A. 2003. 'Britain Is Big Enough'. *Sight and Sound* 13, no. 1: 6–7.

De Grazia, V. 1998. 'European Cinema and the Idea of Europe 1925–95'. In Nowell-Smith and Ricci 1998, 19–33.

European Audiovisual Observatory. 2003. *Focus 2003: World Film Market Trends*. Cannes: Marché du Film.

Everett, W. 1995. 'The Autobiographical Eye in European Film'. *Europa* 2, no. 1: 3–10.

_____, ed. 1996. *European Identity in Cinema*. Exeter: Intellect.

_____. 2003. 'A Sense of Place: European Cinema and the Shifting Geographies of Identity'. In *Schermi della dispersione: Cinema, storia e identità nazionale*, ed. G. E. Bussi and P. Leech, 27–49. Turin: Lindau.

_____. 2004a. 'Between Here and There, Between Then and Now: The Theme of Border Crossings in the Films of Theo Angelopoulos'. In *Border Crossings: Mapping Identities in Modern Europe*, ed. P. Wagstaff, 55–80. Oxford: Peter Lang.

_____. 2004b. 'Leaving Home: Exile and Displacement in Contemporary European Cinema'. In *Cultures of Exile: Images of Displacement*, ed. W. Everett and P. Wagstaff, 17–32. New York and Oxford: Berghahn Books.

Finney, A. 1996. *The State of European Cinema*. London: Cassell.

Forbes, J. and Street, S., eds. 2000. *European Cinema: An Introduction*. London: Palgrave.

Fowler, C., ed. 2002. *The European Cinema Reader*. London and New York: Routledge.

Gaydos, S. 2003. 'European Cinema: The Next Hot Ticket?' *Spectator* 23, no. 2: 5–11.

Heredero, C. 2003. 'New Creators for the New Millennium: Transforming the Directing Scene in Spain'. *Cineaste* 29, no. 1: 32–7.

Hill, J. and Church Gibson, P., eds. 1998. *The Oxford Guide to Film Studies*. Oxford: Oxford University Press.

Hoskins, C., Mc Fayden, S. and Finn, A. 1997. *Global Television and Film: An Introduction to the Economics of the Business*. Oxford: Clarendon Press.

Jäckel, A. 2003. *European Film Industries*. London: British Film Institute.

Lev, P. 1993. *The Euro-American Cinema*. Austin: University of Texas Press.

Mattelart, A. 1998. 'European Film Policy and the Response to Hollywood'. In Hill and Church Gibson 1998, 478–85.

Nowell-Smith, G., ed. 1996. *The Oxford History of World Cinema*. Oxford: Oxford University Press.

Nowell-Smith, G. and Ricci, S., eds. 1998. *Hollywood and Europe: Economics, Culture, National Identity 1945–95*. London: British Film Institute.

Petrie, D., ed. 1992. *Screening Europe: Image and Identity in Contemporary European Cinema*. London: British Film Institute.

Rushdie, S. 2002. *Step Across This Line*. London: Jonathan Cape.

Sadoul, G. 1947. *Histoire générale du cinéma*. Vol. 2: *Les pionniers du cinéma, 1897–1909*. Paris: Editions Denoël.

Said, E. 2001. *Reflections on Exile and Other Literary and Cultural Essays*. London: Granta.

Sorlin, P. 1991. *European Cinemas, European Societies, 1939–1990*. London: Routledge.

Taylor, R. 2000. 'Soviet Union (Former)'. In *The BFI Companion to Eastern European and Russian Cinema*, ed. R. Taylor, N. Wood, J. Graffy and D. Iordanova, 222–30. London: British Film Institute.

Vincendeau, G. 1998. 'Issues in European Cinema'. In Hill and Church Gibson 1998, 440–8.

Wayne, M. 2002. *The Politics of Contemporary European Cinema: Histories, Borders, Diasporas*. Bristol: Intellect Books.

Chapter 7

THROUGH THE LOOKING GLASS OF FOOTBALL

Christian Bromberger

Having first surfaced in the English public schools[1] of the middle of the nineteenth century (and officially recognised since 1863),[2] the sport of football not only was born and nurtured in Europe, but also came to encapsulate the values and contradictions of the European industrial societies that were its cradle.[3] The massive expansion of modern sport, with its competitive calendars and autonomous organisation, was inextricably linked to the emergence of 'free time' and a 'civilisation of leisure' amongst the popular classes. It was in this context of the late nineteenth and early twentieth centuries that a game which was originally played by the aristocratic elite spread rapidly in the new industrial cities. In just 20 years, this sport would become one of the most prominent symbols of British working-class culture with the same resonance as the 'pub', 'fish and chips' and the 'flat cap'. Football clubs sprang up from a variety of sources such as the local parish (Aston Villa and Everton, for example) or enterprises (West Ham and Arsenal) as part of a movement of social reform designed to get young workers off the street or to prevent them from indulging in less salubrious pastimes, while promoting a sense of solidarity.

A striking symbol of this swift popularisation of the sport was provided by the victory of the working-class club of Blackburn Olympic over the aristocratic Old Etonians in the FA Cup final of 1883, a competition first held in 1871. Once established as the people's game, football would quickly come to represent a series of values very different from those of its initial promoters in the public schools. The values of fair play, of an honourable defeat and of playing for the pleasure of the game that were seen as fundamental for an amateur

Notes for this chapter are located on page 139.

creed were replaced by the spirit of competition and professionalism (the first professional championship was held in England in 1888), accompanied by the passionate and turbulent support of the fans of 'our club'. Thereafter football would be intrinsically linked to the industrial milieu, to the town and to the sociability of local pubs and bars where matches were dissected, victories celebrated and defeats drowned in beer amidst the exaltation of local patriotism.

The diffusion of football over the European Continent would follow a pattern similar to that which we have just sketched out for England. An amateur sport that was initially the pastime of aristocrats or the upper bourgeoisie would be transformed into a popular sport, a point of identification for the working-class population of a factory, a district or an industrial town. The employees of British maritime or commercial companies were the pioneers of this rapid spread of the game, which first took root in the northern ports with the founding of Havre Athletic Club in 1872, Antwerp FC of Belgium in 1880 and Hamburger SV in 1887. The new sport was soon to appear in the more distant ports of Southern Europe with the creation of Panionos of Athens in 1890, the Genoa Cricket and Athletic Club (the future FC Genoa) in 1893, the Naples Football and Cricket Club (soon to be Calcio Napoli) in 1904 and finally Athletic Club Bilbao in 1898. Students – whether English in European colleges and universities or their European counterparts in England – would also play an important role in the diffusion of the game. Thus, the famous Juventus of Turin was formed in 1897 as a cosmopolitan student club, while Olympique Marseille was founded in 1899 by the young men of the local bourgeoisie who had completed their studies in Great Britain. The presence in Switzerland of large numbers of wealthy young Englishmen in private educational institutions helps to explain the relatively precocious development of football in that country with the emergence of FC Saint Gall in 1879 and the Grasshoppers of Zurich in 1880. The Swiss themselves would contribute to the further spread of the sport at the beginning of the twentieth century, with FC Barcelona being established by Hans Gamper. According to one of the many local legends regarding the birth of the club, Gamper gave the colours (blue and dark red) of his home canton to the team's jersey. Through the intervention of students and the managers of British enterprises, football was soon established in the cities of the Austro-Hungarian empire (Ujpesti of Budapest in 1885, and Slavia and Sparta Prague in 1893). Likewise, in the Russian empire the Morozov Cotton Mills team, a club that after the revolution would become known as Dynamo Moscow, first saw the light of day in 1887.

Very often, football was originally a symbol of modernity and was adopted by the middle classes who appreciated the novelties spawned by the nation known in the nineteenth century as a country of innovation and leisure – that is, England. As the game became popularised, local industries, anxious to organise the leisure time of their workers, associated their names and their wealth with the growth of football clubs. In 1923, Juventus of Turin became the team of Fiat, led by the director of the enterprise, Edouardo Agnelli. In 1930, Peugeot founded FC Sochaux, the first club in France to be composed of professional players, who would later be known as *les lionceaux* (lion cubs) in reference to the emblem of that make of automobile. As for RC Lens, it was managed from 1934 to 1969 by the Société des Mines, with the club stadium situated in the middle of the mine shafts, between the first and ninth pits, and named Bollaert after the then president of the company. In Holland, FC Eindhoven was linked by contract to Philips, while the German team Bayer Leverkusen was named after the chemical and pharmaceutical company which supported it. It would be easy to multiply these examples of ties between football and industry, a connection that appears clearly not only in the major clubs of the early twentieth century but also those of today. In contemporary Germany, nearly all of the principal clubs are concentrated in the Ruhr, and in England, in the northern cities. Finally, in Italy, too, football is above all a northern affair, with the three great cities, Milan, Genoa and Turin, all possessing two large clubs.

Patrons, Trade Unionists and Patronages

Football's rapid spread across the cities of the Continent was not without conflicts and tensions that highlighted the divisions of European societies. In Germany, it was white-collar rather than industrial workers who first sought to imitate Anglophile students by adopting the game (Eisenberg 1998). The diffusion of the sport clashed perhaps more sharply than in other countries with the major development of the pre-eminent discipline at the end of the nineteenth century, gymnastics, which was intended to foster military and patriotic virtues. Football, this 'foreign' sport, which had the additional disadvantage of being professional, aroused distrust and stigmatisation in conservative circles. The importance of industrial companies in sponsoring football was another source of conflict in an era marked by class struggle. The trade unions and socialists of the period feared that the bosses would use football as a means of defusing social tensions and of suppressing the class-consciousness of their employees. As a result, working-class sporting federations were created, which organised their own competitions with the aim of thwarting the 'capitalist football of the exploiters who excite the workers on the playing field as they strive to increase work production in their factories'.[4] This workers' football, with its own structures, was especially important in Germany in the period before the establishment of the Nazi regime; no less than 140,000 players participated in the competition organised in 1930.

The conflicts between the churches and the partisans of laicity, between Protestants and Catholics, would also leave their mark on the origins of football. The Catholic Church initially looked upon football with suspicion, as it involved bodily contact between players and risked encouraging 'the horrible crime of pederasty'. However, they were also anxious to control an activity which was popular with young people and were therefore quick to create their own associations and competitions. The Fédération gymnique et sportive des patronages de France was founded in 1903. A federation of sporting and gymnastic companions, it could claim having supported more than 1,000 football teams on the eve of the First World War. As for the Federazione delle associazioni sportive cattoliche italiane (FASCI), the Federation of Italian Catholic Sporting Associations, created in 1906, it could claim more adherents in 1914 than its lay counterparts. Confronted by these successes, the lay associations created their own organisations. In France, where the conflict was particularly acute, an association of former pupils of the lay schools was formed and organised its own competitions. In the south-west of the country, state school teachers embraced the sport of rugby, in opposition to the football supported by the local clergy. Religious factors played a significant role in towns or regions that were divided on confessional lines. Thus, in Liverpool, the Blues of Everton (Protestant) opposed the Reds of Liverpool (Catholics). The division was even more marked in Glasgow, where the Celtic Football Club, which was founded by a Marian brother and had the local archbishop as president, was supported by Irish immigrants, who opposed their great rivals, the Rangers (Protestants and unionists), who still celebrate, through their songs and slogans, the victory of William III of Orange over the papists in 1689–90.

The Theatralisation of Modern Society

The growth of leisure time and the desire to provide a structure for the activities of young people and workers in particular encouraged the spread of football, and the properties of the game itself, in tune with the values of industrial society, were powerful ingredients in this process of popularisation. The success of football was no doubt connected to a variety of characteristics unique to this competitive contact sport. It was possible to play football in the working-class outfit of blue overalls or in town shoes, in a public square or in a factory courtyard (unlike rugby, for example, which requires large areas of well-maintained grass), with two players or the regulation 11 (or more), with a ball or a substitute for one. Tall or large, fat or thin, everyone can find a place on the pitch (unlike basketball, where great height is a real advantage).

It could also be argued that football's popularity is founded upon the visual and dramatic qualities that the matches create. A match is a singular event, but one that is repetitive at the same time, comparable to the principal forms of representation that have fascinated Western societies. The classic trilogy is respected: a unity of place, of time (two halves of 45 minutes; the length of time traditionally associated with a play) and of action. The progression of a match is not jerky or interrupted (as with American football), but instead echoes the time of a story that Western societies traditionally prefer, with its period of inertia, its twists and turns, its pauses and dramatic moments. Here one rediscovers the *bonne dimension* (right dimension), which, according to Aristotle in his *Poetics*, was that of the tragic model, that is to say, 'one that includes all the events which move individuals from sorrow to happiness or from happiness to sorrow'. But if football has become 'the most serious trifle in the world' (Bromberger 1998a), it is because it condenses and plays out theatrically, in the manner of the true illusion, the cardinal values of modern industrial societies.

As Alain Ehrenberg (1991) has indicated, the popularity of sports resides in their capacity to represent the ideal of democratic societies by showing us, through the actions of their heroes, 'that anyone can become someone', that status is not acquired at birth but is gained through the course of our existence. If Di Stefano, Kopa, Beckenbauer, Blokhine, Cruijff, Rumennige, Figo and Zidane fascinate, it is, of course, because of the quality of their play, but also because we know that they achieve glory through their own merit and not through the accident of birth. It is revealing that sporting competitions took shape at the points in European history when the democratic ideal had come to the fore – in ancient Greece and in nineteenth-century England – and where social competition meant that the overturning of existing social hierarchies was conceivable. It is unimaginable that in the Middle Ages serfs could participate in chivalric tournaments. Football, on the other hand, exalts competition between equals. It puts before our eyes and in our thoughts, in the most stark and realistic fashion, both the fragility and ever-changing nature of collective and individual status, symbolised by the substitutes on the touchline, the rise and fall of star players, the promotion and relegation of teams, the rigorous rules for classification. These competitions could emerge only in societies that preached the ideal of equality of opportunity, where the most lowly can become the leader. Such is the figure of the champion, this invention of modern society.

Several aspects of the game symbolise the essential characteristics of the industrial societies of which it was the product. On the pitch, to achieve success it was necessary to combine collective planning (tactics), the division of labour (a strict definition of independent tasks) and personal initiative. Each position makes specific demands on the individual player – the strength of a defender, who knows how to make himself respected; the endurance of a midfield dynamo, the heart of the team; the skill of the winger, dribbling on a pocket handkerchief; the organisational skills of a number 10, whose vision of the game makes him the 'leader' of the team.

The club and the team were long thought of in rigidly hierarchical terms as an enterprise in which the players were expected to submit, out of a spirit of solidarity, to the directives of managers and owners. This paternalist disciplinary model was particularly notable in the case of large industrial companies such as Peugeot, whose teams were expected to display the company's *esprit de corps*. The 'Juventus style', invented by the legendary Eduardo Agnelli, was symbolised by three s's – simplicity, seriousness, sobriety. Agnelli thus defined a style of play as well as that of a company. The same rigour was on display at Sochaux. According to the company newspaper of 1954: '[I]t is the responsibility of the team to know intimately each player in order to place him in the position where he can achieve his maximum. In the factory, it is the same story; everyone must be in his place, and it is up to the bosses to keep an eye on their behaviour. One football manager later repeated the same formula in 1976: "No consultation, no disputes, a well-established hierarchy."

A similar and yet very different pattern prevailed under Communism. The pattern was similar in the sense that the clubs were frequently associated with major industrial complexes, but different in that they belonged to the state. We can cite the examples of teams, such as Rotor (previously Traktor) Volgograd and the various Lokomotiv, which were designed to symbolise the 'socialist industry' of Moscow, Sofia, Tbilissi, etc. They were different too because the organisation of many clubs was taken in hand by the police force or the army, and was therefore under the aegis of the Ministry of the Interior or the Ministry of Defence. The famous Dynamos (of Moscow, Kiev, Zagreb and Bucharest) were attached to their respective national police forces, while CSKA Moscow, Steaua Bucarest, Dukla Pragua, Legia Varsovia and Partisan Belgrade were the pride of the army. In Hungary, Honved (Defender of the Fatherland), the team of Puskàs and Kocsis, the stars of the great national sides of the early 1950s, depended directly on the Ministry of Defence, whereas Ujpesti-Dozsa was the official police team, whose badge claimed solidarity with the Dynamos, their brothers in socialism.

The authoritarian model which prevailed in both Eastern and Western Europe has been profoundly transformed in recent decades as a result of the political changes in the East, the restructuring of traditional industries and the emergence of a new generation of club directors. The team owners who had achieved success in the car, textile and other heavy industries have been gradually replaced by a new breed of entrepreneurs whose fortunes derive from media[5] and communications, consumer goods and even public works. Their different management styles are reflected in that of their teams, with risk taking and a high media profile distinguishing them from the older generation of owners, who were content to remain in the shadows. The paternalistic values underpinning the loyalty to the team, with former players being assured of the opportunity to work for the company once their careers were over, have been replaced by a liberal approach emphasising the importance of transfers; stars no longer remain tied to their clubs for life.

The Exaltation of Identities

The rapid spread of football was linked to its capacity, as a team game, to symbolise collective identities as well as local, regional and national antagonisms. Football was created in a Europe that was divided into nation-states, where a sense of collective belonging was part of an atmosphere of patriotic mobilisation. It was also a continent marked by religious differences (between Catholics and Protestants, or in the case of the Balkans, between Orthodox and Muslim) and by ethnic and linguistic divisions within the same state (Flamands and Walloons in Belgium; Basques, Galicians and Catalans in Spain; Czechs and Slovaks in the former Czechoslovakia, etc.). In a fragmented continent, where national sentiments have been so virulently expressed, football has offered a call to action and a means of propaganda for a variety of national, regional and confessional allegiances.

It was above all during the inter-war period, marked by the totalitarianism of both left and right, that matches between nations took on a form of ritualised warfare, with appeals for the mobilisation of the community, the use of bellicose symbols and an insistence upon the lessons of history. The second and third World Cups, which took place in Italy in 1934 and in France in 1938, provided the setting for such nationalist and ideological demonstrations, especially in France. In Mussolini's Italy, the success of the national team (winners of the two competitions) was presented as proof of the superiority of fascism over democracy. After the victory of the Italian team in 1934, *Il Messaggero* informed its readers: 'It is in the name of Mussolini that our team has won in Florence, in Milan and yesterday in Rome for the conquest of the world title.' The players themselves were lauded by *il Duce* as 'soldiers of the national cause'. As for the Italian victory of 1938 in France, where the government of the Popular Front had just collapsed, it was attributed to 'the sporting and intellectual excellence of fascist youth in the very capital of the country whose ideals and methods are anti-fascist'. This rather extreme example demonstrates the role that football could play in the affirmation of a nationalist ideology. More commonly, these international competitions reawaken and amplify traditional animosities, as the often bellicose atmosphere arising from matches between France and Germany, Holland and Germany, Poland and Russia, and England and Ireland attest.

Football has not simply been a form of peacetime mobilisation for nation-states. It has also been, and remains, a powerful catalyst for peoples aspiring to autonomy and independence. The Barça Stadium of Barcelona, with its 110,000 supporters, continues to act as the symbol of Catalan identity. Its eulogists describe it as nothing less than 'the epic sublimation of the Catalan people in a football team', as an 'army without arms', as 'the ambassador of a nation without a state' (Colomé 1998: 82). This is not mere metaphor or hyperbole. During the dictatorship of Primo de Rivera, then during that of Franco, the blue and dark red flag of Barça was waved instead of the *senyera*, the Catalan flag, which was banned. Similarly, in the Basque country, the club of Bilbao, Athletic (renamed Athletico under Franco), has maintained its status as an emblem for the Basques.

In Eastern Europe, the competition between football clubs prefigured the implosion of federal republics. Matches between Slovan of Bratislava (supported by Slovaks) and Sparta Prague (supported by the Czechs) were the scenes of brutal conflicts between rival fans, a pattern repeated when Spartak Moscow and Dynamo Kiev played each other in the Soviet Union. One of the first measures taken by newly independent republics of Central and Eastern

Europe was to organise their own national championships and to demand admission to FIFA (Féderation Internationale de Football Association, the world football governing body). The recent example of Yugoslavia reveals the intensity of the emotions aroused by the game and the continuing association with nationalist ideology. Some particularly grave incidents, involving rival players and supporters of Dynamo Zagreb and Red Star Belgrade, were the precursors of the impeding destruction of the federation. These confrontations saw the emergence of an especially violent and bellicose individual, Zelijko Raznatovic, known as Arkan, the leader of a group of supporters of Red Star Belgrade. Together with his followers, he would subsequently found a Serbian militia, the Tigers, during the Bosnian war. The militia was distinguished by its atrocities and then by its mischief under the protection of the Serbian president, Slobodan Miloševic, before Arkan's death in obscure circumstances.

Football also offers a rich terrain for the expression of religious antagonisms. Thus, in Belfast, Protestants support Lindfield and Glentoran, while Catholics are fans of Celtic and of Cliftonville. The recruitment of players has long posed a problem for clubs with a support base constructed on confessional lines. Thus, in 1989, the Glasgow Rangers signed Maurice Johnston, their first Catholic player in over 80 years, inaugurating a less sectarian era, even if unionist and anti-papist slogans continue to be sung in the terraces. At Lindfield, the persistent opposition to the presence of Catholic players was eventually thwarted by the Irish National Committee, which exerted pressure on Coca-Cola, the US sponsor of the Irish Football Association, which threatened to end its sponsorship unless Lindfield changed its stance. The Irish example leads us to one of the strangest and most significant episodes in the history of European football. There have long been two national teams in Ireland, one based in Belfast, which was created before the independence of Ireland (by treaty in 1921), the other established in Dublin in 1921. The two federations (the Irish Football Association of Belfast and the Football Association of Ireland) both claimed to represent Ireland. Two Ireland teams therefore competed in international competitions, and it was only during the 1970s that the confusion was resolved with the appearance on the sporting scene of Northern Ireland.

Linguistic divisions are no less apparent within the world of football. This is the case in Belgium in particular, where the major cities (which are bilingual) and towns on the linguistic frontiers share their favours between Walloon clubs, of which Standard Liège is the standard-bearer, and Flemish clubs, represented principally by FC Brugge (Bruges).

The legacy of history is also reflected through football. In numerous great cities that have experienced crises and decline, such as Liverpool, Naples, Marseille, and are nostalgic for a grandeur that has passed, the local population clutches with even greater fervour to teams that are seen as representing their struggle. Each confrontation with a team that is reputed to be 'cosseted' is perceived as an opportunity for revenge over the vagaries of fortune and often as a means of expressing a rivalry between north and south, which is another powerful feature of the 'mental map' of Europe. Supporters of Naples are accosted on their arrival in the northern stadiums with the cry 'Benvenuti in Italia' (Welcome to Italy) or 'Africani' (Africans), while they reply after a victory with the chant 'Milano, Torino, Verona, questa e l'Italia? Meglio esere africani!' (Milan, Turin, Verona, is that Italy? It's better to be African!).

The various national religious and regional antagonisms that are such a feature of European societies are therefore expressed in football, to which are added the different legacies of sporting history. On such a canvas, the establishment of various competitions (European Cup, Champions League, Cup Winners Cup, European Nations Cup, etc.) has played an ambiguous role. On the one hand, these competitions have helped to reinforce, even to create, a sense of Europeanness by defining a common geographical space, including the East, with a circulation of common ideas and references. On the other hand, they have created a forum for the expression of hostile sentiments between communities and the perpetuation of stereotypes. The genuine fervour that surrounds these competitions underlines one of the major paradoxes of the times: on a European scale, lifestyles are becoming increasingly indistinguishable, yet the sense of belonging to a particular community within the whole is proclaimed with ever-greater intensity.

Styles and Identities

If football consecrates through the colours that one supports different allegiances and loyalties, it indicates at the same time a variety of styles of play, a geography of behaviour that is unique to each town, region or nation. This style, which is perceived as a badge of common identification, is often far removed from the reality of the game that is actually played by the team; it is instead something of a myth or an ancient image that a community hopes to see in itself and to project upon others. This is therefore less a matter of relating how men play and live than a means of understanding how they like to recount their team's game (and their own existence).

From the 1920s onwards, every major team was conscious of the need to emancipate itself from the British model of 'kick and rush', developing in its stead a unique style that was rapidly perceived and commented upon, by both professionals and spectators, as an illustration of either local or national virtues. The technical proficiency, elegance and precocity of the Austrian 'Wunderteam' of 1928 to 1934, for example, was presented as an expression of national virtues. During the 1930s, on the other hand, the Swiss national team invented the defensive strategy known as the *verrou* (bolt), which was interpreted as that of a neutral state that was falling back on itself in the increasingly threatening international context. Similarly, the Italian *catenaccio*, characteristic of the Squadra Azzurra of both the 1930s and the early 1980s, was, according to some observers, an ideal metaphor for the Italian way of life, founded upon the alliance of the *braccianti del catenaccio* (the hard men of the defensive wall) and the *artisti del contropiede* (the artists of the counter-attack). This, it was believed, symbolised two diametrically opposed aspects of what it meant to be Italian: one negative, the other positive; one displaying an absence of method, the other displaying organisational preparation; one marked by creative genius, the other by generosity of effort.

On a regional scale, every local team imposes its own imprint on the game. The 'total football' preached by Rinus Michels, of which Ajax of Amsterdam was the standard-bearer at the beginning of the 1970s, was, at the same time, the image of a unique urban style and culture – that of a city and a generation breaking with the rigours of tradition and emphasising spontaneity and rhythm, interspersed with hints of nonchalance, impertinence and disrespect for convention. At the same time, in opposition to this festive approach, it was possible to cite the deliberate, almost mathematical precision of the tactics employed by Dynamo Kiev and its trainer Lobanovski. The technical mastery, pre-programmed moves and complementarity of the different lines illustrated the virtues of the 'scientific' football of a Soviet capital.

In every nation, the great teams define themselves with a style of their own, symbolising the personalities of the cities that they represent. Thus, an inexhaustible, laborious bravery was said to be the dominant style of the players of Saint-Etienne, a working-class bastion of the 1970s. It is not surprising that in the list of stars established by their supporters, it was Oswaldo Piazza, an Argentinian feted for his courage, combativeness and continual work rate, even when all hope seemed lost, who came out on top. In opposition to this valorous style, we could cite the *jeu à la nantaise* (the Nantes style), noted for its rapid, short-passing game of geometrical patterns rather than excessive effort. The Marseille style is another that is associated with panache, virtuosity and the spectacular rather than hard labour, and the same could be said of the Neapolitan style in Italy. The players who best encapsulate this local style are the South American stars who have coincidentally arrived in pairs and who have deeply marked the history and memory of the club: Pesaola and Vinicio in the 1950s, Sivori and Altafini a decade later, and Careca and Maradona during the 1980s. As for Juventus of Turin, they have traditionally been associated with a style totally opposite to that preached by Marseille and Naples. Marked by a rigorous, disciplined and measured industrialism, its values, including respect, can bring support from some unexpected quarters. Palmiro Togliatti, the former secretary-general of the Italian Communist Party (PCI) was a *juventino* and was occasionally to be seen watching a match alongside the president of Fiat and of the club. On the pitch, the aim was not to pursue 'art for art's sake' or to dazzle, but rather to win: simple tactics, a strong defence and efficiency in scoring were the dominant features of the local style.

We could provide many other examples of these connections between playing styles and the imagined representation of identities. These bonds, however, have become frayed over the last 20 years. Whereas players and trainers once spent the majority of their career with one club, thus ensuring a sense of continuity, they have now been replaced by the modern professionals who flit across the life of their teams, like footballing meteorites, transforming them in the process.

The Team as a Figure of the Community

The composition of the national team (and, until relatively recently, of local teams) offered another metaphor, both expressive and enlarging, of this collective identity and of different conceptions of belonging in the various European countries. To get an idea of the French conception of the nation, of the right of soil over that of blood, of the republican tradition of integration, one could do no better than consult the make-up of the teams that rendered famous the so-called champagne football. Amongst the most feted French players have been Kopa (of Polish origin), Platini (Italian origin) and Giresse (son of a Spanish mother), and in the team that won the World Cup in 1998 and the Euro 2000 were to be found Zidane (Algerian origin), Pires (Portuguese origin), Djorkaeff and Boghossian (Armenian origin), Trezeguet (Argentinian origin) and Desailly (born in Ghana). Such a team illustrates more effectively that any political speech the ideal of the melting pot *à la française*. This 'tri-colour and multicolour' team can be contrasted with the German team that won the World Cup in 1990, which was an almost perfect example of a nation constructed on a community of blood ties. Only Guido Buchwald (whose Christian name recalls the Italian background of his mother) and Pierre Littbarski introduced an element of discordance into an otherwise homogeneous group. To offer another illustration of how football can act as a barometer of integration, it is worth recalling that in 1979, Viv Anderson became the first black player to represent England in an international match.

At the local level, the team has also long been treated as an idealistic reflection of a population's sense of belonging. Sometimes the choice of a player has been directly subordinate to an ideological project, as we have seen in the case of Glasgow. Indeed, another form of exclusion can be identified in this particular context: despite their wealth, both the Rangers and Celtic were reluctant to buy English players. In the Basque country, Athletic Bilbao, also closely associated with a nationalist movement, was composed, with some remarkable exceptions, of local players. In many other cases, the team does not reflect in such a pronounced way the population of which it is the standard-bearer. However, through the composition of the team, it is possible to read some of the intentions of the organisers. In Turin, the formation of the Juventus team has been thought of over the years as the reflection of the universal image of Fiat, which maintains the club. The team must therefore include major international stars, such as the Welshman Charles in the 1950s; the Pole Boniek, the Frenchman Platini and the Irishman Brady in the 1980s; and the Frenchman Zidane in the 1990s. The team also includes players from the Mezzogiorno, where many of the workers in the company's factories originate. Throughout its history, Olympique Marseille has also featured foreign stars amongst its ranks with whom its supporters have strongly identified. Can we not see in this practice the imprint of a history marked by important waves of migration, the ideal image of a cosmopolitanism characteristic of the city?

In short, until very recently, the team symbolised and rendered tangible, through its playing style and composition, the real and imagined identity of the community that it represented. We are now living through the swan song of this period. The Bosman ruling of 1995 (which in accordance with European Union law forbade the existing practice of limiting the number of players from member countries who could be played by a team) and the transformation of clubs into private enterprises have changed the nature of the identification between star players and the public. The players who, in the past, emerged from the streets and who passed most of their careers with the same club (at the price, it has to be said, of a one-sided contract) have been transformed into shooting stars subject to the forces of the market. This transformation has been spectacular in Spain, Italy and, above all, England, where more than half – even on occasion all – of the players of major teams (Arsenal, Chelsea) are foreigners. The English case is all the more surprising because up until the end of the 1970s, foreign players were not recruited; in 1987, no more than 1.9 per cent of players came from abroad, mainly from Holland, Norway and Denmark, together with a handful from Yugoslavia. If today the fervour of support for the team is undiminished, as the crowds in the stadiums would seem to confirm, its nature has gradually changed in significance: the celebration of a closed community has been replaced by a galaxy of stars brought together under the same colours.

The Public and Football

Who are the stalwarts of the terraces, the fans of the football matches that are today shown almost continually by so many television stations? One initial characteristic of the public in football stadiums is its youth: 70 per cent of the crowd, on average, is under 35. This youthfulness is, however, less marked in two of the great footballing nations: England and Italy. This youthful dominance of football crowds is a recent phenomenon which can be seen through a new placement of age groups within the stadium. The 'youth' (15–25 years old) gather on the slopes behind the goals that were once called in France the *populaires* and that we could rename today the 'juveniles'. The emergence of this group of 15–25 year-olds and their attendant subculture is a characteristic of modern European societies, offering an example of how social change is mirrored on the footballing stage.

Contrary to what is commonly thought, this public is not dominated by the working class. Today, those sitting in the stands or in front of their television sets are a diverse group, and throughout Europe there has been a rise in the numbers drawn from the middle classes. This movement, which has been developing steadily over the last 30 years, is in direct contrast to that which occurred in Victorian Britain. Until the 1880s, spectators of football matches were mainly middle class before being replaced by skilled workers. Today, by contrast, the public is diversifying socially from above rather than below. Should we therefore conclude that football no longer constitutes a 'popular' spectacle? The answer is probably no. These representatives of the middle classes are very often the sons of workers. When compared with basketball, rugby, cricket, tennis or Formula One racing, football has a much more popular base.

The gender base of football crowds has also been gradually modified. Surveys conducted in the 1980s and early 1990s indicated a modest feminisation of the football public (from 7 to 14 per cent, depending on the location). More recent statistics demonstrate a significant increase in the number of female spectators: they currently represent around 20 per cent of the total. If it is now possible to meet many passionate women supporters in the stands, it is still rare to find women who go to the game on their own. More often than not, they accompany fathers, husbands, sons or boyfriends, and this commitment to the game is temporary. It is during the period of adolescence that this type of leisure is preferred. Young female fans are keen to take their places alongside their male friends in the stands behind the goals as part of a common rite of passage. Adult women, on the other hand, especially housewives, are rarely seen at the match. Only those wealthy enough to frequent the executive boxes are likely to attend as part of what is essentially a social gathering. The recent refurbishment of stadiums, the 'Disneyfication' of the spectacle and the willingness of clubs to expel the rowdiest elements from the stands have permitted a feminisation to take place and a more family-orientated public to participate. This change can also be identified if we examine the behaviour of men and women during the broadcast of matches on the television. The image of groups of men watching the match together while drinking beer and eating pizza needs to be treated with caution. According to a recent survey conducted in France, 62 per cent of those watching football matches on television are men, 38 per cent are women and in 35 per cent of the cases they watch the match as a couple. However, the intensity of interest varies, with women being less likely to give their full attention to the action or to make commentaries on technical aspects of the game.

Football stadiums can also present a useful barometer of the extent to which minority groups are integrated into the life of a city. The presence in the stands of immigrants or ethnic minorities can be interpreted as a form of initiation into local society and citizenship. Thus, in the stadium of Olympique Marseille, the presence of young people of Arab descent is an indication of a process of identification with the city. On the whole, however, football stadiums, where a local sense of belonging is often pushed to extremes, are not particularly welcoming to either newcomers or minorities. The stands resound, here and there, with anti-Semitic slogans, in particular at clubs such as Tottenham (in London), Ajax (in Amsterdam), Austria (in Vienna) and MTK (in Budapest) that were either founded by Jews or are popularly believed to have been so. To this can be added the invective against Gypsies in Hungary and Romania and the insults directed at black players or supporters throughout the Continent. Since the 1990s, there have been many initiatives – sponsored by a variety of groups, including European institutions, football associations and supporters groups – designed to stamp out these expressions of racism and xenophobia (Back, Crabbe and Solomos 2001). However, with one or two remarkable exceptions, it is difficult to believe that football is an effective vehicle for integration, especially in states or cities dominated by *communautarisme*, or separation between ethnic or religious communities. In Germany, for example, Turks organise their own competitions, and only very rarely do they support the professional team in the city where they live.

The different backgrounds of spectators can be read within the stadiums as can the forces that unite and divide modern societies. Each part of the ground, which is divided into stands, ends, boxes, curves, etc., forms in itself a sort of territory with a sense of common belonging that expresses itself as being a part of the collective effervescence rather than dissolving itself within it. This process of identification is organised by more than a simple question of ticket prices, and at times the stadium can appear like a map of the town in microcosm or like a mirror that accentuates the lines of division marking our societies. The warm, well-fed and wealthy occupants of executive boxes that dominate the skyline of the stadium look down on the young supporters braving wind and rain from the stands behind the goals to support the team. In all the great stadiums, one of the sections behind the goals provides the rallying point for the most organised and ardent supporters: at Liverpool, it is the famous 'Kop'; in the ground of Standard Liège, 'the Hell side'; at Marseille, the *virage sud*; in Naples, the *curva B*, etc. These macro-spaces, where it is possible to express and to read differences of status and of fervour, can be broken down into subgroups defined by ties of sociability: workmates, regulars of a bar, employees of the same company (whose seats are paid partly or entirely by the company). The row of seats in the stadium is a classic means of cementing ties of friendship, and 70 per cent of the spectators come to watch a match as part of a group, usually with friends (for two-thirds of them), more occasionally as a family (for the other third). Does this mean that those who come alone remain isolated? More often than not, they rejoin other regulars of the same haunts or strike up a conversation with a neighbour in the stands, where it is easier to socialise than in a bar.

Supporters

Today groups of football supporters make their mark very forcibly in urban social life. They can be divided into two broad categories: firstly, associations (with an official status) bringing together mature men on the basis of local or social affinities; secondly, combat groups (associations or loosely formed groups of more or less ephemeral status) of young supporters that have formed in the stands behind the goals.

The associations of mature, respectable supporters first developed in Great Britain at the end of the nineteenth century, becoming sufficiently numerous by 1913 to form a federation. A similar movement, based on the British model, emerged on the Continent slightly later, first in Belgium, where no less than 46 supporters clubs for the one team of Charleroi existed in 1929, and then spreading to other European countries in line with the growth of the professional game. Today, most major professional teams are backed by one or more of these respectable supporters clubs. The phenomenon is particularly strong in Latin countries, especially Italy. At the beginning of the 1990s, the Italian Association of Supporters of Naples could claim 96,000 members, divided into 526 sections, and it is not the largest in the peninsula. Juventus of Turin has more than double that number, while AC Milan is supported by 1,350 sections. Each one of these sections plays the role of a social centre, hosting games, acting as a recreational centre and organising activities, some of which are not even connected to sport, such as family excursions. The associations and many of the sections are administered by local notables (small businessmen, members of the liberal professions, etc.) who have proved their competence and their authority outside as well as inside the football ground.

The battalions of young supporters, who first appeared in England at the beginning of the 1960s (the hooligans), in Italy in the 1970s (the ultras) and in Eastern Europe at the end of that decade, present another face altogether. It is possible to distinguish two main types at both extremes, in the middle of which are a whole variety of groups: at one extreme are frequently short-lived groups of bellicose supporters, while at the other extreme are veritable associations which bring together as many as several thousand members with a clubhouse, membership cards, subscriptions and individual roles carefully divided amongst members who are subject, in theory, to a degree of central control. These two distinct types of organisation are not spread evenly across the European football spectrum. England was the birthplace of the 'crews', a model that has spread to many of the Northern European nations and to the Latin countries, where the associative model remains overwhelmingly predominant.

What are the characteristics of these often violent young supporters, who follow their teams from one side of Europe to the other and appear to consider themselves exempt from the normal rules of partisanship? The conventional image is that of young men from the 'lumpen proletariat', victims of unemployment or social alienation, easily seduced by the ideologies of the extreme-right. Behind the stereotype is a much more complex reality. The only common traits uniting these supporters are their masculinity (to be a violent supporter is interpreted as a stage in a 'virile career'), their age (between 15 and 25 years, occasionally older amongst those who follow the English national team), their fanatical attachment to and support for the team, and their tendency to mass in a particular part of the stadium – behind the goals, on a bend (a *curva* in

Italy), the terraces in England, the sides in Belgium and Holland – which they consider to be their own. That said, neither their social background nor their behaviour or political orientation allows us to create a prototypal portrait of these young supporters.

Sociologically, what is there in common between British hooligans – the young men of the 'rough working class' from depressed former industrial cities – and the Italian, Spanish and French ultras who are recruited from across the social spectrum? Several surveys have demonstrated that these young ultras are ordinary young people. Even amongst the British hooligans, it is difficult to see the link between the skinheads of the 1970s, from the poorest neighbourhoods of the East End, and the 'casuals', who are older and better off, dressed in the latest fashions, infiltrating the stands to launch sudden sophisticated outbursts of violence. With so many national and local variations, even amongst those supporting the same team, the social profile of the violent young supporters cannot be reduced to a single portrait. At most, it is possible to claim that the social origin of these zealous fans is more diversified in the Latin countries than those of Northern Europe, where a working-class identity in crisis continues to reject the prospect of 'embourgeoisement' (trend towards a middle-class outlook) proposed from above.

The behaviour of these militant supporters also varies considerably. In the majority of cases, support for a team and animosity towards an opponent are expressed through a series of highly codified and ritualised forms which only occasionally degenerate into out-and-out violence in a specific context of the game (incidents in the match or the outcome of a decisive game). These sporadic outbursts contrast sharply with the premeditated pursuit of violent confrontations either within the stadium or in the surrounding area, where the sporting context is only a pretext for conflict. Thus, in Germany, it is possible to make a clear distinction between young fans, who passionately support their team, and 'hools', who are in search of a fight, even at matches where their own team is not playing. These forms of gratuitous violence, whose connection to the natural partisanships of sporting confrontation is only tangential, developed strongly during the 1980s in the northern hotbeds of football, but also in the Latin countries, notably Italy.

Given the diversity of their social origins and modes of behaviour, can these groups of football extremists share the same ideology? Xenophobic chants, shaved heads and fascist salutes would appear to suggest that the stands have been infiltrated by the extreme-right. An aggressive, often hateful presence cannot be denied: the ultras, followers of Real Madrid, were nostalgic for *francoisme,* while the skinheads, supporters of East End clubs, attacked the cosmopolitan hippie culture with an exaltation of old community values and hatred of foreigners. In Belgium, Holland, Germany, Italy (especially Lazio of Roma), Greece and France (notably Paris), numerous groups of young fans proclaim racist and anti-Semitic sentiments. They have discovered, on the terraces of the stands, one of the rare public spaces for the expression of 'values' that are not tolerated in society at large. Yet these highly visible and noisy demonstrations can hide much more complex, fluid and ambiguous patterns of behaviour. We can, for example, draw attention to the great variety of ideological claims associated with these ultras: the promotion or defence of a local and regional identity (as in Barcelona, Marseille or Naples), and even the leftist or extreme left-wing protest (the use of the term 'ultras' is born out of the 1968 social movement). It is also important to note that these affiliations, political slogans and gestures are often specific to the context of a football match. Such aggressive symbols are brandished with the aim of provoking or intimidating rival supporters rather than promoting an ideology. In other words, these young supporters are using politics as much as they are being used by politicians, with the exception of the cases cited above of those whose actions are given brutal expression outside the confines of the stadium. So if neither social deprivation nor political ideology can explain the behaviour of these extreme football fans, where should we look for an explanation?

The ultras claim, first of all, the right to be considered as actors and not simply spectators or consumers. They reject the status of consumer which is promoted with ever-greater vigour by the clubs and the football federations, whose motto might best be described as 'Pay up, sit down and behave yourself'. In contrast, these supporters assert through their actions a right to act and react. They are also motivated by a burning desire for recognition: to be seen, they are eager to show off and have to show off, to borrow the apt definition of Alain Ehrenberg (1986), which is at the base of this juvenile subculture. Moreover, these young enthusiasts, with their scarves and banners displaying their names, colours and affiliation, celebrate their own group as much as they do their favourite team, if not more so. Like all enthusiasts, they are tireless collectors, but they cherish press cuttings illustrating their own presence and exploits above all other documents. To be seen, recognised and identified – even through the medium of violence – is the ultimate accolade for this sort of supporter, which goes against the conventional frontiers of representation. Rather than being invisible and anonymous figures watching the exploits of stars, they have succeeded in attracting the attention of the media, in winning the badge of celebrity.

These common characteristics – a passion for football and a particular club, a sense of local pride, the search for excitement and strong emotions, and a desire to demonstrate virility, to do something to be recognised and to conquer the most visible space in the stands – take diverse forms. Such aggressive groups are looking above all for the maximum amount of excitement through violent clashes. Fights take place less often now within stadiums, which are increasingly closely policed; trouble mainly occurs outside in railway stations and on trains or other forms of public transport, where the 'firms' or 'crews' have come to the fore in England, Holland and Germany, as well as ininternational matches staged in Europe. The majority of groups of young supporters, especially in the Latin countries, have an alternative structure and have been transformed over the years into small businesses with their own employees and often sophisticated equipment. (The largest bring together several thousand members and special-ise in selling seats for matches and football merchandise.) Some of these groups have gone even further, adopting a project that goes beyond sport or manage-ment whereby social participation is transformed into a form of political mili-tancy. These *bachelleries* (a name given in earlier times to groups of young single French men) play a role as independent *maison des jeunes* (youth clubs), offering their members an alternative form of socialisation, with its own rites and ideals captured in 'fanzines' that are deliberately anti-establishment or libertarian.

When looked at as a whole, these ties and solidarities that are born of a com-mon devotion offer evidence of a quest for a meaningful life and new forms of social relationships. It is clear that the terraces behind the goals are an excellent position from which to observe the re-emergence of youth as an autonomous age group and new rites of passage to adulthood, as well as existing patterns of sociability which form around a shared passion. In the past, major religious, lay and political institutions, under the control of adults, sought to organise the free time and leisure activities of young people, while shaping their expres-sions of militancy. The organisation of young football supporters is testimony to the changes that have occurred. The desire to run their own affairs and to act independently, the sense of solidarity and the emergence of leaders from outside institutions characterise these groups that the clubs fear, on account of their unruliness and autonomy.

Today, modern groups of organised supporters, both young and old, wish to be more directly involved in the running of the clubs that they support and for which they agree to make important sacrifices. While many clubs are trans-forming themselves into public companies floated on the stock market and are moving away from their public, the fans have organised a counter-offen-sive by becoming shareholders (as was the case at Manchester United, albeit with mixed results, and elsewhere in England) and henceforth making their opinions known within the company and not simply from the stands. This participatory model is particularly understandable if we take into account the evolution of the role of stadiums, which are now replete with shops, cinemas, nurseries, restaurants and even venues for weddings and receptions. They are becoming a *lieu de vie*, or social centre, that recalls, without too much exag-geration, the confraternities of the past.

Between the Ritual and the Show

The fervour of supporters, the cult of star players, the space taken by the stadium as an urban monument and the sentiment of community which is expressed therein make it tempting to draw parallels between a key football match and a religious ritual. It is somewhat of a paradox that a modern secular sport, which flourished in the great industrial cities, arouses and reactivates the grand cere-monial forms. What, then, are these affinities between a big match and a ritual?

For a start, one could highlight the spatial similarities. The large urban stadium has often been presented as 'the sanctuary of the industrial world' (Bale 1993). It has become an essential element of contemporary patrimony. The division of the public in this enclosed space brings to mind the rigorous distribution of different social groups in major religious ceremonies. Indeed, there is a strong bond between spectators and their stadium, as there once was between the peasantry and its church bells. For the most committed fans of a football club, the pitch has all the qualities of holy land (the turf, when acquired, is preserved preciously). We can also identify certain temporal and rhythmic similarities: competitions follow a regular and cyclic calendar which culminates at certain times of the year and mirrors the ineluctable cycle of the seasons, while the linear time frame with its promotions, relegations and uncertainty is combined with the ritual time and its repetitions.

It is also possible to highlight behavioural similarities. The 'faithful', of whom the most fervent are grouped together in what resembles confraternities (such as supporters groups), express their emotional excitement through a form of intense choral and physical participation – collective singing is an inseparable part of the ritual – through highly regulated collective gestures and attitudes or even sometimes by a state that is close to that of a trance. Clothes and other accessories contribute to this metamorphosis of appearance and behaviour that characterises ritualised time. Such practices symbolise the sense of community that one feels (the changing emotional state on arriving in the stadium). The accolades and warm conversations with unknown fellow fans, meals taken together before, during or after a match – these sudden, ephemeral transformations of ordinary social relations result in social cohesion and solidarity.

There is also something about the game and spectacle of football that conjures up a belief in the active presence of supernatural forces, which is the backbone of religious ritual. Football appears, in fact, as a world of refuge, a creator of magical religious practices, a means by which one can believe in the possible efficiency of symbols. The most fervent players and supporters engage in propitious rites to ensure good luck. The former pay particular attention to the choice of their boots, to the way they tie their laces; the latter sport a diverse group of symbols (scarves, badges, etc.) to summon good fortune. The big stadiums also appear as a site for the collection of rites, a place where a variety of customs are performed to avoid bad luck. This fragmented religiosity attests that for those who subscribe, the sense of place and the chain of cause and effect are at least partially beyond the powers of man. Is it necessary to underline the fragility of these beliefs? Not everyone shares them, and those who respect them remain sceptical about their efficiency. 'I know, but one never knows', they say, 'it's better to have everything possible on our side', thus testifying to the ambiguous status of belief today.

It is again the similarities to religious rituals that mark the practices of consecration or veneration in the world of football. Objects such as the cups, shaped like a chalice, which are sacred after being filled with wine, and attitudes of devotion – half-serious, half-parody (in relation to the star players) – testify to the affinities between a big match and a religious ritual. We need only to recall the Maradona mania of the Neapolitans, the 'canonisation' of the star during the celebrations of the Scudetto (the badge symbolising the title of champion of Italy) of 1987 and his transformation into Saint Gennarmando, a cross between the patron saint of the city and that of the star. We could also invoke the pious example of the most devoted supporters who have transformed their homes into a kind of domestic altar, where photographs of players and team emblems take the place of relics.

Whatever the individual nuances, all of these attitudes bear witness to a form of minor religiosity which borrows from the model of conventional devotion and varies in intensity from one set of fans to the next. There exists in the stadium, as in the church, a scale of devotion, from the fanatics ready to employ violence and to risk their lives if their clubs are put in jeopardy to the occasional supporter whose fervour is only lukewarm.[6] Some go to the match as if to a mass; others assist at a religious ceremony as if it was a spectacle. But what is actually being celebrated? In contrast to the great religious festivals, big football matches offer no answers to the key existential questions of where we have come from and where we are going. But they do consecrate and theatralise in a form of dramatic fiction the basic values that shape our societies: individual merit and collective solidarity, competition and performance – the kind of classification that is esteemed in societies obsessed with exam results. Sportsmen have thus become the heroes of our time, a cross between stars and saints, the incarnation of contemporary ideals at the head of which is that of physical perfection. Is it not noteworthy that the fashion model–footballer couple is the pinnacle of the imagination of popular culture?

As we have seen, the different competitions also exalt different allegiances and territorial loyalties, something that is recalled by national anthems and by the flags unfurled on the terraces. They provide a means for a fragmented society to attest to and to reaffirm a sense of continuity and collectivism that is missing from the daily lives of many. The football match illustrates that the gravity of a great ritual, as in a religious ceremony, is never far from derision: tragedy mixes with comedy (there is plenty of laughter in the stands), belief with scepticism, membership with distance, the moral and collective obligation to support one's side with the individual desire to have a good time.

The people's game appears today as a form of hybrid, balanced between ritual and spectacle, between ceremony and entertainment, between the fervour of a believer and the leisure pursuit of a consumer, between passion and the market, with its contracts and its intermediaries. Neither a simple show nor a recognised ritual, it constitutes a new genre, a reflection of the contradictions of our times.

– Translated from the French by Julian Swann

Notes

1. For a British perspective on French football, see Dauncey and Hare (1999) and Dine (2000).
2. This is the date of the creation of the English Football Association and the beginning of the standardisation of the rules of the game.
3. For an introduction on nation and sports, see the following publications: Blain, Boyle and Donnell (1993), Bromberger (1994, 1995, 1998b, 2005), Duke and Crolley (1996) and Holt (1996).
4. See the text of the Fédération sportive du travail, quoted by Wahl (1989: 193).
5. For works done on the media and sports, see Rowe, McKoy and Miller (1998), Wenner (1998), Rowe (1999) and Crolley and Hand (2002).
6. See also the works of Brown (1998), Colomé (1998) and Connelly (2000).

References

Back, L., Crabbe, T. and Solomos, J. 2001. The Changing Face of Football: Racism, Identity and Multiculture in the English Game. Oxford: Berg.

Bale, J. 1993. Sport, Space and the City. London: Routledge.

Blain, N. and Boyle, R. 1998. 'Sport as Real Life: Media Sport and Culture'. In *The Media: An Introduction*, ed. A. Briggs and P. Cobley, 365–76. London: Longman.

Blain, N., Boyle, R. and O'Donnell, H. 1993. *Sport and National Identity in the Media*. Leicester: Leicester University Press.

Bromberger, C. 1994. 'Football Passion and the World Cup: Why So Much Sound and Fury?' In *Hosts and Champions: Soccer Cultures, National Identities and the USA World Cup*, ed. J. Sugden and A. Tomlinson, 281–90. Aldershot: Arena.

_____. 1995. *Le match de football: Ethnologie d'une passion partisane à Marseille, Naples et Turin*. Paris: Editions de la Maison des sciences de l'homme.

_____. 1998a. *Football: La bagatelle la plus sérieuse du monde*. Paris: Bayard.

_____. 1998b. 'Le football: Phénomène de représentation collective'. In *Géopolitique du football*, ed. P. Boniface, 41–8. Brussels: Editions Complexe.

_____. 2005. 'Se poser en s'opposant: Variations sur les antagonismes footballistiques de Marseille à Téhéran'. In *Passions sportives, identifications et sentiments d'appartenance*, ed. R. Poli, 35–55. Neuchâtel: CIES.

Brown, A., ed. 1998. *Fanatics! Power, Identity and Fandom in Football*. London: Routledge.

Colomé, G. 1998. 'La péninsule ibérique dans la tourmente des Ultras'. In *Quels supporters pour l'an 2000?* ed. G. Comeron, 82–90. Brussels: Labor.

Connelly, C. 2000. *Spirit High and Passion Pure: A Journey through European Football*. Edinburgh: Mainstream.

Crolley, L. and Hand, D. 2002. *Football, Europe and the Press: Imagined Identities?* London: Frank Cass.

Dauncey, H. and Hare G., eds. 1999. *France and the 1998 World Cup: The National Impact of a World Sporting Event*. London: Frank Cass.

Dine, P. 2000. 'Sport and Identity in the New France'. In *Contemporary French Cultural Studies*, ed. W. Kidd and S. Reynolds, 165–78. London: Arnold.

Duke, V. and Crolley, L. 1996. *Football, Nationality and the State*. London: Longman.

Ehrenberg, A. 1986. 'La rage de paraître'. *L'amour foot, Autrement* 80 (May): 148–58.

_____. 1991. *Le culte de la performance*. Paris: Calmann-Lévy.

Eisenberg, C. 1998. 'Les origines de la culture du football en Allemagne'. *Société et Représentations* 7 (December): 33–48.

Holt, R. 1996. 'Contrasting Nationalisms: Sport, Militarism and the Unitary State in Britain and France before 1914'. In *Tribal Identities*, ed. J. A. Mangan, 39–54. London: Frank Cass.

Rowe, D. 1999. *Sport, Culture and the Media*. Buckingham: Open University Press.

Rowe, D., McKoy, J. and Miller, T. 1998. 'Come Together: Sport, Nationalism and the Media Image'. In Wenner 1998, 119–33.

Wahl, A. 1989. *Les archives du football*. Paris: Gallimard.

Wenner, L., ed. 1998. *MediaSport*. London: Routledge.

PART III

CHALLENGES TO EXISTENT FORMS OF BELONGING AND CULTURAL VALUES

Chapter 8

Parties, Identity and Europeanisation
An Asymmetrical Relationship?

David Hanley

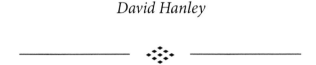

It is generally accepted that political identities are structured via a variety of agencies, yet it is less clear what function political parties play in this process. The literature assigns them a number of roles, principally that of aggregating political demand – seeking to represent, in an overarching way, a swath of opinion across civil society and to obtain from the political process the gratification of desiderata emanating from such support groups. In government, parties are expected to elaborate policy and run the state machinery, while in opposition, to criticise and challenge government, ensuring a healthy political debate. Perhaps their most valuable purpose is the formation and propagation of a political elite; parties are training grounds where political professionals learn their trade. Some analysts see them as enterprises that pursue commercial strategies in a political market and hence need to reward their workforce (activists) and shareholders (voters) at regular intervals (Gaxie 1986; Offerlé 1987). Other accounts dwell on the communitarian nature of parties; they are seen as giving identity or purpose to activists and supporters, who come in from the cold, as it were (Abélès 1992: 155).

None of the above roles connects, on the face of it, with questions of identity building, European or national, that are at the core of this volume. The agencies that helped form the 'imagined communities' (Anderson 1983) of modern nation-states – that is, governments and other parts of the state apparatus, particularly the education system and, in the era of conscription, the armed forces (Weber 1977); the mass media; organic intellectuals (Gramsci 1971) – are not, in the main, party dependent. Political parties have been at the heart of government since the advent of mass democracy, but their direct part in the nation-building process may be modest. Some types of parties may seek to play a bigger role than others; those defining themselves explicitly as nationalist seem an obvious example. Yet the overall contribution of parties to the formation of national identities would need a thorough exploration. So would the contribution of so-called Europarties (we prefer the term 'transnational party', or TNP, used hereafter) to the formation of some hypothetical European demos, a body of citizens or voters which thinks of itself as European more than (or at least as much as) belonging to a specific nation.

First, we will examine the general development of parties in nation-states in relation to the problem of national political identity. Then we will consider the Europeanisation of national party politics, particularly the emergence of TNPs and their relation to national parties. This should enable us to reach a provisional judgement regarding the extent to which parties have helped shape national political identity and modified it in any supranational sense.

Parties in Nation-States

Lipset and Rokkan's (1967) model of party development set the parameters for modern approaches to party scholarship. They saw parties as deriving from a number of recognisable cleavages within nation-states as they developed. A cleavage is understood as a reaction to issues raised at key stages of development, which separates social groups on either side of the cleavage line and provokes their mobilisation, mainly through the organisational mechanisms which we know as parties. The cleavages are principally socio-economic and cultural. Typically, an evolving nation-state will experience a class cleavage as its economy develops towards full capitalism, pitting members of the old order (aristocrats) against the rising bourgeoisie. In their turn, these latter will confront another rising class, that of the industrial workers, which their own entrepreneurial activity has called into being. If these clashes occur in the context of an evolving democracy (with the extension of suffrage), they are likely to be solved not by violence but by politics. Each major social group will tend to form a party or parties to fight for its corner democratically within the new institutions; thus, the bourgeoisie (or, more accurately, some of its political entrepreneurs) will form liberal or 'secular conservative' parties to combat the older conservatives who represent the past order. In their turn, workers will find themselves represented by socialist, later Communist, parties.

One further consequence of economic development is the growing differentiation between town and country. Rural populations, especially the large peasantry found in all Continental states as modernity set in, would soon feel squeezed by market pressures, as they clung to traditional modes of production and lifestyles; their interests were not the same as those of growing urban populations, bourgeois and working class alike. This urban-rural cleavage led to the formation of agrarian and peasant parties, and many scholars see today's Green parties as developments of these, perpetuating or renewing a cleavage which they prefer now to describe as market-nature (Seiler 2000: 144–8; 2003: 154–61).

These socio-economic cleavages run in parallel with cultural clashes. Modern states seek territorial unity and undisputed legitimacy in the eyes of their citizens. To secure unity, centralising, standardising practices are usually applied by the state-builders in the national capital, in order to marginalise older, more distinct cultures on the edge of the new states, which drew in varied populations as they expanded. Peripheral populations, with their own lifestyle, culture and sometimes language, tend to resist centralising imperatives, which they feel threaten their existence. They will usually form parties, described as regionalist or nationalist, to defend their periphery against the big modernising parties (liberals or socialists) of the centre; in some states, this centre-periphery clash can override the class cleavage.

A different cultural cleavage is that of church and state. The Catholic Church in particular stood for a different set of loyalties from the modern state, and was also a holder of power in its own right, owning property and dominating parts of the state apparatus, particularly schools; in many cases, this was reflected in the church's established status. Modern states would launch attacks on what they saw as the privileged position of the church, seeking to reduce its influence in public life, if not to eradicate it; in Scandinavia, the preferred solution was to have an established Lutheran Church, which clearly understood that it had a subordinate role within the state. In the eyes of modernising statists, the church was viewed as a rival focus of loyalty and hence inadmissible. This explains the rise of anti-clerical parties on the state side of the cleavage and, on the other side, of what Seiler (1980: 302–36) calls parties of 'religious defence', epitomised by the Christian Democratic (CD) parties after the Second World War.

Such are the historic cleavages which produced modern party systems across Europe. All states have members of the different party families, to varying extents. In some states, one cleavage overrides others, simplifying the number of parties and thus the nature of partisan competition. Other states boast a vigorous pluralism, sometimes with more than one party from either side of a cleavage. Many analysts believe that another cleavage has emerged forcefully in recent years, namely, that between supporters of European integration and defenders of national sovereignty (Hix 1999: 168–87; Hix and Lord 1997: 26–7).

We turn now to the question of how parties dealt with issues of national identity and culture as they emerged within modernising nation-states. Clearly, any response involves a high degree of generalisation, but it seems possible to distinguish different approaches according to political family. In the period before 1914, all types of party, whether in government or opposition, had to learn how to operate in a distinct set of national institutions. The nation-state was the framework for most political activity, while the framework for the economy was still primarily national, although there was an increasing trend towards what was not yet called globalisation (Hirst and Thompson 1999: 1–62). International relations were carried on, mainly bilaterally, between 'Westphalian' sovereign states in the absence of supranational institutions. This does not mean, however, that all party families necessarily approached the nation in the same way; there is a distinction between recognising the need to work within certain parameters and making an emotional, cultural and identitarian investment in one's nation-state.

Parties on the right of the spectrum, who were most involved in governing and developing nation-states, tended, unsurprisingly, to identify most with ideas of national unity, seeking to portray themselves as key actors in the realisation of national destiny. Typical are the national-liberal parties of Germany and Austria-Hungary, which were centralisers and modernisers of an often reluctant periphery (Seiler 2002). Bismarck, a conservative who allied with liberals against Catholics precisely in order to reinforce national unity in the new German state, came to symbolise a certain definition of German nationhood – confident, tough and expansionist. The British conservatives at the peak of imperial expansion could be seen as occupying a similar position within their political system. Few of the other families, however, invested so heavily in national identity and culture; we could even say that they were not allowed to, as the governing parties of the right sought to make the national space their own and impose their definition of it.

Catholic parties had a particularly difficult time (Mayeur 1980). In the late nineteenth century, modernising governments launched attacks on the Church's positions in public life: *Kulturkampf* in Germany and Austria, Republican drives to separate church and state in France. The modernisers' message to Catholics was clear: loyalty to the church came second to loyalty to the state. Liberals contended that the church's role in the state must be reduced, while the more radical anti-clericals called for its eradication. Catholics mobilised slowly against the attacks, first in voluntary associations and only later in religious parties, as the Vatican belatedly realised that modernity had come to stay and that there would be no rescue by reactionary forces as had happened previously (Kalyvas 1996). When Catholic parties emerged, then, they did so as opponents of a dominant consensus within their political system, which saw them as outsiders and, to varying degrees, illegitimate. This is why formations such as the Zentrum in Germany or the various Catholic groups in France would not be allowed anywhere near government coalitions until after 1918. In the circumstances, it is not surprising that these parties concentrated on assembling their own people and defining a political project for them. The main result of this is the philosophy of personalism, derived from the writings of Jacques Maritain and Emmanuel Mounier, which Christian Democrats still proudly espouse today. A crucial part of this project is to see political identity in anything but nationalist terms. For personalists, national identity is just one of many concentric circles of identity in which all persons share – from the local to the professional to the municipal to the European. At bottom, then the

Catholic, and later Christian Democratic, parties' concept of identity has been largely defined *against* the dominant paradigms of the nation-state.

In some cases, Catholic parties would become strong enough to enter national politics as mainstream players, particularly after 1918. The classic cases are the consociational democracies of the Benelux countries, where for many years politics was conducted by a system of accommodation and compromise in every area of public life between the pillars of communities – Protestant, Catholic, secularist (Lijphardt 1968). But even these parties, which came to be the core of their party systems, retained a supranational dimension.

The socialist family also experienced a conflictual relationship with the nation-state. Divided between revolutionaries and reformists, socialist parties were subjected to varying degrees of state harassment; however, most were primarily concerned with defining (and constructing) their class. The motor force of history was, for most of them, not the nation-state but class; Marxism in particular, the major influence on the European workers' movement, looked forward to a future when producers would be in control and nation-states and their rivalries irrelevant. This focus on identifying and strengthening the class could involve the building of sets of counter-institutions – educational, cultural, leisure – which enabled the class to live almost in a vacuum, cut off from the rest of society. The Sozialdemokratische Partei Deutschlands (SPD, or German Socialist Party) was a model to other parties in this respect. Inevitably, such a class focus took place at the cost of downplaying, if not denying, national identity. Some theorists and leaders such as Jean Jaurès sought to make positive links between national culture (the progressive nature of French Republicanism and radical anti-clericalism) and the socialist project. Others, however, subscribed more aggressively to the growing sense of national confidence based on an expanding economy and empire (e.g. the 'social imperialists' in the SPD and the British Left before 1914). In the main, though, socialist parties tended to stress class ties and minimise or ignore nationalist loyalties. As with Catholics, they were seen to an extent as illegitimate outsiders by governing parties, owing to being based on a problematic of class rather than nation. They, too, were generally kept away from office, even when they were a major force, such as the SPD, or were rising rapidly, such as the French Section Française de l'Internationale Ouvrière (SFIO, or French Branch of the Workers' International) and the UK Labour Party.

The same is true of parties of the periphery, the oldest of which, the Partido Nacionalista Vasco (PNV, or Basque Nationalist Party), recently celebrated its centenary. Representing minorities within powerful centralised states, these parties could only try to group their populations electorally and promote consciousness raising. Within the wider national parliaments, their function was *témoignage* (bearing witness); they could argue for home rule or even outright secession but were unlikely to be heard by those in power. Again, these parties supporting ethnic groups were mobilised on premises different from those of the governing forces, which sought to reinforce nation-states.

Generally, then, we might say that a pattern emerges from the years before 1914, when modern party systems became established across much of Europe. On the right, conservative and some liberal parties provided governing elites who were comfortable with the national framework and strongly identified with national values and culture, which they often helped to define. These parties of the (territorial) centre and the property owners were confronted by other parties who mostly remained peripheral to policy making. In their different ways, Catholic, socialist and regionalist parties remained excluded from mainstream politics and concentrated, logically, on developing their own foci of identification and loyalty: religion, class and ethnicity. In a Europe of nation-states, parties not subscribing to the idea of the nation could only be onlookers.

The First Transnationalism: An Exception Which Confirmed the Rule?

During this period, one highly significant and novel development occurred which adds nuances to, but hardly invalidates, the above picture – the establishment of some transnational party collaboration via the Socialist International (SI). Previous attempts to unify working-class movements had failed, owing to the struggle of revolutionaries and reformers and to personality clashes, but by the mid-1880s, socialists faced a different context. Politically, Europe had been reconfigured; Germany was unified as a powerful empire after the 1870 war, and the Continent settled into a multi-polar balance-of-power system. Social and industrial transformation was rapid, and the working class was increasing in numbers and becoming more organised. Under pressure from below, suffrage was being widened. Many viable socialist parties, albeit not all Marxist, were active in European states, although the SPD, with its big intellectual apparatus and respected thinkers such as Karl Kautsky, tended to dominate ideological debates. The presence of these much stronger constituent elements led in 1889 to the founding of the Second International. Again, this organisation was based on the primacy of class and the inevitability of socialist revolution, which the Second International would try to coordinate.

The SI could never act as a directing centre of world revolution, however, as its parties disagreed on many points. It failed to develop the proper machinery, not getting a general secretary until 1910, along with a small handful of permanent staff (only the Germans had many; the SFIO had but six full-time staff by 1914), while national parties kept control of resources. The SI did achieve some modest gains, such as arbitration between contending parties within one country; thus, the SFIO was formed in 1905 when the SI voted that the Guesdists and Jauresians should merge. This arbitration would become a feature of future Internationals and TNPs. But disagreements on policy, ideology and tactics persisted, with differences often arising between the Germans and the French.

The key issue was the question of war and peace (Haupt 1972). From 1900 on, imperial rivalries intensified, and Europe hardened into two military blocs: the Entente (France, UK, Russia, then Italy) versus the Triple Alliance (Germany, Austria/Hungary, Turkey). Both were unstable, multinational empires with strong demands for autonomy in the Balkans and elsewhere. War seemed highly likely at several points after 1900, and at every stage, SI parties tried to use their leverage to prevent it. The question was, how?

One tactic always surfaced in debates: the general strike against mobilisation. If war threatened, workers in every country were to refuse the call-up. If armies could not be formed or transported to the front, war would not be possible. The SI parties had to decide if such a drastic option was feasible and whether to back it openly, as a deterrent. In fact, the SI split. Some parties – the SFIO especially, but also the British Independent Labour Party (ILP) of Keir Hardie – urged the strike, while the SPD hesitated. The Stuttgart Congress resolution of 1907 showed this underlying ambiguity: parties should do everything to prevent war, but in the event of war breaking out, they should take advantage of the conditions to launch a revolution. This famous text contained, as Joll (1955) remarked, something for everyone while committing no one to anything. It also showed the real dynamics of the SI and hence revealed its impotence as an international actor. When the Serbian crisis erupted in 1914, the SI was again unable to act decisively, despite a flurry of last-minute activity. Once fighting began, all socialist parties swung behind their national governments. The SFIO actually joined the government it had been trying to overthrow, and the SPD voted war credits (opposition to military budgets had been an article of faith in SI parties). The International collapsed overnight.

What does this show? Despite revolutionary rhetoric, socialist parties and voters were slowly becoming integrated into their national societies, to the point that they were willing to side with their governments in wartime against the working class of other states. Various causes have been adduced for this 'negative integration' of workers into their national communities, among them rising affluence, the effects of welfare measures (especially in Bismarckian Germany) and a growing sense that revolution was unnecessary, as unions could bargain for better conditions and reforms could be extracted via parliaments. National parties sensed this, and some realised that they could not actually mobilise 'their' class against a war. It was better, then, not to make verbal promises that could not be fulfilled. Some factions within parties increasingly argued either against revolution (as did Bernstein and his followers in the SPD) or even spoke actively in favour of collaboration with the imperial state (as evidenced by the 'social imperialist' currents).

The failure of the SI showed that national realities were stronger than internationalist, class-based dreams. This experience would mark future attempts to revive the SI. The inter-war Socialist and Labour International and the post-1951 SI have always proceeded on the lowest common denominator; nothing can be done without massive consensus (Devin 1993; Portelli 1983; Van Zyl and Vorster 1997). SI activity has consisted mainly of an exchange of views and platforms, arbitration within the socialist family and modest attempts at diplomacy on issues such as disarmament (Hanley and Portelli 1985) or North-South relations. The socialist family has remained bruised by an overambitious attempt at supranational activity and mistrustful of the whole concept.

Why did early socialists invest so much in transnationalism? Clearly, it was a question of opportunity structure. In no country had socialists been in power, even though they were major forces in some: there were 100 SFIO deputies in 1914, and the SPD was the largest party in the Reichstag. Socialists were either frozen out of the governing clique of parties as in France (Hanley 2002b) or, as in the case of the SPD and the Austrians, operating in authoritarian systems where parliament's role was only consultative. They could achieve little in the domestic arena beyond a politics of imprecation (defending strikers, refusing to vote defence budgets). Yet through the SI, they could perhaps make an impact in one area – international relations. The context was favourable, precisely because Europe was such a dangerous, unstable place. It seemed plausible to see the SI as a genuine international actor, able to influence the behaviour of governments in a way unavailable to individual parties at home, and hence the huge investment.

This episode shows that parties will follow institutional opportunities, even if it means creating a new institution. The tragedy is, however, that the experiment failed, resulting in a legacy of mistrust. Parties were pushed back into their national systems and had to try to seek influence there.

The brief attempt at transnational collaboration of another family, the Catholic parties, mirrors the problems and failures of the socialists (Papini 1988: 25–45). The short-lived, inter-war Secrétariat International des Partis Démocratiques d'Inspiration Chrétienne (SIPDIC) fell apart under Franco-German tension and the rise of fascism. By the Second World War, it seemed that all party families had to operate in a national institutional context, where legitimacy accrued only to parties perceived by electors as soundly anchored within their nation-state and its culture. The parties of the Communist family, which challenged this very assumption, began to make significant progress (e.g. in France and Spain during the Popular Front) only when they moved towards a more national discourse and trimmed their revolutionary internationalism.

Europeanisation

Developments after 1945 began to influence the way in which parties related to nationhood and national identity. We refer to the whole process of Europeanisation, although we stress from the outset that this process is not just top-down, but also bottom-up. Europeanisation is a dialectic. Parties have helped to form European institutions and build some European consciousness, but at the same time they have been forced to adapt to what they have helped to create. This process is, moreover, ongoing and must be understood in a dynamic rather than static way (Featherstone and Kazamias 2001: 1–19; Goetz and Hix 2001).

From a party point of view, the earliest moments of European institutional building remain in some ways the most crucial. The European Coal and Steel Community (ECSC), Euratom and the European Economic Community (EEC) were the result of agreements between coalition governments in France, Italy and Benelux, with a key input from the German Christlich-Demokratische Union/Christlich-Soziale Union (CDU/CSU, or Christian Democratic Union/ Christian Social Union). Without accepting the caricature of the Europe of the Six as 'la petite Europe vaticane', it is clear that CD parties played a major role in the launch of the European project, but so equally did social democrats and liberals. We will investigate shortly the reasons why these forces were ready after 1945 to invest in a transnational – indeed, explicitly federalist – project, but let us note for the moment that by creating institutions of a parliamentary character, these party families laid down parameters for the development of parties at the transnational level. This may not have been entirely clear to the protagonists at the time, but such was the result of their actions.

Right from the start of the Common Assembly of the ECSC, the national delegations of the three main party families constituted themselves as transnational party groups (Kreppel 2002; Murray 2004). They would soon control the running of the Assembly (allotting speaking time, finances, etc.), via the conference of presidents, in a manner typical of multi-party parliaments on the Continent. It matters little that the Assembly's powers and those of the EEC assembly – later, the European Parliament (EP), into which it was subsumed – were modest, involving debate, not control. Genuine transnational groupings had been created, and so had a style of work, based on certain shared assumptions. This pattern of national parties adjusting to new institutional opportunities by devising new forms of transnational collaboration has persisted to this day. As opportunities have grown, so has the degree of transnational collaboration (within limits, however, as will be shown). Yet at the same time, it is the cooperation amongst leaders of national parties (acting in their capacities as heads of government through the European Council and its predecessors) which has created those new opportunities in the first place. Such is the paradoxical dialectic of party Europeanisation, the main phases of which we briefly recall.

So long as the EP remained a debating chamber without a significant role in EC/EU decision making and without the legitimacy of direct election, there was little incentive for transnational groups to evolve. The European Council's agreement on direct EP elections for 1979 led to a flurry of organisational activity. The loosely structured groups tightened up their organisation and even referred to themselves as parties. The European Peoples' Party (EPP) was created by the Christian Democrats in 1976, as was the European Liberal, Democrat and Reform (ELDR) Party (officially it was a federation of parties until 1993, when it adopted the title of party). It would take the confederation of socialist parties until 1992 to adopt full party status as the Party of European Socialists (PES).

Successive agreements on extending EP powers after the Single European Act and the Maastricht Treaty furthered this evolution. The co-decision procedure, since extended, and the EP's role in appointing the Commission have made it a much more important actor in the EU's decision making, even if it is not (as many reproach it), a 'proper' parliament that sustains and controls an executive derived from its ranks (Hix 1999: 74–9).

The EP groups and the national parties of which they are an emanation have followed this evolution of the institutions by gradually moving towards full party status, or at least what they describe as such. After a long passage through EU institutions, regulation (EC) No. 2004/2003 of the European Parliament and of the Council – on the regulations governing political parties at the European level and on the rules regarding their funding – was finally approved on 4 November 2003. Following the override of a legal challenge from the Danish Euro-sceptic leader Jens-Peter Bonde, the regulation came into force in time for the new 2004–9 parliament. In anticipation of the financial and other opportunities granted by this regulation, most of the EP groups had converted themselves into European parties. Thus, in addition to the long-standing TNPs – EPP, ELDR, PES – and more recent additions in the shape of the regionalist EFA-DPPE (European Free Alliance–Democratic Party of the Peoples' of Europe) and the EFGP (European Federation of Green Parties), there have recently emerged the European Democratic Party, affiliated with the liberals within the EP; the Party of the European Left, based on the United European Left-Nordic Green Left (UEL-NGL) group of ex-Communists in the EP; and a party of sovereignists, the Alliance for a Europe of the Nations (based on the Union of European Nations group). At the start of 2006, the Euro-sceptic family, located mainly in the independence and democracy group within the EP, even joined in the act with the fairly cynical creation of not one party but two: Bonde's EUDemocrats and the Alliance des Démocrates Indépendants en Europe (ADIE, or Alliance of Independent Democrats in Europe). It would be unwise to assume, however, that this development of TNPs means that national parties in the EU states have all become converted to European integration and are pushing for that goal through their EP representatives. Examination of the TNPs suggests a much more nuanced picture.

Between the Nation-State and Europe: The TNPs

According to Article 191 (formerly Article 138a) of the Maastricht Treaty, the main justification for a party statute was that '[p]olitical parties at European level are important as a factor for integration within the Union. They contribute to forming a European awareness and to expressing the political will of the citizens of the Union'. Despite the new regulation, which pro-Europeans see as falling well short of a proper party statute, it can be argued that little has changed in the way that national parties see Europe. This can be inferred from an overall analysis of the TNPs themselves, in light of the regulation, and then from considering the main party families in turn (Bardi 2002b; Bell and Lord 1998; Delwit, Kühlaci and van de Walle 2001).

The Structures of TNPs

Panebianco (1988) sees parties in terms of their institutionalisation, that is, the degree to which they control their environment rather than being dependent on it. A key factor in determining how well a party institutionalises is what Panebianco calls its genetic code, which is partly determined by its founding sponsors, or parents, if we are to keep the biological analogy. The TNPs are clearly weakly institutionalised, their ambitious titles hiding fundamental logistic and political weaknesses. These have been programmed into their genetic code by (national) parents with their own agenda. To take the simplest measures of party strength, one might expect a strongly institutionalised TNP to score well on the following counts, in line with the record of most of its various national 'fathers': mass membership, powerful central apparatus, autonomous sources of finance, control of candidate nomination, effective party discipline, programmatic control, strong loyalty from members/supporters/voters. Instead, all existing studies show how poorly the TNPs actually perform on all these counts. In some cases, such as the PES, mass membership was ruled out from the start; with regard to the EPP, it seems mainly a resort for members of organisations in countries who cannot get their group affiliated to EPP.[1]

No TNP can lay claim to a heavy central apparatus; the PES, for instance, has some dozen staff. As a rule, staff support was provided by the parliamentary group, and similar considerations applied to finance. Clearly, the protracted struggle to obtain a party regulation will ease three-quarters of the problem. But this still leaves one-quarter of the monies to be secured elsewhere, and it is hard to see sources other than the traditional ones – namely, national parties – becoming available. EP groups have now presumably been ruled out; the final push towards a party statute was triggered by a Court of Auditors' ruling that group financing of TNPs was illegal. Thus, as regards both elements of infrastructure – staff and finance – parliamentary groups have had a large amount of control and may continue to exert an influence. It should not be forgotten that these groups are emanations of national parties and represent vehicles for aspiring young politicians and sometimes places of rest for the more experienced ('elephants' graveyards', as German members of European Parliament, or MEPs, call them). Such people are not going to cross their national leadership with impunity. Thus, Luciano Bardi (2002a: 298) may have been optimistic when he saw the parliamentary groups as potential building blocks for TNPs; it could be argued plausibly that they are as much growth inhibitors as enhancers.

Turning to candidates, no TNP has hitherto secured the right to draw up its own lists for EP elections, much less to have multinational lists in each country. Candidate provision remains the preserve of father parties and so, to an extent, does discipline. Coercive whipping in the Westminster mode is unknown, and cohesion can be obtained only by agreement. Most studies show relatively high scores for the cohesion of voting within groups. Where there is variance, it is usually along the stress lines between national delegations within a group (Hix 2004; Hix, Kreppel and Noury 2003; Hix, Noury and Roland 2002). Clearly, such delegations are obeying instructions, however oblique, from their home parties. Raunio's (1997) studies of the relationship between home parties and MEPs do not suggest a different picture. Increasingly, the bigger parties are appointing an official exclusively responsible for managing the MEPs and their link to the rest of the party.

It is sometimes suggested that the fact that TNPs now usually have a common electoral manifesto is evidence of their growing integration as genuinely supranational entities; however, caution should be observed here. Generally, a programme is the easiest thing to establish in political organisations at any level; language is always sufficiently elastic to enable conciliation between divergent positions. It is also true that during the actual campaign, it is very much up to the national parties to determine what prominence, if any, is given to a TNP's manifesto or indeed to any other dimension of the TNP's existence (e.g. visits by prominent politicians from other countries, even the use of the TNP logo on campaign literature). The model employed by most TNPs at the approach of the 2004 elections seemed to be that of a two-page campaign letter, very general in character, which home parties could use as they wished. The PES in particular felt that the effort put into past manifestos (and into disguising disagreements between members) was largely a waste of time.[2]

Hitherto, national parties have done very little to promote awareness of TNPs, meaning that another of the above conditions – widespread identification on the part of voters/supporters – has obviously never existed. The European demos for which political scientists hunt amid the statistical debris of the Eurobarometer remains as elusive as the white wolf of French folklore.

Even the use of qualified majority voting (QMV) for certain decisions within the leadership bodies of the TNPs is of limited value (Johansson and Zervakis 2002). Such decisions apply to areas covered by QMV in the European Council. This parallelism reflects the fact that a modest amount of national sovereignty has been pooled over some defined areas, in what is essentially an intergovernmentalist bargain. To put it another way, party leaders in intergovernmental conferences have agreed to a modest measure of integration, which they concede at the same time to the TNPs operating in the EP. This is a small gain, but it needs to be set against the numerous barriers to TNP growth outlined above.

On all the indices of 'partyness', the TNPs rate poorly. Not only are they weakly institutionalised in Panebianco's terms, but it seems that their genetic code makes this inevitable. They were founded by sponsors whose ambitions for them were very limited. The TNPs were simply required to perform a number of coordinating tasks, mainly in an arena (the EP) whose decision-making role was circumscribed; later on, the function of coordinating leaders' actions during the European Council was added on. But neither of those functions requires a strong party (measured by traditional criteria), so no such party was forthcoming.

This pattern of growth inhibition has continued ever since the inception of the TNPs, albeit with some differentiation between families. It can be seen retrospectively that crucial to the determination of growth patterns is the environment in which parties evolve, an environment which implies competition. But a national environment is very different from a transnational one. Within national institutions, a party is in direct contact with those whom it seeks to mobilise, according to long-established cleavages. The parliamentary arena is only one of its levels of action, its presence within civil society being equally important – at least, this was so for many decades, although arguably today what counts is media impact. A party is under constant pressure to raise support and finance in order to combat other parties, also based on societal cleavages, which are similarly battling for control of public policy through government. (This does not exclude collusive behaviour at times, but the dominant mode is one of competition.) In short, the creation of stronger, more vigorous parties (with access to real levers of power) is induced by the higher stakes for which politics is played at the national level.

If the stakes are less, however, as happens at the European level, what incentive is there to create stronger vehicles? Hitherto, the main need at this level for national parties has been to try to influence the workings of the EP, a body whose role involves the modification of policy rather than its initiation. In this case, a loose coordinating body, which provides for reasonably efficient joint action with like-minded parties from other states, when appropriate, is an adequate vehicle. The precedent of the SI is particularly relevant for socialists here. Anything stronger, with possible binding majority decisions on members, is not required; home parties may not always want to agree with other family members. A weak TNP is in fact a perfect intergovernmental vehicle, and the recently acquired function of hosting leaders' summits could be said to make it more so. So long as most national parties that form governments in their own countries wish the TNPs to remain in this weak state, they will do so.

The political environment – that is to say, the stakes available and the type of competition thus engendered – is therefore a major determinant of the degree of institutionalisation which parties can be expected to attain. Such is the logic of the TNPs, and in our view it is unlikely to change fundamentally, despite the real infrastructural opportunities offered by the new legislation. The new structures should simply be seen as a convenient means for national parties to offload some of the costs of running a TNP, without any necessary consequences in terms of increased autonomy for the latter.[3]

The Party Families and Their TNPs

The above judgement might be thought harsh, if applied to all the party families. It is possible, we believe, to nuance the verdict but not to change it fundamentally, even for those parties most committed on paper to European integration. The EPP, for instance, remains pledged to a federal Europe (cf. its Athens programme of 1992), a philosophy of personalism and the social market – three pillars of classic Christian democracy, a term which its energetic president, Wilfried Martens, still employs, even if those around him do so less and less. But EPP behaviour since the early 1990s has done much to belie these values. Not only has its party ideology as a whole shifted towards a neo-liberal market philosophy and uncritical Atlanticism (Hanley 2002a; Hanley and Ysmal 1999), but the group within the EP has, under German aegis, expanded to take in numerous conservative, liberal and nationalist parties, including the British Conservatives, as group allies, known as the ED (European Democrats) (Jansen 1998; Johansson 1997). The ED pole of the EPP-ED alliance has strengthened of late and will do so further with enlargement. Already it is allowed to function as a group within the group, with separate finances and staff; to recruit new members separately; and, most importantly, to preach freely its message of Euro-scepticism (not just of a moderate kind, in the case of numerous MEPs).

By early 2006, David Cameron, the new Tory leader, had signalled his wish to leave the EPP and could be seen in somewhat desperate pursuit of allies from smaller states to form yet another sovereignist–Euro-sceptic party. This gambit owed more to domestic pressures (an electoral challenge from the unforgivingly Euro-sceptic United Kingdom Independence Party) than to real conviction, but there is no doubt that the long-standing conservative presence within the EPP has strongly affected that party's identity. It could be said that the EPP has thus lost most of its identity and cohesion, the benefits for this being deemed hitherto sufficient by its leaders, both in the EP and in the various states (being the biggest EP group, with consequent control of resources and agenda, and furthering the career ambitions of certain leaders). One result of this is the split of the Christian Democratic core of the EP, led by François Bayrou's Union pour la Démocratie Française (UDF, or Union for French Democracy) and the Italian followers of Romano Prodi, to form a new federalist party, the European Democratic Party, with a recognisable CD ancestry. In the aftermath of the June 2004 EP elections, its members sat with the liberals. Once again, opportunity structures within the institutions have determined party behaviour. National leaders of EP parties clearly prize hegemony within the EP at any cost over political rigour, and some of them are not prepared to make sacrifices towards that end even if domestic pressures suggest they should do otherwise.

Similar considerations apply to the socialists. For a long time, European integration promised a new outlet for traditional social democracy, which frequently seemed stalled at the national level, encouraging socialist investment in constructing a 'social Europe'. But successive enlargements have widened the PES membership, and some influential parties (British Labour and the Scandinavians) are clearly reluctant to canvass further integration and are determined to play to national audiences with a sense of their own interest. Labour's feebleness concerning the euro and its latest capitulation – over the draft European constitution – to its friends in the Euro-sceptic press (much of it transatlantically owned) are an eloquent illustration of where it perceives its interests to lie. Even liberalism, with its long-standing commitment to a federal Europe, is less keen to present its message boldly (cf. the much more critical 2004 manifesto of the UK Liberal Democrats). If the regionalists of the European Free Alliance (EFA) remain committed to integration, it is in the hope that the nation-states may thereby loosen their grip and allow peripheral aspirations to flourish; however, they are by definition minorities. The Greens remain split between integrationists, who see their project as depending on political unity and to whom national discourses and identities seem passé (Daniel Cohn-Bendit is a prime exemplar), and jealous guardians of particularisms and differences, which they would be upset to hear described as nationalist (e.g. the UK or Swedish Greens).

In short, there has been a retreat towards a more euro-lukewarm posture across the political spectrum, even by those forces which on paper are the most committed to integration and hence to looking beyond fixed attachment to national identity and a politics based on that. The emphasis clearly varies between party families, but the general trend is visible.

The TNPs and European Identity: A Task Too Heavy?

In light of the hopes expressed for the integrationist role of TNPs, how far should they be blamed for not having inspired greater enthusiasm for European integration among their supporters or for failing to create the fabled European demos? Parties are only one instrument among others for the modification of citizens' attitudes, be it towards Europe or anything else. In many countries, they have to deal with bitterly Euro-sceptic media, and some of the party families have of course always defined themselves as nationalist first and foremost. Their prime task remains the winning of office within their own political system, a necessary prerequisite for influencing European or any other policy. Increasingly, parties sense that for the foreseeable future, Europe will continue to be a set of institutions run by intergovernmental bargaining, in which deals are cut between leaders of national parties who happen to be in government at the time.[4] The decision to put the widening of Europe before its deepening (now privately regretted by some of its foremost apologists) will only accentuate the intergovernmental nature of the EU. Party leaders know, then, that they must be seen primarily as defenders of national interests within an increasingly competitive European space.

Those leaders who feel that national interests are in many cases best understood as European have an arduous task. They have not always argued as boldly as they might have (the leadership of the UK Labour Party being a classic case). The family to which this argument comes most naturally is the Christian Democrats, with their personalist philosophy that downplays the nation as the central reference in public life. Yet this family has the difficult prospect of arguing its case while confronting the decline of two of the pivots of its existence. The social market has been increasingly undermined by neo-liberalism, and the Christian principles behind the CD movement are being eroded by growing religious indifference and secularism. Small wonder that at the European level some CD leaders have been only too ready to ally with conservative and nationalist forces that were once their adversary.

As for the TNPs, it is even more pointless to blame them. They are, to borrow a horticultural metaphor, like bonsai trees; limits have been set to their growth by national parties anxious to keep control. With their meagre resources, visibility and legitimacy, it is unfair to expect them to carry out tasks which their parent-parties are unwilling to do. If more European awareness or identity is to be constructed, perhaps it is to other sources that we must look – the independent media, the universities, even changing patterns of work and leisure mobility. Historically, parties have not as a rule been initiators so much as followers and adapters to circumstance, as the entire chapter of European construction amply illustrates.

Notes

1. Members of the British Christian People's Alliance (formerly, the Movement for Christian Democracy), for instance, see this as the only means of influencing the EPP, access to which is blocked by the Conservative Party, whose size is valued by the EPP leadership despite the difficulties that its association with EPP brings.
2. Interviews in the European Parliament, 21 and 24 November 2003.
3. A number of secretaries-general to whom we spoke were worried that the new system of financing would actually increase their difficulties in terms of paying for staff, premises and other overhead expenses, even though they would now be notionally free of dependency on the group.
4. Some commentators believe that the provisions for enhanced cooperation between states willing to integrate further in certain policy areas will now come into their own. Seiler (2003: 70) suggests provocatively that the states concerned are likely to be those where a strong Christian democracy has inspired European integration since the 1950s.

References

Abélès, M. 1992. *La vie quotidienne au parlement européen*. Paris: Hachette.

Anderson, B. 1983. *Imagined Communities: Reflections on the Origin and Spread of Nationalism*. London: Verso.

Bardi, L. 2002a. 'Parties and Party Systems in the European Union: National and Supranational Dimensions'. In *Political Parties in the New Europe*, ed. K. Luther and F. Muller-Rommel, 293–321. Oxford: Oxford University Press.

_____. 2002b. 'Transnational Trends: The Evolution of the European Party System'. In *The European Parliament: Moving Toward Democracy in the EU*, ed. B. Steunenberg and J. Thomassen, 63–83. Oxford: Rowman & Littlefield.

Bell, D. S. and Lord, C., eds. 1998. *Transnational Parties in the European Union*. Aldershot: Ashgate.

Delwit, P., Kühlaci, E. and van de Walle, C., eds. 2001. *Les fédérations européennes de partis: Organisation et influence*. Brussels: Université Libre de Bruxelles.

Devin, G. 1993. *L'internationale socialiste: Histoire et sociologie du socialisme international*. Paris: Fondation Nationale des Sciences Politiques.

Featherstone, K. and Kazamias, G. 2001. *Europeanization and the Southern Periphery*. London: Cass.

Gaxie, D. 1986. *La démocratie représentative*. Paris: Monchrestien.

Goetz, K. and Hix, S. 2001. *Europeanised Politics? Europeanisation and National Political Systems*. London: Cass.

Gramsci, A. 1971. *Selections from the Prison Notebooks*. Ed. Q. Hoare and G. Nowell-Smith. London: Lawrence and Wishart.

Hanley, D. 2002a. 'Christian Democracy and the Paradoxes of Europeanisation'. *Party Politics* 8, no. 4: 463–81.

_____. 2002b. *Party, Society, Government: Republican Democracy in France*. Oxford: Berghahn Books.

Hanley, D. and Portelli, H. 1985. 'L'IS et le désarmement: Limites et possibilités d'une diplomatie socialiste'. In *Social-démocratie et défense en Europe*, ed. H. Portelli and D. Hanley, 255–76. Nanterre: Institut de Politique Internationale et Européenne.

Hanley, D. and Ysmal, C. 1999. 'Le parti populaire européen et la recomposition des droites européennes'. In *Le vote des quinze: Les élections européennes de juin 1999*, ed. G. Grunberg, P. Perrineau and C. Ysmal, 203–22. Paris: Fondation Nationale des Sciences Politiques.

Haupt, G. 1972. *Socialism and the Great War*. Oxford: Oxford University Press.

Hirst, P. and Thompson, G. 1999. *Globalization in Question*. 2nd ed. London: Polity.

Hix, S. 1999. *The Political System of the European Union*. London: Macmillan.

_____. 2004. 'Electoral Institutions and Legislative Behaviour: Explaining Voting Defection in the European Parliament'. *World Politics* 56, no. 2: 194–233.

Hix, S., Kreppel, A. and Noury, A. 2003. 'The Party System in the EP: Collusive or Competitive?' *Journal of Common Market Studies* 41, no. 2: 309–31.

Hix, S. and Lord, C. 1997. *Political Parties in the European Union*. London: Macmillan.

Hix, S., Noury, A. and Roland, G. 2002. 'Power to the Parties: Cohesion and Competition in the EP, 1979–2002'. *British Journal of Political Science* 35, no. 2: 209–34.

Jansen, T. 1998. *The European Peoples' Party: Origins and Development*. Basingstoke: Macmillan.

Johansson, K. M. 1997. *Transnational Party Alliances: Analysing the Hard-Won Alliance between Conservatives and Christian Democrats in the European Parliament.* Lund: Lund University Press.

Johansson, K. M. and Zervakis, P., eds. 2002. *European Political Parties between Co-operation and Integration.* Baden-Baden: Nomos.

Joll, J. 1955. *The Second International, 1889–1914.* London: Weidenfeld and Nicolson.

Kalyvas, S. 1996. *The Rise of Christian Democracy.* Ithaca: Cornell University Press.

Kreppel, A. 2002. *The European Parliament and Supranational Party System: A Study in Institutional Development.* Cambridge: Cambridge University Press.

Lijphardt, A. 1968. *The Politics of Accommodation: Pluralism and Democracy in the Netherlands.* Berkeley: University of California Press.

Lipset, S. and Rokkan, S. 1967. *Party Systems and Voter Alignment.* New York: Free Press.

Mayeur, J.-M. 1980. *Des partis catholiques à la démocratie chrétienne.* Paris: Colin.

Murray, P. 2004. 'Factors for Integration? Transnational Party Co-operation in the European Parliament, 1952–79'. *Australian Journal of Politics and History* 50, no. 1: 103–16.

Offerlé, M. 1987. *Les partis politiques.* 3rd ed. Paris: PUF.

Panebianco, A. 1988. *Political Parties: Organisation and Power.* Cambridge: Cambridge University Press.

Papini, R. 1988. *L'internationale démocrate chrétienne.* Paris: Cerf.

Portelli, H. 1983. *L'internationale socialiste.* Paris: Editions Ouvrières.

Raunio, T. 1997. *The European Perspective: Transnational Party Groups in the 1989–94 European Parliament.* Aldershot: Ashgate.

Seiler, D. L. 1980. *Partis et familles politiques.* Paris: PUF.

_____. 2000. *Les partis politiques.* 2nd ed. Paris: Colin.

_____. 2002. 'Le paradoxe libéral: La faiblesse d'une force d'avenir'. In *Libéralismes et partis libéraux en Europe*, ed. P. Delwit, 37–56. Brussels: Editions de l'Université de Bruxelles.

_____. 2003. *Les partis politiques en Occident: Sociologie historique du phénomène partisan.* Paris: Ellipses.

Van Zyl, H. and Vorster, S. 1997. 'Transnational Party-Political Movements: Influential Actors or Empty Vessels?' *Politikon* 24, no. 2: 21–39.

Weber, E. 1977. *Peasants into Frenchmen: The Modernisation of Rural France, 1870–1914.* London: Chatto and Windus.

Chapter 9

REMAPPING REGIONALISM

Peter Wagstaff

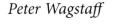

The complex mix of identity and culture that defines life for many in today's Europe is vividly expressed in the first few minutes of British director Ken Loach's recent film *Ae Fond Kiss*, which explores the human impact of ethnic antagonisms in the Scottish city of Glasgow. A teenage girl tries to explain to fellow students in her inner-city school the combination of cultural, social and religious influences that make her what she is: 'I'm a Glaswegian Pakistani teenager woman of Muslim descent who supports Rangers in a Catholic school.'[1] Her declaration is made with a confidence and exuberance (and in a Glaswegian accent) that reflects, no doubt, the defiant optimism of youth, but offers a telling counterpoint to the conflicting and entrenched allegiances that are revealed as the film progresses and as racial, religious and generational divisions deepen. It does not, however, suggest an over-arching European dimension to her identity that would help to heal those divisions. For that we have to wait for an episode later in the film when the main characters – lovers frustrated by race, culture and religion – find respite, albeit briefly, from the controversy that their relationship provokes in a few days' holiday on the Mediterranean coast of Spain. Sunshine replaces the grey streets of the inner city, but not for long.[2] Race, religion, nation, locality, culture, society – all contribute to this combustible mixture, and while there is no mention of a specifically regional dimension, the implication remains that the traditional structures, in terms of nationality and culture, are far too crude and unwieldy to reflect the multifaceted nature of modern identity.

There are perhaps echoes here, however, of some of the more optimistic recent commentaries on prospects for the adoption of multiple identities which might subvert and supplant the single national loyalty. In framing the

Notes for this chapter are located on page 181.

question, how is European identity linked to national, regional and local identities? Gary Marks (1999: 88) underlines William Wallace's argument that while the European project has failed to foster 'a transfer of loyalties from the national to the European level', there has nonetheless been 'a shift towards multiple loyalties with the single focus on the nation supplemented by European and regional affiliations above and below'. He further notes, inter alia, the suggestion by Brigid Laffan that 'the extension of political space beyond the nation-state provides a shelter for multiple identities be they local, regional or national' (ibid.).

What, then, is the role of the region in this perpetual re-evaluation and renegotiation of identities and allegiances? And how have the structures of the European Union (EU) evolved to take account of this re-evaluation? The implication is that the region, poised halfway between the national and the local, can somehow validate the claims of multiple identities while, at the same time, drawing the sting of national allegiance and contributing to the broader objectives of trans- and supranational affiliations. If, however, an understanding of concepts of identity and culture is at the heart of attempts to define what it means to be European in the early years of the twenty-first century, then regionalism, in all its manifestations, appears to occupy a paradoxical, even anomalous position in the debate.

The effort of will and imagination needed to discover mutually compatible threads of identity – the components of a sort of European cultural DNA – among the 15 member states of the European Union over the years has been, to put it mildly, beyond the competence of European leaders and opinion formers, and the more recent accession of a further 12 nations is hardly likely to make the task any easier. Indeed, the enlargement of the EU to encompass Eastern European states formerly under Soviet Communist influence only underlines the paradoxical nature of reflections on national and regional identity. While Western European states have been increasingly preoccupied with the opportunities offered by an erosion of national boundaries – the famous 'ever closer union' – those in the East, following a half-century or more of Communist transnational domination, are no less preoccupied with the assertion and consolidation of those boundaries. How much more challenging, then, to disaggregate Europe still further and seek to reveal, at the sub-national level, a commonality of purpose and understanding that unites rather than divides, that fosters solidarity rather than indifference and incomprehension. The search is for what coheres and unites, whether at the national or transnational level, while regionalism, if it is anything, tends to accentuate uniqueness and difference.

And yet it is clear that recent decades have seen a growing preoccupation with questions of regional identity, a preoccupation which varies in emphasis as well as in place and time. Repeatedly, many of the largest and most influential states of Western Europe – the United Kingdom, France, Spain and Italy – have witnessed some form of challenge to central government from sub-national, regional interests. In this context, it is hardly surprising that the mantra of an 'ever closer union', expressed implicitly or explicitly at intervals since the earliest days of the European Community, appears to run counter to those interests.

It is easy to dismiss challenges to national government from a community or grouping within its own boundaries as something of an aberration, a deviant phenomenon set against the permanent and legitimate status of the nation. It is tempting, also, to assume that the relationship between individual and territory can most easily be defined, in the context of modern Europe as elsewhere, by the relationship between citizen and nation-state. Nationalism is so deeply engrained within modern consciousness that it tends to be seen as the fundamental and permanent constituent of political culture, particularly that of Western Europe. Its roots are, of course, relatively shallow. Its high point, at least in the sense of nationalism-as-national-unification, can be traced to the nineteenth century, with its origins in post-Revolutionary France of the late eighteenth century, and it can be seen in the strong movements for national unification in Italy and Germany in the second half of the nineteenth century. It is also clearly visible, rather earlier, in Britain, where it served to establish a politics of national consensus in a society that might otherwise have been driven by class divisions.

Nationalism is thus viewed in terms of progression towards a cohesion that transforms individuals into citizens in a common allegiance (Smith 1992: 61). It is nonetheless instructive that while the major national elites strove for that consensus from the early nineteenth century, the impact on populations was less clear-cut. Even as little as a century ago, the vast majority of Europe's predominantly rural population remained largely immune to the attractions of nationhood, instead finding both identity and a sense of belonging inscribed within the narrow bounds of a relatively unchanging daily experience (Ignatieff 1984: 138–9). This eruption of nationalist modernity into the circumscribed world of European peasantry is exemplified by the ringing of church bells in France in 1914 to summon peasants from their fields to enlist in the army for the defence of the – for them – hitherto nebulous concept of nationhood. The implicit discrepancy between the establishment of the nation and the creation of a national identity that is meaningful for its inhabitants can be seen, too, in the observation by Massimio d'Azeglio, in the wake of Italian unification in 1870, that 'we have made Italy; now we must make Italians' (Shore 2000: 18). A similar scepticism about the impact of nationhood on peoples can be discerned in Metternich's much-quoted description of Italy as a 'geographical expression' (Woolf 1979: 227).

Nation, Space and Community

Nationalism is seen, then, in terms of progress, as a phenomenon developing in time. It is, moreover, one which, while defending the rights of 'big' nations, paradoxically denied those rights – of unification and self-determination – to lesser groups, both at home and abroad. A telling example can be seen in

English nationalist attitudes to Ireland, attitudes which have been qualified as racist as early as the seventeenth century and which provide a model for attitudes on a wider, European scale to other minority peoples – in Brittany, the Basque Country, Corsica, Catalonia and beyond. The proposition that Ireland was subject to the same colonial and ultimately racist treatment meted out to more distant subject territories by an imperialist power leads not only to the felicitous observation that it was 'long perceived as a country which belonged somewhere else' – as part of England, or latterly the European Union – but also to a sense of Ireland defined in terms of negative values and a problematic status (Mac Laughlin 2001: 7–8). This is an Ireland transformed from a country in its own right into an experiment in plantation, as a prelude to the coloniser's conquest of the New World; an Ireland whose inhabitants are seen as romantic shadows in the background of the self-aggrandising iconography, in paintings and portraiture, of the 'civilised' English settler; an Ireland in which power relations were fundamentally changed by the effects of emigration of the young as they approached the age of political consciousness.

In this nationalist perspective, then, there was no place for small nations or minority nationalities – the Irish, Welsh, Bretons, Basques, Catalans. In such cases, nationalist or separatist tendencies were resisted because they represented a threat to the territorial integrity of the dominant nation-states (the parallels with colonial subordination are self-evident).

The specific instance of migration referred to above is emblematic of a wider trend. The crossing of borders – whether in search of work or in flight from persecution or from the devastation of conflict, or merely as the humdrum consequence of economic and technological advance – is a defining characteristic of what it means to be European: 'Emigration, forced or chosen, across national frontiers or from village to metropolis, is the quintessential experience of our time' (Berger 1984: 55). Migration therefore brings to the definition of nationalism and national allegiance the possibility of ambivalence: multiple allegiances may co-exist, emphasising the porosity of borders and the permeability of cultures.

There is perhaps a utopian tinge to the assertion that 'we all embody several overlapping identities; it is bad faith to attach ourselves too exclusively to any one of them, such as national identity' (Kumar 2003: 42), and while there may equally be interest in considering that 'in this sense, migrants and migrant communities are the outriders of the emerging postnational society' (ibid.), every migrant is also an exile, whether by choice or necessity. But the need to reconnect in some way with the past, to re-establish a sense of origin and continuity, survives. The memory of a lost home persists and is part – a large part – of what it means to be human: 'Identity is a question of memory, and memories of "home" in particular' (Morley and Robins 1995: 91). It is perhaps to be expected, then, that the existence of a diaspora prompts a definition of nationhood less rooted in territory than in ethnic solidarity, expressed in terms of culture, language, shared history. In this context, territorial borders tend to lose something of their distinctiveness, to be replaced by the potentially mobile boundaries of ethnicity. These are surely the values that underpin the declaration, in 1991, by Josef Antall that he was not prime minister of Hungary but of 15 million Hungarians, and the assertion by his successor Viktor Orban in 1999 that every Hungarian living beyond the borders of Hungary belonged to a single, indivisible nation (Malfliet 2000: 66–7).

These uncertainties call into question hitherto unchallenged theories of the nation-state and the allegiances that bind people to the communities of which they form a part, although here the notion of community itself cannot be left unexamined. In one sense, the nation-state is perhaps best expressed in terms of theory since it can ever be, in Benedict Anderson's famous phrase, only an 'imagined community'. Its existence depends on the willingness of its inhabitants to make the imaginative leap that connects them to each other, even though their compatriots remain largely unknown to them and there is no guarantee that they share the same conception of nationhood. National-ism has traditionally been embedded in myths of permanence and security: individuals seek relief from insecurity by identifying with community, and it is self-evident that the cohesiveness of the concept of nationhood is facilitated by the homogenising impact of modern communication technologies. The dissemination of information and the transmission of mutually reinforcing self-images, released in the wake of the Industrial Revolution, provide fer-tile ground for the establishment of common identities securely linked: 'To date, the nation state thus becomes the optimal "identity-securing interpretive system" which man has created for himself' (Spiering 1996: 110). This is the nation as family, enshrined in the etymologies of fatherland, mother country and mother tongue and in myths of kinship and ancestry.

The nation and nationalism therefore offer both psychological and eco-nomic security. Once that security is called into question, the legitimacy of the nation-state is threatened. There is evidence of this in many of the major European nation-states in the second half of the twentieth century for a variety of reasons, including the dilution of concepts of national sovereignty within the broader boundaries of the EU, the collapse of the Soviet Union, the relative failure of states to fulfil expectations of continuous and equitable economic development. The result is a sense of the remoteness of the state and a recourse to more local, culturally homogeneous allegiances

One evident consequence of this turbulence is a re-evaluation of the rela-tionship between individuals and the physical territory they inhabit. From a social science perspective, the importance of spatial relationships – 'the funda-mental spatiality of social life, the adhesive relations between society and space, history and geography' (Soja 1994: 128) – has received much attention. All this contributes to an understanding of the ways people relate to the world around them. The social space they inhabit, their landscape, is more than a simple backdrop to their activity; like them, it is subject to an evolving, dynamic confrontation of state and citizen. This recognition underlies David Harvey's

(2000: 78) assertion that 'geographical differences are much more than mere historical-geographical legacies. They are perpetually being reproduced, sustained, undermined and reconfigured by political-economic and socio-ecological processes occurring in the present'. The potential for change, seen for so long in terms of the linear predictability of historical progression in time, is transferred to the variability of 'a network that connects points and intersects with its own skein' (Foucault 1980: 70).

This is perhaps how the evolving relationship between individual, state and territory is best considered. Notwithstanding the efforts of a 'Europeanising' elite to project an inclusive vision of what it means to be European – efforts which are frequently seen as 'inherently circular and self-reinforcing' (Shore 2000: 27) – it is precisely the nature and detail of that vision that remains elusive. Indeed, the very recourse to a vocabulary of 'vision' suggests as much (ibid.: 26), and in the balance between idea and reality, it is the former that has long had the more visible role: 'Europe has always been a promise, an ideal, even an ideology, as much as it has been an achieved reality' (Kumar 2003: 49). An approach to the unresolved question of 'Europeanness' may therefore prove more fruitful if based on the realities of 'human experiences of spaces' (Middleton and Woods 2000: 282).

State Formation in Europe: The Regional Dimension

Yet these human realities are far removed from the historical reality of nation-state formation, which, throughout much of Europe at least, has tended to conform to the 'centre-periphery' model in which a powerful centre comes to dominate its surrounding territory, imposing not only political and economic but also cultural and linguistic control over what may be a variety of ethnically diverse smaller national identities, thus creating a reasonably cohesive state and society. The application of the model to many of the countries of Western Europe is persuasive: cities such as London, Paris, Madrid, Lisbon, Rome, Vienna and Dublin have clearly performed that function – in political, economic and sometimes cultural terms – by assimilating their peripheral regions. It is problematical in the case of Brussels, a capital sitting uneasily at the heart of a country that is driven by the stark distinction between two cultures and communities, Dutch and French. And in the case of Germany, with its polycentric – or polycephalic – federal structure, the model remains largely inappropriate, irrespective of unification and the restoration of capital status to Berlin.

These variations on the theme of the relationship between centre and periphery suggest the limitations inherent in an attempt to apply a single definition to the multiplicity of sub-national entities. If the nation-state defines itself by the control it exerts over its constituent parts, then those parts in turn elude a simple definition, not merely because of their cultural and territorial diversity, but also in terms of the extent to which their existence is acknowledged, from outside or from within. If the definition of 'nation' in a European context is itself problematical (with, for example, the Spanish state encompassing the historic nations of Catalonia and the Basque Country, while, on the French side of the Pyrenees, Catalan and Basque territory is seen as simply a constituent part of the French state), then 'region' is that much more difficult to define. As Dunkerley et al. (2002: 67) make clear:

> When employed to analyse empirical conditions at the sub-national level across Europe the concept of 'region' has a chameleon-like quality. There are, for example, considerable differences between the Austrian and German *Länder* on the one hand, and the nominal regional entities that are the focus of regional development bodies in Greece or the Republic of Ireland on the other. Indeed, the fact that some regional polities, such as North Rhine-Westphalia in Germany, manage budgets larger than the national state budget of Denmark or Greece underscores the considerable disparities between regions across Europe. Even without drawing attention to such extremes of difference, the most cursory evaluation of conditions across Europe reveals that there exist varying levels of administrative, economic and political decentralisation between countries, as well as, in a number of cases, within them.

While the region is perhaps most easily defined, then, primarily as a unit smaller than the state which contains it, the state itself may range from the federal, such as Austria or Germany, to the unitary, such as Greece or Poland, with varieties of devolving (France, Portugal) and regionalised (Italy, Spain) unitary states between the two extremes. Largely irrespective of the precise mode of regional administration, the term 'region' may also indicate a territory given the status of a region for administrative purposes, simply occupying an intermediate position between central and local government, or a territory having a claim to a cultural and political individuality of its own, marked out by ethnic, historical and linguistic features, and moulded by shared myths and traditions. The aspirations and activism of the concerned inhabitants of a region, and the pursuit of the specific interests of such a unit, can usefully be labelled 'regionalism', in contrast to the process of regionalisation, which is rather the pursuit of state-centred policies designed to impose top-down remedies (especially economic ones) to regional problems and imbalances. To this extent, it may be argued that regionalism and regionalisation are mutually contradictory, or at least require an uneasy compromise subject to periodic reassessment. Evidence of this uneasy compromise and of the wide variation in centre-periphery relationships is not hard to find, as the following contrasting examples indicate.[3]

In the United Kingdom, a political culture founded on the belief in firm central government as a necessary condition for both the survival of the state and the maintenance of British power overseas left very little room, until recently, for the institutional expression of regional diversity. A protracted debate on the devolution of power away from Westminster during the 1970s, prompted in part by the growth of electoral support for 'minority' parties with some form of commitment to regional devolution, proved inconclusive. Since the 1997 election, however, the long-standing recognition of the distinctiveness of Scotland, Wales and Northern Ireland has been translated into the establishment of a Scottish Parliament with significant legislative powers, an elected Welsh Assembly (with fewer such powers) and, after long and complex negotiations, a power-sharing executive in Northern Ireland.

This recognition of regional diversity within the quite clearly defined Celtic nations that form part of the United Kingdom has tended to mask, however, considerable diversity in terms of origins, geography, religious observance and popular culture in England, where a superficial homogeneity is underscored by nationally organised mass media. In this context, it is tempting to suggest that the overwhelming rejection, in a referendum in November 2004, of central government proposals for an elected regional assembly in the north-east of England – and the subsequent abandonment of plans for similar referendums in other regions – was prompted as much by scepticism about the very limited range of powers on offer as by a lack of belief in regional specificity. It remains the case, however, that the absence of a sharply defined regional administration in any part of the English regions – an absence unlikely to be remedied in the near future – masks the existence of age-old local identities rooted in administrative and socio-cultural traditions that can be traced back for a thousand years.

Throughout Continental Europe, too, examples abound of the variety of subnational regional entities. The fundamental importance of Germany's carefully balanced federal system as a defence against the repetition of past mistakes is underlined by the fact that the federal principle is unalterably enshrined in the constitution or Basic Law (*Grundgesetz*). The federal state system in Germany offers a settled pattern of vertical power distribution through localities, *Länder* and the state, plus horizontal attributes of self-government at each level as appropriate. The allocation of responsibilities within this system is complex and carefully regulated, with clearly delineated powers for each level, as well as an element of concurrent legislation that permits shared decision making in some areas. In addition, the redistributive nature of the tax regime ensures that those *Länder* which are the least well developed economically are, in effect, subsidised by the more prosperous. This measure is particularly significant at a time when the old north-south economic divide has been altered by the decline of traditional industries, and when the severely underdeveloped *Länder* of the former East Germany have been absorbed into the Bundesrepublik.

In political terms, too, federalism is seen as a crucial element in the building and reinforcement of the democratic process. From the origins of the Bundesrepublik, a deliberate policy of education through democratisation was adopted, with citizens made familiar with the electoral process first at the local level, then in the *Länder* and finally nationally, at the level of the *Bund*. In addition, with the allocation of responsibility for, in particular, education policy to the intermediate level of the *Länder*, a plurality of systems and programmes was encouraged. This plurality is in itself viewed as a positive value, working against any tendency to the despotic and the authoritarian. It could be argued that in the search for new models of political and institutional structures to buttress European integration, Germany offers a pertinent example of a possible way forward for strengthening the diversity of regional identities within a wider institutional framework.

In Italy, the perception, following the Second World War, that the rise of fascism had been aided by the centralised nature of the state led to a new involvement with the idea of decentralisation. Paradoxically, the re-emergence of federalism as a strand of political thought coincides with the attainment by Italy of a greater sense of cultural and linguistic homogeneity than at any previous period. Other factors, therefore, create a specifically Italian environment in which federalism and regional preoccupations can flourish. These include, above all, the corrupt nature of the relationship between the political and business worlds, organised crime and the general deterioration of political institutions, all serving to induce cynicism on the part of the electorate and a desire for systematic institutional change. In the early 1990s, the Northern League's proposal for a federal state made up of three macro-regions (north, centre and south) won an unexpected level of electoral support, setting the political agenda in the face of Socialist and Christian Democratic parties' disarray brought about by corruption scandals.

The historic underdevelopment of southern Italy, prompting a two-way process of state subsidies in return for electoral support, has long been a feature of the political scene. Attempts to help first agriculture and then industry, through the centralised agency of the Cassa per il Mezzogiorno, had limited success, with problems blamed on excessive centralisation; yet subsequent attempts to devolve responsibility became mired in the ever-present corruption and clientelism. Accordingly, the concept of regional development itself has been called into question by northerners resentful of the need to subsidise the south, and this resentment can be seen as responsible in part for the federalist proposals of the Northern League. Legislation enacted in 1990 to regulate relations between central, regional and local government appeared to assign superior powers to the regions in planning terms, and yet federalist demands persisted. Popular support for institutional change, embracing regional reform, was indicated by the results of a number of referenda held in the mid-1990s, and laws enacted during 1997 both enhanced the responsibilities of regions within the unitary state, introducing the concept of subsidiarity, and decreed that local or regional autonomy should vary according to the competence of the authorities concerned.

European integration receives broad support from the Italian population as a whole – indeed, political groupings such as the Northern League see the European dimension as an ideal context for the renewal of contact between northern Italy and its transalpine neighbours. Transnational and interregional collaborative agreements have met with wide support and seem to suggest 'the coexistence of multiple political identities, no one of them necessarily replacing all others' (Agnew 2003: 230). The conclusion is, however, unavoidable that

Italian enthusiasm for many or all aspects of European integration may have less to do with transnational solidarity and idealism than with a widespread distrust of and frustration with central government. It is the perceived inadequacies of a particular – Italian – form of the nation-state that explain the appeal of an as yet ill-defined federal Europe.

One of the main factors inhibiting regional development in Greece has been the extreme centralisation of the Greek state, while regional disparities remain very pronounced. Since the early 1980s, centralism has been seen as a cause of the clientelism that bedevils the relationship between the capital, Athens, and regional urban and rural centres in what is a largely agrarian country. Gradual rationalisation of administration is attributable less to pressure from the grass roots than to the need to conform to European directives and demonstrate probity. The movement towards consolidation of local authority structures, to be followed by the creation of an elected regional tier, suggests that Greece's unitary state is obliged to contemplate a process of regionalisation in response to external (i.e. European Union) requirements.

The regional question in the Iberian Peninsula offers two sharply contrasting images – a contrast explicable in terms of the difference in the process of state formation in Spain and Portugal, respectively. In more than 500 years, the supremacy of the Portuguese state has remained virtually unchallenged by any of its regions. This is attributable to the fact that the state, formed by military conquest over the Moors in the fourteenth century, preceded the nation, which duly found its identity and created its myths in the challenge and opportunities of its Atlantic seaboard. Discovery, conquest and the founding of colonies brought unity and a sense of shared purpose. Furthermore, the ubiquity of the Portuguese language throughout the territory cemented that unity, underlining once more the central importance of a distinctive language as an indicator of cultural limits and thus of national identity. The half-century of dictatorship under Salazar confirmed and reinforced this seamless national identity, with its high degree of centralised, corporatist control and minimal financial power at the local government level. Even after the transition to democracy in the mid-1970s, however, tentative plans for a regional administration remained in the shadow of a reinvigorated local, municipal government, fostering the view that the size and uniformity of the country as a whole does not justify an additional, intermediate tier. The sole exception to the state's unquestioned supremacy has been evident periodically in the Atlantic islands, but the granting of directly elected assemblies to the Azores and Madeira, with the power to raise local taxes, in the post-Salazar era has largely defused the impact of their regionalist movements, despite the islands' reliance on Lisbon for budgetary supplementation.

In Spain, however, successive waves of separatist activity since the early nineteenth century have formed a backcloth for modern regionalist aspirations. State formation in Spain has a long history rooted in both military conquest and alliances through royal marriages. This latter feature ensured, in contrast to the situation in Portugal, the persistence of a variety of regional identities outside centralised Castille. Ancient rights, notably in the Basque Country and Catalonia, coupled with uneven economic development from the very beginnings of industrialisation, led to the restoration of a measure of autonomy in the three historic minority nations – Catalonia, the Basque Country and Galicia – in the early decades of the twentieth century. Subsequently, the Franco regime eradicated all traces of regionalism, but failed to expunge the desire for it; as a result, on Franco's death, demands for regional recognition and reform re-emerged. The most fundamental explanation of these demands is cultural difference, exemplified by the language factor, which differentiates Catalans, Basques and Galicians. Castillian Spanish is spoken by no more than three-quarters of the population of Spain, so that the three minorities and, in particular, large cities such as Barcelona or Bilbao exert a centrifugal force, encouraging the growth of regionalisms.

Cultural difference was amplified in the mid-twentieth century by starkly uneven economic development. With the country's political centre, Madrid, relatively lacklustre in economic terms, two of the three industrially active regions – the Basque Country and Catalonia – had formed the powerhouse of early industrial development. Much of western, central and southern Spain remained undeveloped and poor. The negative effects of this pattern of development were multiple: imbalances were accentuated by migration from poor to prosperous regions, the poorest posed problems of regional equity and successful regions such as Catalonia objected to subsidising their less successful neighbours. Paradoxically, Franco's regime itself offered succour to the regionalist movements, as its heavy-handed suppression of regional activity encouraged a spirit of anti-government solidarity between regionalist groups. With the post-Franco return to democracy, a measure of autonomy was seen as an essential element of constitutional reform, but its implementation posed a number of problems. Not least was that some regions were obviously self-defining and eager to assume an autonomous role, while elsewhere it was by no means clear what, in precise territorial terms, constituted a region. The principles of state unity, regional autonomy and interregional solidarity enshrined in the 1978 Constitution represented an attempt to deal pragmatically with widely divergent levels of concern. Subsequent legislation and regional elections have gone some way towards producing an equitable settlement which, despite its lacunae and drawbacks, has brought about, in only a quarter of a century, an astonishing degree of regional reform.

Finally, in France, the regional question has to be seen in the context of a rigid centralisation that characterised the administrative, economic and social structure of the country for the best part of two centuries. The mould of Republican uniformity – with its doctrinal opposition to the notion that any one part of the state within mainland France or, for that matter, in any of the far-flung overseas territories might display characteristics at variance with that uniformity – ensured that the potential varieties of political, cultural and linguistic expressions of Frenchness were deprived of formal judicial recognition.

An element of ad hoc flexibility, which allowed local politicians to negotiate adjustments in light of local circumstances, could not conceal the impact of a rigidly bureaucratic central control (Cole 2003: 87). The concentration of political and economic power in Paris, and the consequent centralisation of decision making, expressed through the prefectorial system of administration, held sway throughout the nineteenth and much of the twentieth centuries. Only gradually, with the growth of industrialisation and the consequent unevenness of development, did the disadvantages of a rigidly hierarchical system of administration and centralised planning make themselves felt.

The dearth of reliable information about economic progress in a vast, varied and relatively underpopulated country led also to an element of inertia – complacency, even – which was not shaken until the years after the Second World War. This period witnessed a dawning realisation that the growth and prosperity of Paris had drained the French provinces of resources and manpower, leaving an enfeebled network of provincial towns and an impoverished agriculture. Policy thereafter was directed at a realignment of economic activity, so that the traditional, if oversimplified, demarcation line between a relatively prosperous and dynamic north, east and south-east and an underdeveloped and stagnant west and south-west became less clearly defined. During the 1950s and 1960s, the reassertion of regional identities began to be felt, predominantly in the more outlying provinces. Regionalist movements in Brittany, Corsica, Occitania and, to a lesser extent, the Basque Country and Alsace claimed attention with demands for varying degrees of cultural, political and economic autonomy. The twin pressures of political and economic demands led to a gradual process of regional reform emanating from the centre, highlighting the paradox inherent in a situation in which central government takes decisions relating to matters of regional autonomy.

Arguably, the most significant reforms were set in train in the early 1980s, when, for the first time, the principle of direct election to regional assemblies was conceded. Conclusive evidence of the effectiveness of these assemblies in improving the lot of their populations and in fostering the development of regional identity and allegiance has yet to be provided. Two of the examples mentioned above provide interesting contrasts in terms of an accommodation between regional and central government interests. In the case of Brittany, a centuries-old cultural, religious, social and linguistic tradition underpins what has become a relatively relaxed acceptance of existing measures of decentralisation. Apparently confident in their regional identity, in which their Celtic language and cultural (and Catholic) vitality play a part, few Bretons would wish to return to the rigid central control that pre-dates the reforms of the 1980s, while only a small minority favour the autonomous status that was the aspiration, in the late 1960s and early 1970s, of a vociferous and briefly active minority. The tendency of most Breton political actors to close ranks in the interests of the region – what Cole (2003: 96) has called 'a deeply rooted territorial solidarity' – rather than to exploit political differences has led Bretons as a whole to accept existing regional institutions while remaining receptive to the possibility of enhanced decision-making powers at the regional level in the future.

Regionalist political parties attract relatively little support in Brittany, and potentially contentious issues, such as the status of the Breton language, are not seen as seriously divisive. Even the long-standing argument over the exclusion of the fifth Breton *département* of Loire-Atlantique (including Nantes, the historic capital of Brittany) from the Breton region does not threaten what remains, in effect, a consensual political arrangement, despite significant popular support for the *département*'s reincorporation (Charlet 2003: 157). It may be significant that, unlike much of the rest of mainland France, where the relationship between *capitale* and *province* is articulated at the local level largely through the multiplicity of *départements* and *communes*, Brittany enjoys a cohesive and secure regional identity, which makes it possible for the regional council to be the natural focus, not only for state-region interaction and negotiation, but also for liaison between the region and the European Commission. It may also be significant that revision of regionalisation legislation was undertaken by a government led by a former (Poitou-Charentes) regional council president, Jean-Pierre Raffarin, prime minister of France from 2002 to 2005.

In surveys of national and regional identification among the French population, it is no surprise to discover that geographical disparities determine the relative significance attached to the two allegiances. In particular, it is to be expected that in regions such as Ile de France, at the centre of power, and Centre, an arbitrarily delineated region with little or no social or cultural specificity, most people identify with the nation rather than with their region. This preference, however, extends to most other regions, including some, such as Alsace, where regional identification might be expected to be stronger. The only regions in which the pattern of preference is reversed are Brittany and Corsica. In the latter case, the disparity is by far the more marked – almost twice as many Corsicans give priority to their regional, as opposed to national, allegiance, while the ratio for Brittany is far more evenly balanced (Schrijver 2004: 201) – and this is reflected in the performance of autonomist or separatist political parties at elections.

It perhaps goes some way to explain, too, the persistence of a strain of violent political action over the last three decades, sparked initially by an incident in August 1975 at Aleria on the east coast of Corsica. Two gendarmes died in an assault on a wine cellar that was occupied by Corsican separatists in protest against what they perceived as the colonisation of Corsican land and property by *pieds-noirs* (descendants of French settlers from Algeria). This militant action also marked a split between separatist nationalists and autonomist nationalists, who, despite a number of shared policy positions ranging from the practical to the largely symbolic, including the protection and promotion of the Corsican language and recognition of the separate and specific identity of 'le peuple corse' (the Corsican people), differed in their attitudes to the use of violence. While the autonomists abjured its use, the separatists adopted it as a legitimate means to further their objectives. This perhaps needs to be seen in the context of a deeply embedded historical reliance on violence (in particular, the vendetta) as a means of conflict resolution in Corsica.

Whereas the long-established model of republican uniformity in theory precludes any asymmetrical development in the institutions of government and administration in France, it is notable that an exception was made, in the wake of the regional reforms of the early 1980s, in the case of Corsica. Of the 22 regions of metropolitan France, 21 were endowed with an elected *conseil régional* (regional council), while the comparable Corsican body became the Assemblée de Corse (Corsican Assembly). The Assembly was validated for the first time by elections in 1984, two years earlier than its equivalents on the mainland. In 1998, the Assembly affirmed the existence of 'le peuple corse' as 'a historically and culturally living community', but despite recognition by the French parliament in 1991, the supreme arbiter of constitutional propriety, the Conseil constitutionnel, immediately declared this recognition unconstitutional (Charlet 2003: 162). A decade of sporadic violence culminated in the assassination, on 6 February 1998, of the government's principal representative on the island, Préfet Claude Erignac – 500 years to the day after the birth of Sampiero d'Ornano, better known as Sampiero Corso, the contentious historical figure most closely associated with alliance with mainland France (Andreani 1999: 56). In Corsica, historical memory has very deep roots.

By the end of the 1990s, however, separatist and mainstream parties alike were edging towards negotiations. Following a ceasefire in 1999, Prime Minister Lionel Jospin initiated a series of discussions referred to as the 'Matignon process'.[4] Negotiations revolved around four key proposals: new and enhanced competences for the Assemblée de Corse in territorial management and economic development; new legislative powers of a very limited nature; the suppression of the two existing Corsican *départements*; and guaranteed teaching of the Corsican language in *maternelle* and primary schools (Charlet 2003: 163). These proposals received a cool reception, not least from President Jacques Chirac, and were effectively vetoed by the Conseil constitutionnel when, by declaring the transfer of legislative powers to the Corsican Assembly unconstitutional, it undermined the nationalists' key demand. The subsequent defeat of Jospin and re-election of Chirac in the presidential election of 2002 left little prospect of implementation of the Matignon agreements, and the rejection by a slim majority, in a referendum in Corsica in June 2003, of the proposed merging of the two *départements* and of a limited increase in the Assembly's powers lessened the likelihood of further progress in the short term.

European Regions and the Committee of the Regions

It should be clear from the foregoing that the variation in the status, function and historical foundation of regions from one state to another is so great as to preclude a meaningful over-arching definition. And yet the currency of the phrase 'Europe of the Regions' is a recognition of the fact of regional allegiance, however unevenly spread, as well as of the value, in both socio-political and economic terms, of an intermediate level of responsibility and decision making, an interface between the local and the national or supranational. It is in this latter context that the decision taken at Maastricht in 1992 to set up the Committee of the Regions of the European Union is significant. Indeed, the lengthy debates and negotiations which led to its inauguration themselves reveal something of the variety of motives and interests at issue. The German *Länder* and, more recently, the Belgian and Austrian federal provinces had expressed reservations about the way in which the distribution of EU regional support was increasingly held to be the responsibility of governments at the national level, therefore limiting their own room for manoeuvre. The pressure for some sort of regional representation at the Council of Ministers grew as a result. In a parallel development, the movement from the mid-1980s towards greater integration in the EU as a whole – evident from the Single European Act of 1987 to the Maastricht Treaty of 1992 and beyond to the Treaty of Amsterdam in 1996 – has, it is argued, not only increased the complexity of inter-state relations but also, by eroding the autonomy of individual member states, brought regional factors to the forefront (Loughlin 1997: 148).

Pressure for a regional level of representation was chiefly felt in those states where the federal principle was already firmly established. Nevertheless, there was support, in varying degrees and for a variety of reasons, from the regional components of other EU member states. For some, notably in Spain and, to a lesser extent, Italy, the regional agenda reflected aspirations towards internal political settlements. In France, newly empowered regions in a centralised state were attracted by the idea of a direct conduit to the European institutions, particularly in view of the resource implications of a growing EU regional policy budget, now second only to the Common Agricultural Policy in size. Elsewhere, in centralised states such as the United Kingdom and Ireland, regions that had either atrophied through neglect or been emasculated by centralisation began to recognise that the EU offered opportunities for regional funding and therefore a certain legitimacy denied them by their own governments. Other factors came into play as well, so that, for example, it has been in the interests of a highly centralised Greece to consider some measure of decentralisation in order to justify EU regional funding. Scandinavian countries, with a strong local government tradition, see the advantages of both inter- and intra-state cooperation. Finally, the piecemeal growth of transnational European associations, such as the Atlantic Arc and the Mediterranean Arc, testifies to a willingness to explore networks of relationships that go beyond national boundaries. The Assembly of European Regions, whose membership includes regions from Eastern Europe beyond the borders of the newly enlarged EU, such as Bosnia-Herzegovina, Albania and Ukraine, had also, since its inception in the mid-1980s, sought to lobby in favour of greater influence for regional forces in European policy making.

The establishment of the EU Committee of the Regions as an outcome of the Maastricht Treaty negotiations was therefore timely, although it was overshadowed by the two main agenda items: the preparations for European Monetary Union and the debate over the concept of 'subsidiarity'. The importance of this concept to the issue of regional levels of responsibility cannot be overstated. The provision in the Maastricht Treaty (Article 198a) calls for 'an advisory committee of representatives of regional and local authorities, hence to be called the Committee of the Regions'.

Two apparently conflicting views of the role of the Committee of the Regions can be seen in the respective positions of the United Kingdom and Germany at the time of its inception. The British government, wishing at all costs to avoid the empowerment of a regional or sub-national level of government that could be seen as a step towards a federal Europe, endorsed the creation of an exclusively consultative body devoid of legislative powers so that it could claim to be cooperating with European partners without endangering its own role as a member state. For the German *Länder*, in contrast, the Committee of the Regions represented the opportunity to put into practice, on a European-wide scale, experience in decentralised government that had served the Bundesrepublik well for more than 40 years (Collins and Jeffery 1997: 6). The restraining influence of the British government's attitude may, however, have served the interests of a federal government in Bonn anxious to check the ambitions of its own *Länder*.

When the Committee of the Regions (CoR) was first constituted in 1994, it was made up of 189 members, allocated according to the size of the member state (24 each for France, Germany, Italy and the UK; 21 for Spain; 12 for Belgium, Greece, the Netherlands and Portugal; 9 for Denmark and Ireland; 6 for Luxembourg). In the subsequent enlargement of the EU at the start of 1995, the number of members rose to 222 with the accession of Austria and Sweden (12 members each) and Finland (9). With the further expansion of the EU in May 2004 to a total of 25 member states, representation on the CoR rose to 317 (with 21 members for Poland; 12 each for the Czech Republic and Hungary; 9 each for Lithuania and Slovakia; 7 each for Estonia, Latvia and Slovenia; 6 for Cyprus; and 5 for Malta). Following the accession of Bulgaria (12 members) and Romania (15) in January 2007, the current membership is 344.

An aspect of the CoR's constitution that led to vigorous debate in its early stages was the freedom accorded to member state governments in deciding how to fill their allocated seats. The result was what has been termed 'a highly heterogeneous body' (Collins and Jeffery 1997: 6), although this was in any case inevitable: to have subjected the term 'region' to a strict interpretation would have excluded well over half the member states on the grounds that they did not have sub-national tiers of government above the local or municipal level (Loughlin 1997: 157). The principal point at issue was the status in their home countries of the members nominated by national governments. It was the clearly expressed wish of the European Commission, and subsequently of the European Parliament, that CoR members should be elected representatives within their own regions, so that they could be seen to have legitimate democratic credentials. The Council of Ministers, on the other hand, merely advised that states should choose members according to their suitability to represent local and regional authorities.

The initial response from the UK and from Greece, for example, was to attempt to nominate unelected civil servants, although subsequent shifts in policy led to the appointment of a variety of elected representatives of local authorities. An interesting insight into the functioning of European institutions can be gained from the fact that the pretext for bypassing elected representatives in the first instance in the UK and Greece arose from tendentious English- and Greek-language versions of the Maastricht Treaty. References in English to 'representatives of regional and local bodies' and in Greek to 'regional administrations' provided the loophole to justify the appointment of unelected members. Faced with these anomalies, the Commission rapidly closed the loophole to bring the two aberrant versions into line with those in other languages (Féral 1998: 28). Virtually all nominated CoR members are now therefore directly elected or politically accountable to an elected assembly within their own regional or local constituencies, in keeping with the stipulations of the 2000 Treaty of Nice. They are, nonetheless, expected to devote their energies while in office to the interests of the CoR and the EU as a whole, and not to narrow regional or sectoral interests. It is therefore salutary to note the widely held view that 'the primary divisions within the CoR have so far been overwhelmingly along national lines' (Collins and Jeffery 1997: 15).

In territorial terms, the origins of CoR members are also subject to immense variation according to country. In the simplest case – Luxembourg, which has no regional tier of government – a single level of representation at the local authority level suffices. Most other states have opted for a mixture of regional, local/municipal and intermediate representation with, for example, a communal, departmental and regional distribution in France and a complex pattern for the UK, with representation following differing patterns in England, Scotland, Wales and Northern Ireland.

In view of this involved system of nomination and representation, it was to be expected that decisions about the workings of the CoR, and in particular its presidency, would prove to be sensitive. For its first four-year term (1994–8), agreement was reached that led to the election of Jacques Blanc, the president of France's Languedoc-Roussillon region, with Pasquall i Maragall, the mayor of Barcelona, as his deputy, on the understanding that the positions of president and deputy would be reversed after two years. Maragall was thus elected to the presidency in March 1996. This arrangement served the purpose of guaranteeing equal influence at a high level to representatives of both regional and municipal/local authorities. It also produced a political balance between the centre-right (Blanc) and the left (Maragall). A similar delicate balancing act has governed each successive election to the presidency.

From the inception of the CoR, a certain number of policy areas of direct regional interest – education; culture; public health; trans-European networks for transport, telecommunications and energy; economic and social cohesion – were designated as those on which it is obligatorily consulted by the decision-making bodies of the EU. The CoR was entitled to offer opinions on any other subject that it deemed relevant to regional concerns; however, there was no obligation on any other European institution to take account of the opinions expressed. In view of its relatively limited sphere of influence, both in terms of the range of subjects on which it was initially entitled to produce opinions and of the weight attached to those opinions, the CoR was predictably keen to increase its purview and to gain greater influence. The series of consultations and negotiations which took place under the heading of the Inter-Governmental Conference (IGC), culminating in the Treaty of Amsterdam signed in June 1997 and brought into force two years later, provided the opportunity for intensive lobbying on the part of the CoR. The Catalan prime minister, Jordi Pujol, oversaw the preparation of a report, subsequently submitted as an official opinion for the IGC, which sought to defend and reinforce the CoR's status among the European Community institutions.

Among the measures adopted as a result was an extension of those areas in which the CoR is obligatorily consulted on matters of policy to include an additional five: employment, social policy, environment, vocational training and transport. Perhaps most significant was a proposal put forward for the benefit of regional and local tiers of government rather than in the interests of the CoR itself. This was an attempt to reformulate the principle of subsidiarity so that it would extend automatically to the sub-national level of responsibility: 'The Community shall take action, in accordance with the principle of subsidiarity, only if and so far as the objectives of the proposed action cannot be sufficiently achieved by the Member States, or by the regional and local authorities endowed with powers under the domestic legislation of the Member State in question' (quoted in Collins and Jeffery 1997: 20). The final element of the lobbying process that preceded the culmination of the IGC was a 'summit' conference organised by the CoR in Amsterdam one month before the European Council meeting which was to complete the revision of the Community treaties in that city in June 1997. This conference – which had as its basic text a report, *Regions and Cities: Pillars of Europe*, prepared by the prime minister of Bavaria and the mayor of Oporto – was designed to underline the importance of local and regional authorities.

In the event, the Amsterdam Treaty produced modest gains for the CoR. In addition to the extension of the range of subjects on which it must be consulted, it was also granted the status of 'expert' on matters concerning cross-border cooperation. Furthermore, it gained a greater measure of administrative freedom to the extent that is now permitted to develop its own internal regulations. It may be claimed, therefore, that by a process of accretion of very limited powers and influence, the CoR has become firmly embedded among the institutional structures of the EU.

Conclusion

Although the role of the Committee of the Regions within the architecture of the European Union is exclusively consultative and advisory – and despite the fact that the regions for which it provides a platform and an outlet for opinion vary enormously in size, status and influence – the CoR embodies an important acknowledgement of the significance of sub-national territories and identities. It represents, too, an attempt to merge cohesiveness and diversity, while making visible the perpetual tension that governs relationships between state and region. Not the least of the merits of the attention which the CoR has focused on the regions has been the encouragement of the development of regional networks that transcend traditional national affiliations. In the context of EU funding initiatives, an example is Interreg III, which is financed under the European Regional Development Fund and is intended to foster 'the balanced development of the continent through cross-border, transnational and interregional cooperation.'[5] Other developments include efforts that seek to bring together in partnership regions which share common, but not national, characteristics and interests.

The formation of regional and transnational networks has struck a chord particularly in those regions occupying an outlying or peripheral position in relation to their own states or to Europe as a whole. The Mediterranean Arc, which links Catalonia with Piedmont and Lombardy via the southern French territory of Occitania; the Atlantic Arc, which brings together Wales, Brittany, Aquitaine and Galicia and establishes common cause between the maritime towns of Oporto, Bilbao, Nantes and Milford Haven; Anglo-Franco-Flemish declarations of common economic and social interest – all of these ventures bear witness (despite their occasionally implausible connections) to the desire to create new ways of belonging. In some cases, the theories – for example, that inhabitants of the Atlantic seaboard of the EU have common interests to balance against their national interests – appear to be some way ahead of the day-to-day reality.

Unlike the nation or the region itself, these newly conceived transborder regional networks suffer from more than one serious shortcoming. For one thing, regional networks are vulnerable to the accusation that they lack the legitimacy that comes with democratic accountability; their leading figures are, at best, genuinely representative only of their own constituencies. Furthermore, their very newness deprives them of a clear identity and makes it hard for them to arouse in their populations any sense of belonging or allegiance. Attempts to forge new identities, new patterns of allegiance, must take these needs into account (Smith 1992: 73). Transborder regions have no easily reconstituted history, no common language or shared mythology, and the idea of identity stretching even more thinly to take on a European aspect creates its own dangers. The attempt to encourage a sense of pan-European identity risks the creation of an identity vacuum that reduces the sense of belonging to the level of tribalism, an atavistic instinct which finds itself through the identity of the Other. Growing support in recent years for the extreme right throughout Western Europe – particularly in France, Belgium and Germany – has been stimulated in part, at least, by the perceived threat of mass migrations from the south and east, not least from those countries in Eastern Europe whose recent accession to the European Union has facilitated economic migration.

However, the same mobility which brings about the clash of cultures and living standards also ensures that, increasingly, individuals have an interest or a stake in a variety of communities, both large and small. Migration is not the prerogative of the incoming Other. Even the most clearly delineated cultures and communities evolve and cross borders: the Corsican diaspora is at least as large as its home population, and physical frontiers are, in the end, no barrier to economic and social imperatives. The porosity of borders creates overlapping circles of allegiance, networks of belonging, and these are perhaps the most appropriate way to describe the formation of European identity in the twenty-first century: 'It is possible that the nature of European identity is more in tune with post-modern patterns of identification, i.e. it functions in a matrix of "multiple identities", where each of us may be many, many things – baker, railway enthusiast, mother, conservative, from Hamburg, etc. Of course, people always were many things, but in the epoch of nationalism, one identity was the trump card.... This might now be changing, dissolving into a true multiplicity of identities' (Waever 1993: 207).

One of the consequences of globalisation is the realisation that the shapes and contours of the world we inhabit, the boundaries which define our culture and sense of belonging, are increasingly fluid rather than fixed. These boundaries remain the means by which we classify and impose meaning on our world and define our own identity – collectively and as individuals. Yet we may, in acknowledging their fluidity, open up new modes of belonging which supplant the binary oppositions of here and there, them and us: 'An authentically migrant perspective would, perhaps, be based on an intuition that the opposition between here and there is itself a cultural construction, a consequence of thinking in terms of fixed entities and defining them oppositionally. It might begin by regarding movement, not as an awkward interval between fixed points of departure and arrival, but as a mode of being in the world' (Carter 1992: 101). The resulting patterns and relationships may then lead to multiple allegiances which enable, for example, a native of Brittany to be Breton, French and European; a Corsican to have a similarly tripartite allegiance; and a Glaswegian – whatever her ethnic origin – to be Scots, British and European.

Notes

1. *Ae Fond Kiss* (UK 2004) is the third Ken Loach film set in or around Glasgow, following *My Name Is Joe* (1998) and *Sweet Sixteen* (2002). In each, Loach portrays inner-city life, with its varying degrees of social deprivation, as the background for a characteristically humane exploration of human resilience and indomitability. Rangers, one of Glasgow's two major football teams, is traditionally supported by the city's Protestant community; the Catholic community supports Celtic.
2. An interesting, if oblique and strictly extra-diegetic commentary on the film's hidden European dimension can be seen in the final credits, which reveal that it was produced with funding from the UK, Belgium, Germany, Italy and Spain.
3. For a fuller account of the experience of regionalism in the pre-enlargement 15 member states of the EU, see Wagstaff (1999), from which these details have been adapted.
4. For a detailed analysis and assessment of the Matignon process, see Daftary (2003).
5. See http://europa.eu/scadplus/leg/en/lvb/g24204.htm (accessed 20 April 2007).

References

Agnew, J. 2003. 'Territoriality and Political Identity in Europe'. In Berezin and Schain 2003, 219–42.

Andreani, J.-L. 1999. *Comprendre la Corse*. Paris: Gallimard.

Berezin, M. and Schain, M., eds. 2003. *Europe Without Borders: Remapping Territory, Citizenship, and Identity in a Transitional Age*. Baltimore: Johns Hopkins University Press.

Berger, J. 1984. *And Our Faces, My Heart, Brief as Photos*. London: Writers and Readers.

Carter, P. 1992. *Living in a New Country: History, Travelling and Language*. London: Faber and Faber.

Charlet, F. 2003. 'France's Peripheral Parties: Nuanced Demands'. In Ruane, Todd and Mandeville 2003, 144–66.

Cole, A. 2003. 'Beyond Exceptionalism: Changing Regional and Local Government in France'. In Ruane, Todd and Mandeville 2003, 84–100.

Collins, S. and Jeffery, C. 1997. *Whither the Committee of the Regions? British and German Perspectives*. London: Anglo-German Foundation.

Daftary, F. 2003. 'The Matignon Process and Insular Autonomy as a Response to Self-Determination Claims in Corsica'. In *European Yearbook of Minority Issues, Volume 1, 2001–2002*, ed. European Centre for Minority Issues, 299–326. The Hague: Kluwer Law International.

Dunkerley, D., Hodgson, L., Konopacki, S., Spybey, T. and Thompson, A. 2002. *Changing Europe: Identities, Nations and Citizens*. London and New York: Routledge.

Féral, P.-A. 1998. *Le Comité des régions de l'Union européenne*. Paris: PUF.

Foucault, M. 1980. 'Questions on Geography'. In *Power/Knowledge: Selected Interviews and Other Writings, 1972–1977*, ed. C. Gordon, 63–77. New York: Pantheon.

Harvey, D. 2000. *Spaces of Hope*. Edinburgh: Edinburgh University Press.

Ignatieff, M. 1984. *The Needs of Strangers*. London: Chatto and Windus.

Kumar, K. 2003. 'The Idea of Europe: Cultural Legacies, Transnational Imaginings, and the Nation-State'. In Berezin and Schain 2003, 33–63.

Loughlin, J. 1997. 'Representing Regions in Europe: The Committee of the Regions'. In *The Regional Dimension of the European Union: Towards a Third Level in Europe*, ed. C. Jeffery, 147–65. London: Frank Cass.

Mac Laughlin, J. 2001. *Reimagining the Nation-State: The Contested Terrains of Nation-Building*. London: Pluto Press.

Malfliet, K. 2000. 'Identités nationales, minorités et citoyenneté dans une Europe élargie'. In *L'Europe et ses citoyens*, ed. L. le Hardÿ de Beaulieu, 65–96. Brussels: Peter Lang.

Marks, G. 1999. 'Territorial Identities in the European Union'. In *Regional Integration and Democracy: Expanding on the European Experience*, ed. J. J. Anderson, 69–91. Lanham: Rowman and Littlefield.

Middleton, P. and Woods, T. 2000. *Literatures of Memory: History, Time and Space in Postwar Writing*. Manchester: Manchester University Press.

Morley, D. and Robins, K. 1995. *Spaces of Identity: Global Media, Electronic Landscapes and Cultural Boundaries*. London: Routledge.

Ruane, J., Todd, J. and Mandeville, A., eds. 2003. *Europe's Old States and the New World Order: The Politics of Transition in Britain, France and Spain*. Dublin: University College Dublin Press.

Schrijver, F. J. 2004. 'Electoral Performance of Regionalist Parties and Perspectives on Regional Identity in France'. *Regional and Federal Studies* 14, no. 2: 187–210.

Shore, C. 2000. *Building Europe: The Cultural Politics of European Integration*. London: Routledge.

Smith, A. D. 1992. 'National Identity and the Idea of European Unity'. *International Affairs* 68, no. 1: 55–76.

Soja, E. 1994. 'Postmodern Geographies: Taking Los Angeles Apart'. In *NowHere: Space, Time and Modernity*, ed. R. Friedland and D. Boden, 128–45. Berkeley: University of California Press.

Spiering, M. 1996. 'National Identity and European Unity'. In *Culture and Identity in Europe: Perceptions of Divergence and Unity in Past and Present*, ed. M. Wintle, 98–132. Avebury: Aldershot.

Waever, O. 1993. 'Europe since 1945: Crisis to Renewal'. In *The History of the Idea of Europe*, ed. J. van der Dussen and K. Wilson, 151–214. London: Routledge.

Wagstaff, P., ed. 1999. *Regionalism in the European Union*. Exeter: Intellect.

Woolf, S. J. 1979. *A History of Italy, 1700–1860: The Social Constraints of Political Change*. London: Methuen.

Chapter 10

CULTURAL IDENTITIES AND THE EUROPEAN CITY

Susan Milner

The city as a form of organisation is seen by many as central to Europe's cultural identity (Bagnasco and Le Galès 2002). Historically, the development of European identities is linked to Christianity and the rise of a secular bourgeoisie which often came into conflict with it; these expressions of identity and conflicts were given physical form in towns and cities (Le Goff 2005). In other words, Europe's buildings and the organisation of its towns and cities reflect its history. Little wonder, then, that French historians (e.g. Halbwachs 1994; Roncayolo 1997) have identified cities as 'places of memory'. Europe's cultural identity is therefore closely bound up with that of its historic cities and their architectural heritage, as portrayed, for example, on euro notes.

Cities are also seen as the bedrock of Europe's political culture, with Greek democracy originating in city-states before nation-states were invented. Moreover, Europe's cities are held to have particular characteristics linked with their historical origin and development, notably their density and their organisation around a central public space. It has been argued that because of this shared history and sense of collective belonging, Europeans are more attached to their cities than North Americans are: 'Europeans are more likely to consider their cities to be national treasures, whereas Americans are more likely to abandon theirs at a moment's notice or to treat them as commodities or investment opportunities whose value is, at best, fleeting' (Beauregard and Body-Gendrot 1999: 21).

At the same time, the city has become a prime site of the tensions created by the rescaling of the economy and politics in late capitalism (Jessop 2002). Global trends – worldwide urbanisation, mass migration, new conditions of international economic competition, socio-cultural change linked to mass communications media – appear to be leading towards a convergence of urban development, at least in the developed world, and to be diminishing the specificity of Europe's urban model. In particular, there are signs that the American way of life is becoming the model with which all European cities will sooner or later catch up. Nevertheless, due to Europe's heritage, it may be expected that common trends would be experienced differently in different settings, and that cities themselves could become actors shaping this process of globalisation. As cities are increasingly expected to compete amongst themselves, urban identities become marketing tools. The shift from industrial to service economies requires cities to redefine their identities in order to build coalitions for growth and development. Political decentralisation also creates pressures for local identity building. Cultural policies have therefore increased in importance.

European regional integration also plays a part in this twin process of convergence and differentiation. Through its economic policies, the European Union (EU) contributes to the direction of socio-economic change, encouraging or mitigating the effects of global competition and convergence. Through its specific policies aimed at urban centres, notably in the structural funds and associated programmes, it helps to define the place of Europe's cities in the world and their relationship to each other. Conversely, cities have become a key component of the EU's attempts to forge a common European identity.

This chapter seeks, first, to review the impact of contemporary economic, political and social trends on European cities; second, to examine the ways in which Europe's cities have attempted to develop or create specific cultural identities, in the face of these global trends; and, finally, to evaluate the contribution made by EU policies and programmes. It will show that European cities are in flux. The EU as a policy actor tends to encourage global trends by equipping cities with leverage to enhance their position as autonomous actors in new conditions of international competition. Cultural policies are a major vehicle for these changes.

Globalisation and the Post-industrial City

There is no doubt that economic restructuring, deindustrialisation and the erosion of post-war political institutions and practices (state restructuring) have affected cities in the developed world. However, there is considerable disagreement about the scope and impact of economic, social and political changes on the city.[1]

In a recent collection of essays on the city, urban scholars Robert Beauregard and Sophie Body-Gendrot (1999: 3) begin by noting the fragility of the democratic city: 'In a world becoming simultaneously disarticulated and rearticulated under the onslaught of corporate globalization, ethnic social movements, state violence, massive waves of immigration, and intellectual upheaval, the city itself has become unstable as an object of thought and action.' One consequence of this flux, they argue, is that urban scholars have distrusted meta-narratives of urban theory; instead, '[a]mbiguity and complexity take the place of grand theory's traditional infatuation with the formal, the unequivocal, and the parsimonious' (ibid.). At the extreme, this postmodern view of the city invites us to read the city as meaning different things to different people, or perhaps as a series of cameos or disconnected parts.

Some scholars argue that the study of the city itself has become meaningless because – in the Western world at least, where urban lifestyles dominate society – 'the city is no longer the basis for association (Weber), the locus for the division of labour (Durkheim) or the expression of a specific mode of production (Marx), in which case it is neither fruitful nor appropriate for the sociologist to study it in its own right' (Saunders 1981: 13). Anthony Giddens (1999) similarly seems to deny a special place to the city in the modern era, when its functions and power to attract loyalty have been taken over by the nation-state. According to these arguments, the city has lost its meaning in that the social and cultural realities of the city and its components are no longer connected with actual physical locations.

However, the prediction that information technologies would dissociate businesses from specific places has not been proved true – at least not yet. Internet businesses tend to emerge in particular urban settings, creating information technology clusters such as the area around Lyon in France or Hamburg in Germany (Moriset 2003), both being cities with a long industrial tradition. This is not only because innovative businesses depend on proximity to higher education and research centres, but also because they need to be close to the large corporations that are their main clients.

Other observers agree that cities have become more important as a result of trends associated with economic globalisation, which is usually viewed rather broadly as engendering new forms of capitalist restructuring that give greater power to financial markets, extend the reach and influence of multinational corporations, and loosen ties with national territories and states. Many scholars argue that globalisation takes place primarily in cities, especially large metropolises, because it is cities rather than countries that become integrated into the global network, and because cities are especially open to global trends (Short and Kim 1999). 'Global' cities, or those aspiring to this status, play a strategic role as command points within the global economy, as sites of production, investment and innovation.[2] Cities are seen not as passive recipients of the effects of globalisation but rather as actors in the process.

One effect of economic globalisation is spatial restructuring – a new clustering of activities linked to the information economy and especially to financial power. These clusters reflect a loss of national control over the economy. Another effect is increased competition between cities ('place wars').[3] The new competition is characterised by an emphasis on the specific traits of cities and a neo-liberal discourse of entrepreneurialism. Large metropolises aspire to the rank of world city through civic booster projects. Competition to host world events, particularly the summer Olympics or international exhibitions (Barcelona managed both in 1992), provides an important focus for this activity.[4]

Deindustrialisation and the shift towards the informational society also have an impact on the specific urban forms which have characterised Europe. Many writers have contrasted Continental European urban development with the United States model, the latter being constructed around the industrial city of the late nineteenth and early twentieth centuries: compact cities built around the business district (also the locus of administrative and cultural activity), with low-income neighbourhoods 'woven into manufacturing districts and adjacent to commercial cores and its middle income neighbourhoods beyond' (Beauregard and Body-Gendrot 1999: 5). In the US, suburbanisation occurred as more privileged, then professional, groups moved out towards the periphery to form the 'prototypical metropolis' (ibid.). The decentring of US cities was accentuated by deindustrialisation and by increased car ownership and use. The European model, on the other hand, has been characterised as the creation and preservation of a vibrant historic centre radiating outwards. However, there is arguably a trend towards suburbanisation ('edge cities') and decentring in Europe (Cheshire and Hay 1989), although a comparative case study of France and the UK indicates that European edge locations have dynamic political cultures and administrative practices which help to insulate them from complete deregulation and unplanned sprawl (Phelps and Parsons 2003). Sir Peter Hall (1998) has argued that suburbanisation and population shifts from old industrial centres to the 'sunbelt' will be a general trend in the Western world, with the UK following closely behind the US, and Southern European countries lagging behind. For him, this development is positive, because cities are places of creativity and innovation. Thus, attempts by European states to keep their city centres strong by locating new commercial and leisure developments there may be contributing to the very problem they are trying to solve, because it reinforces suburban dwellers' dependence on the car.

The idea of the public space is under severe pressure with, again, the trend coming from the United States, where, as Sharon Zukin (1991, 1995) has shown, public areas such as parks are being taken over by private interests keen to gentrify particular districts and make them safe for up-market buyers. In Europe, the trend is less evident but nevertheless growing (Bianchini and Parkinson 1993). There is also a fear that the US pattern of events – the abandonment of areas by commercial and residential functions leading to the creation of 'zones of discard' which are then conserved through public or more likely private initiatives – may be reversed in Europe, where the heritagisation of city centres pushes businesses and residences out (Graham 2002).

As Hall (1993) makes clear, however, such trends are not autonomous but are largely determined by coalitions of interests and implemented by planning policies. In France, Hall notes, public policies have attempted to contain suburbanisation within certain limits and improve transport infrastructures within cities, particularly in Paris. The new territorial competition is driven not solely by economic restructuring but also by political agency and organised interests (Cox 1993).

Cities remain important as organisers of social relations, too. Although the new mobility linked with the informational age (Castells 1993, 2000) and with mass migration undoubtedly changes the relationship between society and city space, it is not true that one can have equally dense relations by email as with someone living close by.[5] Moreover, many urban populations are still, in David Harvey's (1987) term, 'trapped in space', that is, locked into particular residential locations and unable to move or, less dramatically, unable to work from home, despite the promises of new technologies, or they are forced to use local bus routes because they do not have a car or are unable to park it once they reach their destination. The reality of cities as organisers of social exclusion means that cities remain salient as political forums (ibid.).[6]

The boundaries of the city in the global economy have become blurred as competences are shared or divided up with regions, as the relationship with central government changes and as the European Union mediates relationships between cities (Amin 2004; Amin and Thrift 2002; Massey 2004). This leads some scholars to question whether the city retains any distinctiveness as a political space. Ash Amin (2004: 42) argues that 'what goes on in cities is about questions of political choice and democracy that could be found anywhere, which makes the politics of cities and regions no different from the politics of, say, the household, the nation or the Internet'. However, Amin, like Paquot (2001), goes on to argue that the city retains some specificity as a connective, cosmopolitan formation – 'the forcing ground for challenges that are thrown up when difference is gathered so visibly in one place and when a globality of myriad flows and connections is temporarily halted in one place' (Amin 2004: 43).[7] Global restructuring leads not only to new forms of inequality in cities but also to new spaces for action (Hamel, Lustiger-Thaler and Mayer 2000).[8]

But new urban social movements also depend on the opportunity structures opened up by political rescaling, which suggests that, due to global restructuring and the decline of nation-state regulation, cities matter *more* as spaces of political agency, rather than *less*. Local governments appear to be 'at the forefront of the process of management of new urban contradictions and conflicts' (Castells 1993: 255). The new urban politics has focused on the development of public-private partnerships and other forms of new contractual relations, particularly as part of an agenda of regeneration of inner-city zones (MacLeod, Raco and Ward 2003). New modes of urban governance seek to recast the relationship between central and local government, on the one hand, and between political authorities and citizens, on the other, particularly through a discourse of civic participation and a shift of service delivery to voluntary and community associations – the 'new localism' (Cars et al. 2002).[9] As Patrick Le Galès (Bagnasco and Le Galès 2002) in particular has argued, the new urban governance is linked to changes in European states, with the erosion of the post-war European welfare state but at the same time renewed demands for social policies. As the city becomes more entrepreneurial, and the provision of social services is restructured, local government now involves a greater array of non-governmental actors in a series of contractual relationships.

Cities play a crucial role 'as political actors in the construction of social groups and often in the leadership of local authorities, defining agendas, bringing alliances of public, private and voluntary sector organisations together, and overcoming internal conflict' (Le Galès 2002: 197). Urban governance is thus differentiated, complex and contingent, with no single model dominant. In some cases, urban growth regimes will be created that reflect strong and well-organised business interests which are well integrated into political networks (as in Stuttgart, Bologna, Milan, Lyon, Rennes, Birmingham, Barcelona and Valencia). In other cases, strong governance systems may give rise to conservative, anti-development coalitions which rein in economic interests (as in Strasbourg and Bordeaux in the 1980s).[10]

To sum up, globalisation leads to a deterritorialisation and a reterritorialisation around new centres of power which may well be geographically the same centres as before (but reflecting new powers), or not. An already leading position will give some cities – particularly capital cities – a head start; however, their power is not coming from the nation but from the global flows of capital or information. Similarly, cultural globalisation has an effect of deterritorialisation and reterritorialisation. Migration and the homogenisation and commodification of culture have deterritorialised cultural attributes, particularly on the national level. But empirically it can be seen that although there is much borrowing of trends and consumption practices across countries, there is also much adaptation of what is borrowed to suit local tastes and practices.

Cities and Cultural Policies

Increasingly, attention is being paid to cultural aspects of the city, whether as explanations for specific types of urban development, or as a growing policy area in which 'culture' (i.e. the arts or creative production) is an important and contested resource in the new 'place wars' (Sennett 1999). The 'cultural turn' in city politics is, however, open to interpretation. On one hand, it is pointed out that cultural policies form an important part of Europe's heritage and that they therefore represent a bulwark against global homogenisation, as well as a source of local identity: 'For many centuries European cities were breeding grounds for artistic creation' (Smiers 2000). Commenting on Europe's success in maintaining and exporting its identity through 'soft' policies, as opposed to the US's reliance on military presence, political scientist Joseph Nye identifies cultural and education policies as an important element in this success.[11] In terms of expenditure, European countries generally spend more on cultural policies as a percentage of GDP and per capita than does the United States.[12]

On the other hand, the increasing investment in culture by cities is seen as a product of economic change, particularly post-industrialism. Castells (2000: 18) analyses the city as part of a network in an informational society where 'there is an especially close linkage between culture and productive forces, between spirit and matter' – in other words, between human capital and economic capital. Thus, the new 'culturisation' of economics means a shift towards the local level, the location of cultural production and consumption at the level of urban governance rather than regional or national (ibid.). Postmodernists would also point to the importance of cultural policies in defining the post-industrial city as a place of consumption rather than production. Mike Featherstone (1991: 96) draws on Baudrillard to point to the 'increasing salience of forms of leisure consumption in which the emphasis is placed on the consumption of experiences and pleasure (such as theme parks and tourist and recreational centres) and the ways in which more traditional forms of high cultural consumption (such as museums, art galleries) become revamped to cater for wider audiences'.

Cultural policies may be seen as an instrument, rather than a product, of broader economic and political change. Cities possess cultural capital – in the form of treasure houses containing accumulated artefacts or cultural production including new mass culture industries – which they can deploy as part of this shift. As Hall (1998: 640) argues, 'Culture is now seen as a substitute for all the lost factories and warehouses, and as a device that will create a new urban image.' Civic boosterism, originally a US phenomenon, has increased in Europe, as part of a policy response to the need to regenerate decaying inner cities and to attract inward investment. City marketing campaigns, based on images and representation of a city, typically include four elements: (1) world image (skyscrapers, postmodern architecture, international airports, prominent architects, spectacles such as the Olympics); (2) post-industrialism (rebranding through abstract logos, makeovers, reuse of former industrial buildings and docks as artistic centres); (3) city for business; and (4) capitalising on culture (major art gallery, preferably of modern art and preferably designed by a big-name architect, the archetype being the Guggenheim Museum in Bilbao, designed by Frank Gehry).

As well as inward investment, such campaigns also tend to be aimed at attracting professional middle classes and thus form part of a 'gentrification' or sanitisation programme for urban areas (Featherstone 1991). Unsurprisingly, then, cultural diversity and the arts figure prominently in quality-of-life rankings of European cities.[13]

Not only have cultural policies increased in terms of volume of spending and number of projects, they have also become more fine-tuned and administratively complex. As all major cities now have their large prestige projects (state-of-the-art museums or modern art galleries and arts festivals),[14] local leaders have become more interested in cultural clustering strategies that aim to create durable artistic centres, often in former industrial settings (Mommaas 2004; see also Florida 2002).[15] The archetype for this new type of regeneration through culture was the transformation of SoHo in New York City into an artistic quarter (Zukin 1991: 221–4). Since then, cultural clusters – such as the Temple Bar area in Dublin and museum quarters in Frankfurt, Rotterdam and Vienna – have been promoted in many European countries. Although many of the early cultural clusters emerged as the result of changing populations (a bottom-up development), Mommaas (2004: 508) has observed that 'the conscious creation or nourishment of cultural sites, clusters or "milieux" is rapidly becoming something of an archetypal instrument in the urban cultural planning toolbox'.

Cultural entrepreneurship is closely linked to political decentralisation and to the rise of an entrepreneurial style of city politics.[16] Generally, in those European countries with relatively high aggregate spending on the arts, regional and local governments share between a third and a half of the total expenditure.[17] The Netherlands probably represents the most decentralised model of cultural policy, with local authorities accounting for around two-thirds of total cultural spending. The Scottish case also throws light on the relationship between political decentralisation, identity building and cultural policies. The reorganisation of local government in Scotland in the mid-1990s saw the abolition of middle-tier authorities, which had been important arts providers, and a subsequent drop in arts expenditure.[18] However, following devolution, the Scottish Executive, in a series of policy-shaping statements, defined culture as a major policy priority and set a series of targets for artistic excellence and international profile in order to 'talk Scotland up'.[19] Cultural policy is here seen as a political resource aimed at embedding the new political institutions and fostering a regional identity.

The new regeneration-through-culture agenda has been complex, unstable and contested. Some authors warn against cultural entrepreneurship on economic grounds, particularly cautioning against large-scale projects which may be no more than white elephants. Economist Paul Krugman (1996) has argued that places cannot be competitive and therefore should not attempt to compete as places. According to this analysis, quality-of-life rankings, urban welfare rankings and other local marketing indices of attractiveness are useless because they do not address the real reasons why companies relocate or why they are competitive once they are there (ibid.; see also Camagni 2002). Geographer Ivan Turok (2003) also warns against expecting too much from cultural policies as drivers of economic regeneration. In particular, one-off landmark projects often fail to deliver the anticipated economic benefits, as CABE (the Commission for Architecture and the Built Environment, the organisation set up to implement the recommendations of the 1999 Urban Task Force report chaired by the influential architect Lord Rogers) found when it analysed the impact of Britain's millennium projects, which had sought to emulate the Guggenheim effect in Bilbao.[20]

Institutions are also an important factor in the new cultural governance (Le Galès 1998). Comparisons of Lyon, Lille and Barcelona, whilst highlighting the extent to which European cities have been able to use booster projects to assert their identity, particularly as niche business centres, draws attention to the problems caused by institutional fragmentation (McNeill 2001). Political decentralisation provides a spur and a rationale for civic boosterism but does not always ensure adequate institutional support. In the case of Barcelona, strong support from the national government was key to the success of the initiative. There is often a fear that the aim of projecting an 'international city' image can lead to a loss of city distinctiveness.[21] Cultural clusters may also be beset by poor institutional coordination or conflicting sets of values, most obviously between bohemian artistic values and economic development interests (Mommaas 2004).[22]

France, recognised as one of Europe's high spenders on the arts, exemplifies the multiple processes at work in the new cultural politics. After the 1981 elections, the socialist government identified cultural policy as a key component of its project to 'change society' and set a target of 1 per cent of GDP for arts expenditure. Since then, expenditure has been in the area of 0.7 to 1 per cent of GDP. Part of the reason for this relatively high level of spending may be found in the competition between politicians at the national level, with Paris in particular becoming a battleground between rivals François Mitterrand and Jacques Chirac in the 1990s (Collard 1998). Cultural policies became a political resource in a highly personalised political system. At the same time, expenditure in cultural resources may be seen as a rational investment for a country that is both highly integrated into the world economy (and therefore a site for inward investment) and dependent on tourism.

Cultural policies also formed an integral part of reforming the state through new modes of urban governance.[23] The delivery of cultural policy in France in the 1990s involved a network of partnerships between local, regional and state bodies, and between these bodies, decentralised government agencies and local associations. It was thus the vehicle for a new contractualism in politics, with the development of public-private, sponsor-artist partnerships. Guy Saez (2003), in his analysis of the delivery of cultural policies at the local and regional levels in France, particularly in the Rhône-Alpes region, argues that cities played a crucial role in creating 'regimes of cooperation' with other actors at all levels. At the same time, they are also competing with each other outside the region for the financing of their projects. Thus, the national policy and funding regimes have encouraged, more or less explicitly, a race between regional capitals.

French municipal authorities quickly seized on this new role. Cultural policies became an integral part of local identity building, promoted by mayors in the context of decentralisation. As a result, most major cities and many large towns have developed ambitious cultural policies which serve a variety of social, economic, political and artistic goals simultaneously. Cultural policy accounted for over 10 per cent of the municipal budget in towns with over 10,000 inhabitants in the 1990s.

Cities like Lyon and Lille have used cultural policies to promote their international aspirations – most recently Lille, under the banner of the European Capital of Culture. Initiatives such as the European Capital of Culture can provide an opportunity to bring together large-scale projects and horizontally linked clusters, but they are not the only programmes supporting cultural entrepreneurship, as we shall see in the following section. These policies reproduce the tensions noted above between economic and artistic or social values, between local and global identities, between internal and external consumption.

Europeanisation and the European City

Europeanisation has been defined in many different ways (Featherstone and Radaelli 2004). Broadly, it denotes the impact of European policies and ways of working on domestic policies and practices. In particular, it focuses on the process through which domestic actors are realigned in relation to each other as a result of policies at the European level or of new ways of working promoted by the European Union (particularly through its transnational networks). This process has a particular relevance to the relationship between national government and sub-national authorities. As noted earlier in this chapter, European integration affects cities both indirectly, notably through its economic policies, and directly, through its redistributive policies, through programmes aimed specifically at promoting certain types of urban development and, last but not least, through cultural policies for which the city is the main vehicle. At the same time, many cities themselves have found new roles – or have found support for existing roles – within the political space opened up by European integration. Cities are seen as performing at least four roles on the European stage: twinning, transnational networks, cross-border collaboration and participation in the advisory committees of European institutions (Ercole, Walters and Goldsmith 1997). European funding is often viewed as a measure of cities' success in carrying out these roles and amplifying their voice and resources.

Globalisation and the Formation of a 'New Urban Hierarchy' in Europe

Hall (1993: 894) has suggested that the progress towards a single market 'must inevitably lead to a certain centralisation of these functions in a super-capital or capitals', whilst on the other hand a resurgence of nationalism, particularly in East Central Europe, would work in the opposite direction. The result of these two contradictory shifts was to create a new triangle of power – Brussels-Bonn-Frankfurt – in the middle of Europe, with the possibility of northern and southern nodes also arising over time. The overall result could be a new urban hierarchy, based on the following:

- global cities (with London being challenged by Brussels, Paris, Amsterdam and/or Frankfurt, depending on decisions regarding the site of financial and monetary institutions);

- city regions in a global fringe or corridor zones with niche functions in the information economy, defined by the siting of technology or conference centres (Birmingham, Dortmund, Reading, Lyon, Nantes);
- remote regional cities at the periphery of the national economy (Glasgow, Belfast, Clermont-Ferrand, Saarbrucken, Cadiz);
- national and regional capital cities (Bristol, Norwich, Bordeaux, Toulouse, Hanover, Stuttgart, Bologna, Amsterdam, Brussels, Copenhagen, Stockholm, Dublin), where the lack of an industrial base is an advantage;
- county towns (Durham, Preston, Roubaix, Charleroi, Essen), often in older industrial regions.

Short and Kim's (1999) indices of global networkedness – based on the presence of multinational corporations, financial centres and stock markets (command centre classifications), and nodal position in global air traffic – confirm Hall's argument, although the authors note that Europe's cities still lag behind in global terms. Frankfurt and Paris in particular appear to be up-and-coming centres. But generally, Europe's networks remain regional rather than global. The effect of economic integration thus seems to have been to accentuate the hierarchy of cities within Europe, without necessarily boosting the position of the most densely networked cities (Paris, London, Frankfurt, Amsterdam) internationally. In fact, the relative position of Europe's cities has declined, in terms of both global urban population and significance as mega-cities (Thorns 2002: 54).

Most analysts agree that the likely effect of economic trends is to create an 'archipelago economy' of fragmented centres, in which inequalities between cities will be increased, even as specialisation decreases. For historical reasons, Europe's regional contrasts are far more marked than in the United States. In the post-war period these differences were mitigated by welfare and other redistributive spending, but as welfare states contract, disparities are seen to be spreading. If anything, it is argued that the effect of European structural funding may be to exacerbate inequalities (Braunerhjelm et al. 2000; Veltz 2002). EU policies have introduced their own dynamics of territorial competition (Cheshire and Gordon 1995).

European Regional Policy and the European Dimension of Spatial Planning

From the late 1980s onwards, EU regional policy has helped to reshape relationships between European, national and sub-national levels of governance, giving rise to a new conceptualisation of the EU as 'multi-level governance' (Hooghe 1996).[24] European cities have been key actors in this process, identifying opportunities to secure funding and extend political influence. Cities, rather than regions, were not explicitly mentioned in the EU treaties until Maastricht (1992), when urban planning became a focus of the chapter on environmental policy (subject to unanimity voting). The new interest in cities was sparked by a concern partly about inequalities within regions and more specifically about the regeneration of industrial sites under Objective 2 of regional policy, but it was also a response to the emergence of cities as policy actors. For example, by the 1990s, it was apparent that in the UK, Glasgow, Birmingham, Manchester and Liverpool were better than other cities at 'playing the game', whilst Barcelona used European funding to prepare for holding the 1992 Olympic Games (Goldsmith 2004: 123; see also Bache and Jones 2000).[25] INTERREG (an initiative that aims to encourage interregional cooperation) in particular helped cities to link up with partners in other European countries to secure access to funding for infrastructure projects (see table 10.1).

It has been argued that cities are changing from being 'policy takers' to 'policy makers', partly because the EU has moved towards more participative modes of governance, but also largely because the cities themselves have become forceful actors. For example, around 30 of the 200 regional offices in Brussels explicitly represent the interests of cities or groups of cities, in addition to the 20 or so offices of local authority organisations and city networks

TABLE 10.1 EU and Urban Development Policies and Programmes (Structural Funds)

1991	Committee on Spatial Development formed
1997	Communication 'Towards an Urban Agenda in the European Union'
1998	Green Paper 'Sustainable Urban Development in the European Union – A Framework for Action'
1998	'Urban Forum' in Vienna (November)
1998	'Urban Exchange Initiative' (benchmarking on national urban policies)
1999	Adoption of the 'European Spatial Development Perspective' (ESDP)
2000	Establishment of two urban expert groups within the Committee on Spatial Development (Tampere Council, 1999)
1989	INTERREG set up to assist border regions to overcome development problems related to their peripheral position and to encourage cross-border cooperation and city networking
1994–9	INTERREG II included energy networks and spatial planning cooperation initiatives
2000–6	INTERREG III had a budget of 4,875 million euros and emphasised the EU's external border regions, in the context of eastward enlargement
1989–99	URBAN: 164 million euros spent on 59 pilot projects developed by the European Regional Development Fund
1994	URBAN established to coordinate structural funds initiatives in urban areas with a high concentration of social, environmental and economic problems
1994–9	URBAN I: 900 million euros spent on 118 projects
2000–6	URBAN II: 730 million euros spent on 70 projects (mainly in Germany, France, Spain, Italy and the UK), with an emphasis on 'sustainability'

such as EUROCITIES (Schulze 2003). The URBAN II programme (see table 10.1) was agreed to because of lobbying by big cities, particularly those within the EUROCITIES group. This reflects the importance of EU funding for these cities, which have been helped in their lobbying efforts by the national governments of some member states, particularly the Netherlands. Associations of regional and municipal authorities are now so influential that the European Commission has formalised its dialogue with them.[26]

Nevertheless, the resources of cities as actors at the EU level should not be overestimated, since very few cities are influential enough to have a major impact. Also, local government is not particularly good at implementing EU programmes. At the same time, urban policy has become mainstreamed into EU policy making: with the exception of foreign and security policy, there are hardly any policy areas where cities are not recognised as stakeholders and consulted by the European Commission. The Constitutional Treaty, signed in November 2004, commits the EU to the promotion of 'economic, social and territorial cohesion and solidarity among member states' as one of its key objectives.

The inclusion of a specific commitment to territorial cohesion has been attributed to French attempts – spearheaded by President of the European Commission Jacques Delors and then European Commissioner Michel Barnier – to extend the French concept of *aménagement du territoire* (territorial planning) to the EU (Faludi 2004). Strategic spatial planning, which has been pursued since 1991 with the establishment of the Committee on Spatial Development (see table 10.1), represents an attempt to provide a strategic framework for regional policy. It may be seen as a pragmatic response to concerns about unequal development as well as to the increasingly strong voice of municipal government (Healey 2004). However, despite strong support from France and Germany, it remains to be seen whether the EU has the institutional capacity or the political will to move from an ad hoc, responsive mode (under structural funding) to a more strategic approach. Meanwhile, there is evidence that a bottom-up Europeanisation is taking place, at least in the bigger and richer member states: sub-national actors are taking the initiative from national governments in forging European alliances and securing access to European funding. In the UK, for example, British planners are increasingly involved in transnational cooperation facilitated by EU membership, in terms of an exchange of ideas and practice, and by a broadening of the knowledge base. There is also evidence of an impact on administrative structures, in terms of the delegation of tasks to agencies outside local authorities, the appointment of European officers and the direct Europeanisation of planning departments through the creation of a corporate team (the county of Kent being the most advanced in this respect) (Tewdwr-Jones and Williams 2001).

Arguably, a more strategic approach is needed to overcome the fragmentation evident in the EU's policies, which is likely to be exacerbated with enlargement. As noted above, EU actions have been criticised by several analysts for increasing rather than reducing inequalities between and within regions.

There are several reasons why this might be the case. As we have just seen, cities themselves have differential resources, and the more that the successful cities are able to 'capture' policy making, the greater the share of funding they will continue to take. Urban initiatives within the structural funds tend to be concentrated in the larger countries, with a relatively small number of cities receiving several millions of euros (to be matched by national funds). The unequal ability of cities to meet the co-financing criteria tends to reinforce this concentration.[27] EU regional and cohesion policy is also often undermined by other policies, particularly agricultural policy (Braunerhjelm et al. 2000). For other analysts, the EU's regional and cohesion policy can never be more than a palliative to the destructive effect of its neo-liberal economic policies (Allen, Massey and Cochrane 1998).

European Cultural Policy

We have seen that EU regional policy tends not only to accompany but to reinforce territorial competition. Cultural projects have been an important focus of local entrepreneurialism, and local authorities have naturally looked to the EU for part-funding.[28] The argument here is that while EU policies do not shape local strategies (not least because the amounts of money involved are often relatively small), they can serve as leverage for local coalitions. At the same time, the cultural policies promoted by the EU are not immune to the tensions already noted in our discussion above. Since the EU is also using cultural policies to promote a sense of 'Europeanness' – to 'brand' Europe, as it were – these tensions are amplified.

This branding is most apparent in the European Capitals of Culture initiative (Evans 2003). Formerly known as the European Cities of Culture, the programme was launched in June 1985 'as a means of bringing EU citizens together', at the initiative of Melina Mercouri, then Greek Minister of Cultural Affairs. The choice of city is made in the Council of Ministers on proposals from member states (see table 10.2 for a list), but starting in 2005, a new selection procedure is used on the basis of national rotas (one city per member state, in turn) and the national choice presented to the Commission, the European Parliament and the Committee of the Regions. The Capitals of Culture initiative forms part of the EU's recently developed cultural policy, codified in Culture 2000 (for the period 2000–4, subsequently extended to 2006) and Culture 2007 (for the period 2007–13). Culture 2000 had a budget of 167 million euros over five years and worked on the basis of funding individual projects, whilst Culture 2007 has a proposed budget (as of January 2007) of 408 million euros over seven years. Within this programme, spending on Capitals of Culture has increased significantly.

Community cultural policy has a very ambitious remit since its goals cover social and economic outcomes (employment creation, social inclusion and participation), information and knowledge (technologies, means of communication), citizenship and dialogue between generations and between cultures,

TABLE 10.2 European Cities of Culture/Capitals of Culture

European Cities of Culture, 1985–2004
- 1985 Athens (Greece)
- 1986 Florence (Italy)
- 1987 Amsterdam (Netherlands)
- 1988 West Berlin (West Germany)
- 1989 Paris (France)
- 1990 Glasgow (United Kingdom)
- 1991 Dublin (Ireland)
- 1992 Madrid (Spain)
- 1993 Antwerp (Belgium)
- 1994 Lisbon (Portugal)
- 1995 Luxembourg (Luxembourg)
- 1996 Copenhagen (Denmark)
- 1997 Thessaloniki (Greece)
- 1998 Stockholm (Sweden)
- 1999 Weimar (Germany)
- 2000 Reykjavík (Iceland), Bergen (Norway), Helsinki (Finland), Brussels (Belgium), Prague (Czech Republic), Krakow (Poland), Santiago de Compostela (Spain), Avignon (France), Bologna (Italy)
- 2001 Rotterdam (Netherlands), Porto (Portugal)
- 2002 Bruges (Belgium), Salamanca (Spain)
- 2003 Graz (Austria)
- 2004 Genoa (Italy), Lille (France)

Capitals of Culture, 2005–10
- 2005 Cork (Ireland)
- 2006 Patras (Greece)
- 2007 Luxembourg (Luxembourg), Greater Region – Sibiu (Romania)
- 2008 Liverpool (United Kingdom), Stavanger (Norway)
- 2009 Linz (Austria), Vilnius (Lithuania)
- 2010 Essen (Germany), Pécs (Hungary), Istanbul (Turkey)

Cultural Months (1992–9)
- 1992 Krakow (Poland)
- 1993 Graz (Austria)
- 1994 Budapest (Hungary)
- 1995 Nicosia (Cyprus)
- 1996 St Petersburg (Russia)
- 1997 Ljubljana (Slovenia)
- 1998 Linz (Austria), Valletta (Malta)
- 1999 Plovdiv (Bulgaria)

both within and outside of Europe. The objective of the Capitals of Culture programme is rather broad – 'to highlight the richness and diversity of European cultures and the features they share, as well as to promote greater mutual acquaintance between European citizens' (Decision 1419/1999/EC of the European Parliament and Council, 25 May 1999). The criteria for the selection of projects include the following:

- promotion of shared artistic movements and styles in which the city has played a particular role;
- organisation of artistic events (music, dance, theatre, visual arts, cinema, etc.) and improvement of the promotion and management of the arts;
- promotion of European public awareness of the figures and events which have marked the history and culture of the city;
- organisation of specific activities to encourage innovation;
- special measures for young people;
- multimedia and multilingualism (for broader access);
- contribution to local economy (employment and tourism);
- development of links between architectural heritage and strategies for new urban development;
- dialogue with cultures of other parts of the world.

Projects are intended to underline and encourage cultural diversity whilst at the same time also reinforcing a common European cultural heritage and a 'European dimension'.

Academic interest in the Capitals of Culture programme has burgeoned recently, reflecting its growing importance to city authorities.[29] However, the impact of cultural initiatives is notoriously difficult to measure, especially given the breadth of objectives.[30] The European Commission has also commissioned a series of evaluations of its actions. The first of these, by John Myerscough (1994), was particularly influential. It suggested a positive impact of the early projects in terms of visitor numbers (the easiest criterion to evaluate) and total funding for local initiatives. Myerscough's (1991) earlier evaluation of Glasgow had noted a 40 per cent rise in attendance at all types of event. Evaluations of specific cities' cultural programmes also tend to note a positive balance between boosting tourism and local involvement, contrary to the risks of tensions highlighted by some authors.[31] Later reports on the Culture 2000 initiative indicated a high degree of satisfaction on the part of participating bodies, who reported that the events had been 'positive in terms of media resonance, the development of culture and tourism and recognition by inhabitants of the importance of their city being chosen' (Cogliandro 2001). City officials evidently look on the Capitals of Culture programme as a means to develop infrastructure, upgrade a city's image, attract tourists and tackle social problems by bringing people together, particularly through ambitious prestige events such as festivals.

However, more recent evaluations have cast doubt on the capacity of European cultural initiatives to tackle economic regeneration. Reports by independent consultants have noted the limited socio-economic impact of the Capitals of Culture programme, with negative legacies, such as political rivalries and conflicts over capital spending, resulting in some cases.[32] The reports have led to discussions about how best to ensure longer-term sustainability of the projects, particularly at the city government level, where cultural policies need to be integrated into other aspects of urban development. In Lille in 2004, this tension between short-term mobilisation and visibility, on the one hand, and long-term community regeneration, on the other, was resolved mainly through innovative *maisons folies*, former industrial buildings recycled for community arts use, although it remains to be seen how successfully these buildings will be incorporated into local arts strategies in the future.

Finally, evaluation of the impact of cultural initiatives on territorial identities presents something of a challenge. In adopting the Culture 2000 proposal, the ministers also claimed that the Cities of Culture programme had helped to strengthen local and regional identity, as well as fostering European integration. Unfortunately, there is a dearth of hard evidence, which Eurobarometer, for example, might have been expected to supply. Part of this difficulty may stem from the ad hoc, responsive nature of the programme to date, which is reflected even at the level of funding, with cities applying for and receiving widely varying amounts of money for ostensibly similar objectives (Richards, Goedhart and Herrijgers 2001). The problems faced by Southern European countries in accessing EU structural funds, discussed above, apply also to cultural programmes. Applications for cultural funding come disproportionately from the wealthier, northern member states, although the discrepancy is ironed out at the selection stage.[33] Differential resources also apply to co-funding possibilities, which for most participants constitute the main benefit of EU cultural programmes.

As already noted, the 'European dimension' of the programme is one of the main criteria for selection. However, this dimension is nowhere defined and is difficult to identify in the projects to date.[34] In many cases, the local dimension also appears to be overshadowed by a universal ambition (for 'high' culture and classicism) or by references to national culture. The nine cities selected to mark the millennium programme, for instance, had little in common. They differed markedly in size, from 1.25 million inhabitants in Prague to only 88,000 in Avignon. Some were capital cities, others not. Nor did the choice of themes necessarily provide a good indication of local identity: they tended to be bland and universal, as did the logos chosen to represent the cities' programmes. However, some significant differences stood out in the way that the funding was used locally, ranging from Avignon's classical and traditional programme, reinforcing its existing festival rather than providing added value, to Krakow's heavy emphasis on history and national cultural identity, particularly the influence of various Christian Orthodox and

Jewish musical traditions, to Brussels's rather inward-looking city regeneration project. Bergen, a relatively small regional capital, offered a distinctive, youth-oriented and very broad-based cultural programme, with something for everyone (Sjøholt 1999).

The two cities selected for 2001, Porto and Rotterdam, also differed in terms of levels of funding, the scale of the projects and their impact. Whilst Porto strove to associate the city with futurism, Rotterdam's aim was to promote the city as international and culturally diverse (Richards, Goedhart and Herrijgers 2001). What both cities' programmes had in common was a desire to present themselves as outward-looking, international and dynamic.

The approach of Bergen and Rotterdam, with its heavy emphasis on diversity and cosmopolitanism, represents a newer phase of the Capitals of Culture programme. For Amin (2004: 42), this initiative represents a form of 'consumer' cosmopolitanism, which 'celebrates cities and regions as cultural gateways, and plays on the virtues of world music, minority ethnic food and festival, regeneration based on multi-cultures and multi-ethnic public spaces, and the exoticism of the stranger'. Here we find again the tension between a Europe of places and a Europe of flows, a Europe which is rooted and a Europe which is finding its place in the world.

Conclusion

We have seen in this chapter that cultural events matter to city authorities as they engage in competitions for funding, which is largely public, in the quest to 'brand' their cities as distinctive places for business investment and tourism and also as places to live. This quest has coincided with the European Union's own agenda for the promotion of a European identity. As a result, the Capitals of Culture initiative has grown in importance, becoming integrated into cities' own development strategies and also appearing in mainstream press and public discussions in the member states.[35] In this sense, it could be argued that cultural policy has contributed to an emergent European civic space. At the very least, the signposting of events as 'sponsored' by the European Union gives a sense of the material and cultural benefits to be gained from membership, an effect already noted for the EU's regional policy.

However, the EU's programmes serve as a lever for existing strategies rather than an entirely new creation. They amplify existing trends. As such, they are not immune to tensions already identified between local and global, roots and networks, places and flows. They tend to exacerbate rather than alleviate existing inequalities between places. As a result, it is unlikely that a 'European' identity could come to replace or rival existing territorial identities. On the other hand, cities are emerging as important actors, thanks at least in part to the action of national and European public authorities. Although not all of them are able to do so, some European cities have the institutional capacity to use the resources available to them, including those provided by the EU, in order to boost their position relative to other cities and, in some cases, to national authorities. However, the evidence suggests that those cities which can take part in the global race without exacerbating internal inequalities will be the exception rather than the rule. Cultural policy can promote collective mobilisation but by itself is a rather weak tool – albeit arguably an indispensable part of the toolkit – of wider socio-economic regeneration.

Notes

1. For a useful overview of the debates, see MacLeod, Raco and Ward (2003). For an introductory text, see Thorns (2002).
2. This is the 'global city' developed by Sassen (2001); see also Scott (2001).
3. On the competition between European cities to attract foreign investment, see the 1999 special issue of *Urban Studies*, 'Competitive Cities', edited by W. F. Lever and I. Turok.
4. There are numerous case studies of this process. See, for example, Cochrane, Peck and Tickell (1996).
5. This claim is made by Paquot (2001: 79–95).
6. On social exclusion and the city, see Andersen (2003).
7. See also 'Geographies of Responsibility', *Geografiska Annaler B* 86, no. 1 (2004): 11: 'Local place ... is the locus of the production of heterogeneity. This is its role in life.'
8. See especially Mayer's (2000) overview chapter.
9. For some recent case studies, see Coaffee and Healey (2003).
10. Several studies identify the quality of urban governance as a key variable explaining economic performance and the attractiveness of cities in Europe. See Cheshire (1999) and Harding (1997). On growth coalitions in Europe, particularly applied to the case of Lille, see Cole and John (2001) and Matejko (2000).
11. J. Nye, 'Europe's Soft Power', *Globalist*, 3 May 2004 (http://www.theglobalist.com/ DBWeb/StoryId.aspx?StoryId–3886).
12. It is notoriously difficult to compare countries' spending on cultural policies, and within the EU figures vary widely. Figures given by the respective arts ministries are compared in a report by the Arts Council of Ireland, *A Comparative Study of Levels of Arts Expenditure in Selected Countries and Regions* (Dublin, 2000). They show the US as having spent 0.019 per cent of GDP on arts and museums at the end of the 1990s, compared to 0.14 per cent spent by the UK, 0.27 per cent by Finland, 0.35 per cent by Sweden and 0.07 per cent by Ireland. Germany was not included because the available figures were for an earlier date (1993), but spending was relatively high: 0.36 per cent of GDP.
13. See, for example, the ranking in Rogerson (1999: 978), in which cultural products and the arts are cited as key attributes of quality of city life in four of the seven rankings reviewed.

14. The more that cities seek to stress their distinctiveness by using the toolkit of flagship projects and spectacular events, the more they come to resemble each other. Thus, the heritage waterfront has become something of a cliché (see Graham 2002).

15. Florida's work, based on the US but also looking at comparable European developments such as Dublin's Temple Bar, has received close attention from policy makers in Europe.

16. On Leeds and Manchester as the archetypal entrepreneurial cities, see Haughton and Williams (1999) and Quilley (2000).

17. Council of Europe/ERICarts, *Cultural Policies in Europe: A Compendium of Basic Facts and Trends*, 2003.

18. Arts Council of Ireland, *A Comparative Study of Levels of Arts Expenditure*, 12.

19. A. Scallion, paper for the Scottish Arts and Culture Policy Forum, University of Stirling, 2 February 2004.

20. See M. Weaver, 'Urban Design: The Issue Explained', *The Guardian*, 21 November 2004. For the Urban Task Force recommendations, see Rogers (1999).

21. Author Gordon Burn has made this point in his commentary on the regeneration of northern England ('Knickers to fancy-pants ideas', *The Guardian*, 13 November 2004): 'Now Bradford, in common with Leeds, Liverpool, Newcastle and other famous "manufacturing places", has been re-branded a world city and has been rewarded with the kind of post-modern trophy buildings which betoken this new status.... The irony of course is that all the great Victorian cities of the north of England, thanks to the Lottery bounty, are beginning to look the same.'

22. Mommaas's (2004) discussion of five Dutch projects draws on Zukin's (1991) critique of SoHo.

23. In 1996, 38.6 per cent of cultural expenditure came from the French municipal authorities, compared to only 7.1 per cent from departments and 2 per cent from regions.

24. For a useful summary of the policies and concepts of multi-level governance, see Goldsmith (2004).

25. It is noteworthy that many studies of the impact of regional policy focus on major cities rather than regions as such. This mirrors the tensions within European integration itself between a logic of places (territoriality) and a logic of flows (fluidity). See Jonsson, Tagil and Tornqvist (2000).

26. Commission Communication of 19 December 2003, 'Dialogue with Associations of Regional and Local Authorities on the Formulation of European Union Policy', COM (2003), 811 (final).

27. For an acute analysis of the problems faced by Spanish, Greek and Portuguese cities in this competition for funding, see Chorianopoulos (2002).

28. For example, the study of cultural clustering in the Netherlands, cited above, shows that at least one of these projects (the Tilburg Museum Quarter) was partially funded by the European Regional Development Fund.

29. Glasgow is probably the city which has been most studied in this respect. See in particular Booth and Boyle (1993), Gomez (1998), Myerscough (1991), Richards, Goedhart and Herrijgers (2001) and Sayer (1992).

30. For a useful review of the literature relating to the link between cultural policies and urban marketing, see Richards and Wilson (2004).

31. The risks are outlined by Bianchini and Parkinson (1993). However, studies of Glasgow and Rotterdam, for example, show that although tourist numbers

increase as a result of the cultural programmes, the vast majority of participants are local and that the objectives of increased external awareness and internal cohesion can be achieved at the same time.

32. PLS Ramboll, *Interim Evaluation of the Culture 2000 Programme: Final Report*, 2003; Palmer/Rae Associates, *European Cities and Capitals of Culture*, Brussels, 2004. The Palmer/Rae report in particular received a great deal of media and political attention. See 'The European Capital of Culture – an Event or a Process? Issues on Sustainability and Long-Term Impact', *ArtsProfessional Magazine*, November 2004; C. Jonas, 'City Pledge on Capital of Culture', *Liverpool Echo*, 1 November 2004.

33. GMV Conseil, *Evaluation ex-post des programmes Kaleidoscope, Ariane et Raphaël, 1996–1999*, Brussels, European Commission, 2003.

34. British cities, particularly when competing for European funding, are apt to describe themselves as 'European', but struggle to define this Europeanness other than in terms of pavement cafés and late-night entertainment.

35. In the UK, for example, the competition for the 2008 nomination saw a mass media campaign, involving thousands of citizens in local mobilisations and culminating in a telephone vote.

References

Allen, J., Massey, D. and Cochrane, A. 1998. *Rethinking the Region*. London: Routledge.

Amin, A. 2004. 'Regions Unbound: Towards a New Politics of Place'. *Geografiska Annaler B* 86, no. 1: 33–44.

Amin, A. and Thrift, N. 2002. *Cities: Reimagining the Urban*. Cambridge: Polity.

Andersen, H. S. 2003. *Urban Sores: On the Interaction between Segregation, Urban Decay and Deprived Neighbourhoods*. Aldershot: Ashgate.

Bache, A. and Jones, R. 2000. 'Has EU Regional Policy Empowered the Regions? A Study of Spain and the UK'. *Regional and Federal Studies* 10, no. 3: 1–20.

Bagnasco, A. and Le Galès, P., eds. 2002. *Cities in Contemporary Europe*. Cambridge: Cambridge University Press.

Beauregard, R. and Body-Gendrot, S., eds. 1999. *The Urban Moment: Cosmopolitan Essays on the Late 20th Century City*. London: Sage.

Bianchini, F. and Parkinson, M., eds. 1993. *Cultural Policy and Urban Regeneration: The West European Experience*. Manchester: Manchester University Press.

Booth, P. and Boyle, R. 1993. 'See Glasgow, See Culture'. In Bianchini and Parkinson 1993, 21–47.

Braunerhjelm, P., Faini, R., Norman, V., Ruane, F. and Seabright, P. 2000. *Integration and the Regions of Europe: How the Right Policies Can Prevent Polarization*. London: Centre for Economic Policy Research.

Camagni, R. 2002. 'On the Concept of Territorial Competitiveness: Sound or Misleading?' *Urban Studies* 39, no. 13: 2395–411.

Cars, G., Healey, P., Madanipour, A. and Magalhaes, C., eds. 2002. *Urban Governance, Institutional Capacity and Social Milieux*. Aldershot: Ashgate.

Castells, M. 1993. 'European Cities, the Informational Society, and the Global Economy'. *Journal of Economic and Social Geography* 84, no. 4: 247–57.

———. 2000. *The Rise of the Network Society*. 2nd ed. 3 vols. London: Blackwell.

Cheshire, P. 1999. 'Cities in Competition. Articulating the Gains from Integration'. *Urban Studies* 36, no. 5/6: 843–64.

Cheshire P. and Gordon, I. R. 1995. 'European Integration: The Logic of Territorial Competition and Europe's Urban System'. In *Cities in Competition: Productive and Sustainable Cities for the 21st Century*, ed. J. Brotchie, M. Batty, E. Blakely, P. Hall and P. Newton, 108–26. Melbourne: Longman.

Cheshire, P. and Hay, D. G. 1989. *Urban Problems in Western Europe: An Economic Analysis*. London: Unwin Hyman.

Chorianopoulos, B. 2002. 'Urban Restructuring and Governance: North-South Differences in Europe and the EU URBAN Initiative'. *Urban Studies* 39, no. 4: 705–26.

Coaffee, J. and Healey, P. 2003. '"My Voice: My Place": Tracking Transformations in Urban Governance'. *Urban Studies* 40, no. 10: 1979–99.

Cochrane, A., Peck, J. and Tickell, A. 1996. 'Manchester Plays Games: Exploring the Local Politics of Globalisation'. *Urban Studies* 33, no. 8: 1319–36.

Cogliandro, C. 2001. *European Capitals of Culture for the Year 2000: A Wealth of Urban Cultures for Celebrating the Turn of the Century*. Brussels: European Commission.

Cole, A. and John, P. 2001. *Local Governance in England and France*. London: Routledge.

Collard, S. 1998. 'Architectural Gestures and Political Patronage: The Case of the Grands Travaux'. *European Journal of Cultural Policy* 5, no. 1: 33–47.

Cox, K. 1993. 'The Local and the Global in the New Urban Politics: A Critical View'. *Environment and Planning D: Society and Space* 11: 433–48.

Ercole, E., Walters, M. and Goldsmith, M. 1997. 'Cities, Networks, Euroregions, European Offices'. In *European Integration and Local Government*, ed. M. Goldsmith and K. Klausen, 219–36. Cheltenham: Edward Elgar.

Evans, G. 2003. 'Hard-Branding the Cultural City – from Prado to Prada'. *International Journal of Urban and Regional Research* 27, no. 2: 417–40.

Faludi, A. 2004. 'Territorial Cohesion: Old (French) Wine into New Bottles?' *Urban Studies* 41, no. 7: 1349–65.

Featherstone, K. and Radaelli, C. M., eds. 2004. *The Politics of Europeanization*. Oxford: Oxford University Press.

Featherstone, M. 1991. *Consumer Culture and Postmodernism*. London: Sage.

Florida, R. 2002. *The Rise of the Creative Class*. New York: Basic Books.

Giddens, A. 1999. *Runaway World: How Globalisation Is Reshaping Our Lives*. London: Profile.

Goldsmith, M. 2004. 'Variable Geometry, Multilevel Governance: European Integration and Subnational Government in the New Millennium'. In Featherstone and Radaelli 2004, 112–33.

Gomez, M. 1998. 'Reflective Images: The Case of Urban Regeneration in Glasgow and Bilbao'. *International Journal of Urban and Regional Research* 22, no. 1: 106–21.

Graham, B. 2002. 'Heritage as Knowledge: Capital or Culture'. *Urban Studies* 39, no. 5/6: 1003–17.

Halbwachs, M. 1994. *Les cadres sociaux de la mémoire*. Paris: Albin Michel.

Hall, P. 1993. 'Forces Shaping Urban Europe'. *Urban Studies* 30, no. 6: 883–98.

———. 1998. *Cities in Civilization*. London: Weidenfeld and Nicholson.

Hamel, P., Lustiger-Thaler, H. and Mayer, M., eds. 2000. *Urban Movements in a Globalising World*. London: Routledge.

Harding, A. 1997. 'Urban Regimes in a Europe of the Cities?' *European Urban and Regional Studies* 4: 291–314.

Harvey, D. 1987. 'Flexible Accumulation Through Urbanization: Reflections on "Post-Modernism" in the American City'. *Antipode* 19, no. 3: 260–86.

Haughton, G. and Williams, C., eds. 1999. *Corporate City? Partnership, Participation and Partition in Urban Development in Leeds*. Avebury: Aldershot.

Healey, P. 2004. 'The Treatment of Space and Place in the New Strategic Planning in Europe'. *International Journal of Urban and Regional Research* 28, no. 1: 45–67.

Hooghe, L., ed. 1996. *Cohesion Policy and European Integration*. Oxford: Clarendon Press.

Jessop, B. 2002. *The Future of the Capitalist State*. Cambridge: Polity Press.

Jonsson, C., Tagil, S. and Tornqvist, G. 2000. *Organising European Space*. London: Sage.

Krugman, P. 1996. 'Making Sense of the Competitiveness Debate'. *Oxford Review of Economic Policy* 12, no. 3: 17–25.

Le Galès, P. 1998. 'Regulations and Governance in European Cities'. *International Journal of Urban and Regional Research* 22, no. 3: 482–506.

_____. 2002. 'Private-Sector Interests and Urban Governance'. In Bagnasco and Le Galès 2002, 178–97.

Le Goff, J. 2005. *The Birth of Europe*. London: Blackwell.

MacLeod, G., Raco, M. and Ward, K. 2003. 'Negotiating the Contemporary City: Introduction'. *Urban Studies* 40, no. 9: 1655–71.

Massey, D. 2004. 'Geographies of Responsibility'. *Geografiska Annaler B* 86, no. 1: 5–18.

Matejko, L. 2000. 'Quand le patronat pense le territoire'. In *Les nouvelles politiques locales*, Cahiers lillois d'économie et de sociologie, 95–110. Paris: L'Harmattan.

Mayer, M. 2000. 'Urban Social Movements in an Era of Globalisation'. In Hamel, Lustiger-Thaler and Mayer 2000, 141–57.

McNeill, D. 2001. 'Embodying a Europe of the Cities: Geographies of Mayoral Leadership'. *Area* 33, no. 4: 353–9.

Mommaas, H. 2004. 'Cultural Clusters and the Post-industrial City: Towards the Remapping of Urban Cultural Policy'. *Urban Studies* 41, no. 3: 507–32.

Moriset, B. 2003. 'The New Economy in the City: Emergence and Location Factors of Internet-Based Companies in the Metropolitan Area of Lyon, France'. *Urban Studies* 40, no. 11: 2165–86.

Myerscough, J. 1991. *Monitoring Glasgow 1990*. Report for Glasgow City Council. Glasgow: Strathclyde Regional Council and Scottish Enterprise.

_____. 1994. *European Cities of Culture and Cultural Months: Summary Report*. Glasgow: Network of Cultural Cities.

Paquot, T., ed. 2001. *Le quotidien urbain: Essais sur les temps des villes*. Paris: La Découverte.

Phelps, N. A. and Parsons, N. 2003. 'Edge Urban Geographies: Notes from the Margins of Europe's Capital Cities'. *Urban Studies* 40, no. 9: 1725–49.

Quilley, S. 2000. 'Manchester First: From Municipal Socialism to the Entrepreneurial City'. *International Journal of Urban and Regional Research* 24, no. 3: 601–15.

Richards, G., Goedhart, S. and Herrijgers, C. 2001. 'The Cultural Attraction Distribution System'. In *Cultural Attractions and European Tourism*, ed. G. Richards, 71–89. Wallingford: CAB International.

Richards, G. and Wilson, J. 2004. 'The Impact of Cultural Events on City Image: Rotterdam, Cultural Capital of Europe 2001'. *Urban Studies* 41, no. 10: 1931–51.

Rogers, R. G. 1999. *Towards an Urban Renaissance*. London: Urban Task Force.

Rogerson, R. J. 1999. 'Quality of Life and City Competitiveness'. *Urban Studies* 36, no. 5/6: 969–86.

Roncayolo, M. 1997. *La ville et ses territoires*. Paris: Fayard.

Saez, G. 2003. 'L'action des collectivités territoriales en matière culturelle'. *Cahiers Français* 312: 12–18.

Sassen, S. 2001. *The Global City: New York, London, Tokyo*. Princeton: Princeton University Press.

Saunders, P. 1981. *Social Theory and the Urban Question*. London: Hutchinson.

Sayer, C. 1992. 'The City of Glasgow, Scotland: An Arts Led Revival'. *Culture and Policy* 4.

Schulze, C. 2003. 'Cities and EU Governance'. *Regional and Federal Studies* 13, no. 1: 121–47.

Scott, A., ed. 2001. *Global City-Regions: Trends, Theory, Policy*. Oxford: Oxford University Press.

Sennett, R. 1999. 'The Spaces of Democracy'. In Beauregard and Body-Gendrot 1999, 273–85.

Short, J. R. and Kim, Y.-H. 1999. *Globalization and the City*. London: Macmillan.

Sjøholt, P. 1999. 'Culture as a Strategic Development Device: The Role of "European Cities of Culture" with Particular Reference to Bergen'. *European Urban and Regional Research* 6, no. 4: 339–47.

Smiers, J. 2000. 'European Cities – First Sow, Then Reap'. In *The City Cultures Reader*, ed. M. Miles, T. Hall and I. Borden, 111–17. London: Routledge. [First published 1997.]

Tewdwr-Jones, M. and Williams, R. H. 2001. *The European Dimension of British Planning*. London: Spon Press.

Thorns, D. C. 2002. *The Transformation of Cities*. London: Palgrave.

Turok, I. 2003. 'Cities, Clusters and Creative Industries: The Case of Film and Television in Scotland'. *European Planning Studies* 11, no. 5: 549–65.

Veltz P. 2002. 'European Cities in the World Economy'. In Bagnasco and Le Galès 2002, 33–47.

Zukin, S. 1991. *Landscapes of Power: From Detroit to Disney World*. Berkeley: University of California Press.

_____. 1995. *The Cultures of Cities*. Oxford: Blackwell.

CONTRIBUTORS

Christian Bromberger is Professor of Ethnology at the University of Provence and presently director of the French Institute for Iranian Studies in Tehran. Since 1995, he has been a member of the Institut Universitaire de France (Chair of General Ethnology) and, since 1998, Chairman of the Council of Ethnological Heritage (Ministry of Culture). He has published extensively on collective identities in Iran and Southern Europe, and his recent publications are devoted to the ethnography of football in France, Europe and Iran.

Marion Demossier is Senior Lecturer in the Department of European Studies and Modern Languages, University of Bath, where she taught a postgraduate module on politics, culture and identity in Europe. Her research focuses on French and European societies, and she is currently writing a book titled *Wine and National Identity: Drinking Culture in France*. She has published extensively on French rural societies, French politics and French heritage.

Wendy Everett is Senior Lecturer in French and Film at the University of Bath. Published books include *Terence Davies* (2004), *Cultures of Exile* (2004), *The Seeing Century: Film, Vision and Identity* (2000) and *European Identity in Cinema* (1996). Recent articles and chapters include studies of Theo Angelopoulos, Léos Carax, Terence Davies, Fridrik Thor Fridriksson, Ken Loach, film and music, postmodern fractal films and the contemporary European film industry. She is a member of the editorial board of the *Literature/Film Quarterly* and co-editor for Peter Lang's *New Studies in European Cinema* series.

Ralph Grillo is Research Professor of Social Anthropology at the University of Sussex, and formerly Dean of the School of African and Asian Studies and Director of the Culture, Development and Environment Graduate Research Centre. He has published extensively on immigrants in France and Italy, on the politics of language and on plural societies. Currently, his work focuses on the relationship between transnational migration and multiculturalism and on debates about cultural difference in Europe.

David Hanley is Professor of European Studies and former Head of School at Cardiff University. He has held teaching posts at Ulster and Reading Universities as well as at Nanterre and Sciences Po in Paris. His work is on French and comparative European politics, especially with relation to parties and party systems. His books include *Party, Society, Government: Republican Democracy in France* (2000). His monograph *Beyond the Nation State: Parties in the Era of European Integration* will appear in 2007.

Ullrich Kockel is Professor of Ethnology and Folk Life at the University of Ulster. In 2001–3, he convened the Economic and Social Research Council (ESRC) Research Seminars in European Ethnology. His research interests include endogeneous regional development, cultural encounters, human ecology and philosophical anthropology. Recent books include *Negotiating Culture* (2006, ed. with Reginald Byron), *Cultural Heritages as Reflexive Traditions* (2006, with Máiréad Nic Craith) and *Culture and Economy* (2002). An Academician of the Academy of Learned Societies for the Social Sciences, and an executive board member of the Société Internationale d'Ethnologie et de Folklore, he is editor of the *Anthropological Journal of European Cultures* and also edits the series *Progress in European Ethnology* and *European Studies in Culture and Policy*.

Susan Milner is Reader in European Studies at the University of Bath. She is interested in the social impact of economic change in Europe, in the workplace and in the community. One of her main areas of research is urban and regional governance in Europe, with a particular focus on France and the UK. She recently coordinated an ESRC seminar series on urban and regional governance and the role of the voluntary and community sector. Related publications include *Reinventing France: State and Society in the Twenty-First Century* (2003, with Nick Parsons).

Anne-Marie Thiesse is Director of Research at the French National Centre for Research. She has published extensively on the cultural and social history of France and Europe. Her publications include *La création des identités nationales: Europe XVIII–XXèmes siècle* (1999) and *Ils apprenaient la France: L'exaltation des régions dans le discours patriotique* (1997).

Richard Vinen is Reader in French History at King's College. He has worked on French history with special reference to the Vichy regime of 1940–4, the politics of the Fourth Republic and the Algerian War. His publications include *A History in Fragments: Europe in the Twentieth Century* (2000), *France, 1934–1970* (1996), *Bourgeois Politics in France, 1945–1951* (1995) and *The Politics of French Business, 1936–1945* (1991). He is also interested in European history and in Britain during the twentieth century.

Peter Wagstaff is Senior Lecturer in French in the Department of European Studies and Modern Languages at the University of Bath. His research interests lie chiefly in questions of identity in a cross-national context. He is co-editor of *Cultures of Exile: Images of Displacement* (2004, with Wendy Everett) and editor of *Border Crossings: Mapping Identities in Modern Europe* (2004) and *Regionalism in the European Union* (1999).

Select Bibliography

General Bibliography on European Identity

As the bibliography on European identity is unlimited, I have chosen to select the principal articles and books which I have read and which are relevant to an interdisciplinary approach to the topic. I have presented them under the key headings below in order to facilitate an introduction to the issue of European identity in an interdisciplinary context.

– Marion Demossier

Theoretical Approaches to Identity/Identities

Abbott, D. 1998. *Culture and Identity*. London: Hodder & Stoughton.

Ackelsberg, M. A. 1996. 'Identity Politics, Political Identities: Thoughts towards a Multicultural Politics'. *Frontiers*: 87–100

Bauman, Z. 2001. 'Identity in the Globalising World'. *Social Anthropology* 9, no. 2: 121–9.

Bourdieu, P. 1991. *Language and Symbolic Power*. Cambridge: Polity Press.

Cederman, Lars-Erik, ed. 2001. *Constructing European Identity: The External Dimension*. London: Lynne Rienner.

Cohen, A. 1999. *Signifying Identities: Anthropological Perspectives on Boundaries and Contested Values*. London: Routledge.

Eagleton, T. 2000. *The Idea of Culture*. London: Blackwell.

Gellner, E. 1987. *Culture, Identity and Politics*. Cambridge: Cambridge University Press.

Kuper, A. 1999. *Culture: The Anthropologists' Account*. Cambridge, MA: Harvard University Press.

Neumann, I. B. 1999. *Uses of the Other: 'The East' in European Identity Formation*. Manchester: Manchester University Press.

Ross, M. 2000. 'Culture and Identity in Comparative Political Analysis'. In *Culture and Politics: A Reader*, ed. L. Crothers and C. Lockhart, 39–70. New York: St. Martin's Press.

Shore, C. 2000. *Building Europe: The Cultural Politics of European Integration*. London: Routledge.

Van Ham, P. 2001. 'Europe's Postmodern Identity: A Critical Appraisal'. *International Politics* 38, no. 2: 229–52.

Wikan, U. 1999. 'Culture: A New Concept of Race'. *Social Anthropology* 7, no. 1: 57–64.

Woodward, K., ed. 1997. *Identity and Difference*. London: Sage.

Wright, S. 1998. 'The Politicization of Culture'. *Anthropology Today* 14, no. 1: 7–15.

Debates on European Identity

Alibhai Brown, Y. 1998. *Islam and European Identity*. Demos Collection 13: 38-41.

Bellier, I. and Wilson, T. M., eds. 2000. *An Anthropology of the European Union*. Oxford and New York: Berg.

Delanty, G. 1995. *Inventing Europe: Idea, Identity, Reality*. London: Macmillan.

———. 1996. 'Beyond the Nation-State: National Identity and Citizenship in a Multicultural Society – A Response to Rex'. *Sociological Research Online* 1, no. 3. http://www.socresonline.org.uk/1/3/1.html.

De Witte, B. 1987. Building Europe's Image and Identity. In *Whither Europe. Borders, Boundaries, Frontiers in a Changing World*. Edited by Rutger Lindhal. Gothenburg: Cergu.

Dunkerley, D., Hodgson, L., Konopacki, S., Spybey, T. and Thompson, A. 2002. *Changing Europe: Identities, Nations and Citizens*. London and New York: Routledge.

Farrell, M., Fella, S. and Newman, M. 2002. *European Integration in the 21st century*. London: Sage.

Garcia, S., ed. 1993. *European Identity and the Search for Legitimacy*. London: Pinter Publishers.

Habermas, J. 1992. 'Citizenship and National Identity: Some Reflections on the Future of Europe'. *Praxis International* 12, no. 1: 1–19.

Hedetoft, U. 1994. 'National Identities and European Integration "from Below": Bringing the People Back In'. *Journal of European Integration* 18, no. 1: 1–28.

———, ed. 1998. *Political Symbols, Symbolic Politics: European Identities in Transformation*. Aldershot: Ashgate.

Herb, G. H. and Kaplan, D. H., eds. 1999. *Nested Identities: Nationalism, Territory and Scale*. Lanham: Rowman & Littlefield.

Ifversen, J. 2002. 'Europe and European Culture: A Conceptual Analysis'. *European Societies* 4, no. 1: 1–26.

Kohli, M. 2000. 'The Battlegrounds of European Identity'. *European Societies* 2, no. 2: 113–37.

Laffan, B. 1996. 'The Politics of Identity and Political Order in Europe'. *Journal of Common Market Studies* 34, no. 1: 81–102.

Rex, J. 1996. 'National Identity in the Democratic Multi-Cultural State'. *Sociological Research Online* 1, no. 2. http://www.socresonline.org.uk/socresonline/1/2/1.html.

Schlesinger, P. 1997. *From Cultural Defence to Political Culture*. Oslo: Arena.

Smith, A. D. 1992. 'National Identity and the Idea of European Unity'. *International Affairs* 68, no. 1: 55–76.

———. 1995. *Nations and Nationalism in a Global Era*. Cambridge: Polity Press.

Stråth, B., ed. 2002. *Europe and the Other and Europe as the Other*. Brussels: Peter Lang.

———. 2002. 'A European Identity: To the Historical Limits of a Concept'. *European Journal of Social Theory* 5, no. 4: 387–401.

Tassin, E. 1992. 'Europe: A Political Community?' In *Dimensions of Radical Democracy*, ed. C. Mouffe, 169–93. London: Verso.

Taylor, R. 2001. *Unity in Diversity*. Brussels: European Quality Publications.

Wilson, K. and van der Dussen, J., eds. 1993. *The History of the Idea of Europe*. London: Routledge.

Zetterholm, S., ed. 1994. *National Cultures and European Integration*. Oxford: Berg.

Citizenship and European Integration

Alsayyad, N. and Castells, M. 2002. 'Introduction'. In *Muslim Europe or Euro-Islam: Politics, Culture and Citizenship in the Age of Globalization*, ed. N. Alsayyad and M. Castells, 1–6. Lanham: Lexington Books.

Castles, S. and Davidson, A. 2000. *Citizenship and Migration: Globalisation and the Politics of Belonging*. London: Macmillan.

Cesarani, D. and Fulbrook, M., eds. 1996. *Citizenship, Nationality and Migration in Europe*. London: Routledge.

Ferrera, M. 2003. 'European Integration and National Social Citizenship: Changing Boundaries, New Structuring?' *Comparative Political Studies* 36, no. 6: 611–52.

Geddes. A. 2000. *Immigration and European Integration*. Manchester: Manchester University Press.

Habermas, J. 1992. 'Citizenship and National Identity: Some Reflections on the Future of Europe'. *Praxis International* 12, no. 1: 1–19.

Kymlicka, W. 1998. *Multicultural Citizenship*. Oxford: Clarendon Press.

Leveau, R., Mohsen-Finan, K. and Wihtol de Wenden, C., eds. 2002. *New European Identity and Citizenship*. Aldershot: Ashgate.

Neveu, C. 2000. 'European Citizenship, Citizens of Europe and European Citizens'. In *An Anthropology of the European Union: Building, Imagining and Experiencing the New Europe*, ed. I. Bellier and T. M. Wilson, 119–36. Oxford: Berg.

Randall, H. and Weil, P., eds. 2001. *Towards European Nationality: Citizenship, Immigration and Nationality Law in the EU*. London: Palgrave.

The Anthropology of Europe

Abélès, M. 1996. 'La communauté européenne: Une perspective anthropologique'. *Social Anthropology* 4, no. 1: 33–46.

Bellier, I. and Wilson, T. M., eds. 2000. *An Anthropology of the European Union*. Oxford: Berg.

Borneman, J. and Fowler, N. 1997. 'Europeanization'. *Annual Review of Anthropology* 26: 487–514.

Douglas, H. 2000. *Integral Europe*. Princeton: Princeton University Press.

Goddard, A., Llobera, J. R. and Shore, C. 1994. *The Anthropology of Europe: Identity and Boundaries in Conflict*. Oxford: Berg.

Macdonald, S., ed. 1993. *Inside European Identities*. Oxford: Berg.

McDonald, M. 1996. 'Unity in Diversity: Some Tensions in the Construction of Europe'. *Social Anthropology* 4, no. 1: 47–60.

Shore, C. 1993. 'Inventing the "People's Europe": Critical Approaches to European Community "Cultural Policy"'. *Man* 28, no. 4: 779–800.

_____. 1998. 'Creating Europeans: The Politicization of "Culture" in the European Union'. *Anthropology in Action* 5, no. 1/2: 11–16.

_____. 2000. *Building Europe: The Cultural Politics of European Integration*. London: Routledge.

_____. 2004. 'Whither European Citizenship? Eros and Civilization Revisited'. *European Journal of Social Theory* 7, no. 1: 27–44.

Stolcke, V. 1995. 'Talking Culture: New Boundaries, New Rhetorics of Exclusion in Europe'. *Current Anthropology* 36, no. 1: 1–24.

The History and Politics of Europe

Gilbert, M. 2003. *Surpassing Realism: The Politics of European Integration since 1945.* Lanham: Rowman & Littlefield.

Hobsbawm, E. and Ranger, T., eds. 1983. *The Invention of Tradition.* Cambridge: Cambridge University Press.

McCormick, J. 1999. *Understanding the European Union: A Concise Introduction.* London: Palgrave.

Wilson, K. and van der Dussen, J., eds. 1993. *The History of the Idea of Europe.* London: Routledge.

Index